# THE PLACE OF MEDIA POWER

*The Place of Media Power* focuses on an area neglected in previous studies of the media: the meetings between 'ordinary people' and the media. Nick Couldry's fascinating study explores what happens when people who normally consume the media witness media processes in action, or even become the object of media attention themselves. Such encounters, Couldry argues, tell us a great deal about our attitudes towards the media world. They also offer a new way of thinking about the media's impact on contemporary social life, the basis of their social authority, and the possibility of challenging it.

Nick Couldry uses perspectives from anthropology, discourse analysis, sociology and geography as well as media studies to develop a wide-ranging theory of how the media's special status – as storytellers and as presenters of 'facts' – is maintained. He goes on to explore the implications of this theory in two detailed case studies – of visitors to the Granada Studios Tour, Manchester, home of the outdoor set of the long-running soap *Coronation Street*, and of protestors against live animal exports at the port of Brightlingsea – to offer fresh insights into media institutions' impact on everyday lives.

**Nick Couldry** is a Lecturer in the Department of Media and Communications, Goldsmiths College, University of London. He is the author of many articles on the social impact of the media. He is also active as a musician and as a curator.

# COMEDIA
## Editor David Morley

MIGRANCY, CULTURE, IDENTITY
*Iain Chambers*

THE PHOTOGRAPHIC IMAGE IN DIGITAL CULTURE
*Edited by Martin Lister*

SPECTACULAR BODIES
Gender, Genre and the Action Cinema
*Yvonne Tasker*
*Stuart Hall*

CRITICAL DIALOGUES IN CULTURAL STUDIES
*Edited by Kuan-Hsing Chen and David Morley*

TEACHING THE MEDIA
*Len Masterman*

TELEVISION AND COMMON KNOWLEDGE
*Edited by Jostein Gripsrud*

TELEVISION, AUDIENCES AND CULTURAL STUDIES
*David Morley*

TELEVISION, ETHNICITY AND CULTURAL CHANGE
*Marie Gillespie*

TELEVISION MYTHOLOGIES
*Len Masterman*

TIMES OF THE TECHNOCULTURE
From the Information Society to the Virtual Life
*Kevin Robins and Frank Webster*

TO BE CONTINUED ...
Soap Opera Around the World
*Edited by Robert C. Allen*

TRANSNATIONAL CONNECTIONS
Culture, People, Places
*Ulf Hannerz*

VIDEO PLAYTIME
The Gendering of a Leisure Technology
*Ann Gray*

# THE PLACE OF MEDIA POWER

## Pilgrims and witnesses of the media age

*Nick Couldry*

London and New York

First published 2000
by Routledge
11 New Fetter Lane, London EC4P 4EE

Simultaneously published in the USA and Canada
by Routledge
29 West 35th Street, New York, NY 10001

Routledge is an imprint of the Taylor & Francis Group

© 2000 Nick Couldry
The right of Nick Couldry to be identified as the Author of this Work has
been asserted by him in accordance with the Copyright, Designs
and Patents Act 1988

Typeset in Bembo by Bookcraft Ltd, Stroud
Printed and bound in Great Britain by Biddles Ltd,
Guildford and King's Lynn

*British Library Cataloguing in Publication Data*
A catalogue record for this book is available from the British Library

*Library of Congress Cataloguing in Publication Data*
CIP data have been applied for

ISBN 0-415-21314-2 (hbk)
ISBN 0-415-21315-0 (pbk)

TO MY PARENTS:
PHILIP COULDRY
AND
LILIAN COULDRY

particularly Johan Fornäs and Göran Bolin, for helpful comments on earlier
versions of my work. My friends and colleagues, Dave Hesmondhalgh and
Jonathan Burston, have also throughout been vital sources of encouragement and humour when most needed. Many thanks and admiration to
Barbara Croucher for compiling the index so effectively.

Last, but certainly not least, I want to thank my wife, Louise Edwards, for
the insight without which I would never have embarked upon this project,
and for her unfailing love and support throughout its writing.

London, January 1999

# CONTENTS

# PLATES

# ACKNOWLEDGEMENT

First, I want to thank those without whom there
research: the Economic and Social Research Counci
Research Studentship R00429534066; and all thos
interviewed by me.

I am also grateful to Granada Studios Tour, part
their support of the fieldwork for Part Two; M
Against Live Exports for her help during the fie
the women of Yellow Gate, Greenham Comm
being most generous with their time. Thanks t
*Coronation Street* for allowing me to publish a r
out charge. Thanks also to the following (in al
documents or other help: Olive Allum, W
Camauer, Uma Dinsmore, Helen Edwards
Beth Junor, Ian Kilburn, Norma Langley,

An earlier version of some of the mate
'The View from Inside the Simulacrum: \
*nation Street'* in *Leisure Studies* volume 17
Greenham Common from Chapter Eig
Media Frame at Greenham Common
Mediations?' in *Media, Culture and So*
respectively, of the publishers, E  &
acknowledged.

A book such as this could never ha
support and friendship of many pe
ticular. David Morley, as the super
the most supportive and subtle cr
very grateful to him. I also owe
thesis, Kevin Robins and Ro
Routledge's other, anonymous
criticisms, from which the fina'
Thanks also to Bill Schwarz
University's Department of

# Part 1

# A NEW THEORY OF MEDIA POWER

# 1

# LOCATING MEDIA POWER

A television producer tells a visitor how excited his team will be to see her at the studio. 'Oh, the studio!' says the woman to her husband. 'That's where all the magic happens.' The producer smiles disdainfully: 'Oh, you've worked in television?' 'No,' replies the woman, 'but I've watched a lot of it.'

The dialogue comes from *Wayne's World*,[1] a film about how a talk programme produced by Wayne and Garth in their basement and broadcast on public access television, gets adopted by a commercial channel. The channel's sponsor proudly takes his wife one day to the studios to see the new acquisition being rehearsed. There she meets the producer's professional disdain. The short encounter crystallises in fictional form the question from which this book starts: what do non-media people's encounters with the media world (whether 'magical' or not) tell us about the symbolic power of media institutions?

More broadly, how is media power – the particular concentration of symbolic power that the media represent – reproduced as legitimate? The aim is not to criticise symbolic power as such: all aesthetic production involves boundaries and hierarchies around the fictional world it creates. Nor is it to argue that the mediation of social life is necessarily bad, requiring a return to an idealised world 'before' mediation (if one ever existed).[2] I am interested instead in questions about the particular concentration of symbolic power in contemporary media institutions: how is it legitimated and naturalised, and what is its social impact?

I approach these questions by exploring how non-media people interact with media institutions, and how they talk about those interactions. We know a lot about the media's institutional structures, and about how people interact indirectly with them through consuming media texts, but direct interactions between non-media people and media institutions remain something of a mystery. What happens, for example, when people witness media production? What are people's experiences of appearing in the media themselves? These questions remain underresearched.[3] Yet it is in such cases – when people see the media process close up – rather than in the relaxed, but distanced, context of everyday domestic consumption, that the media's

3

symbolic power is most likely to be contested. People's talk about these interactions offers insights into what is perhaps the most fundamental question for media theory: why do we place any value, or credence, in media outputs at all?

To emphasise non-media people's direct interactions with media institutions is also to focus on the *spaces* where those interactions take place: studios, filming locations, sites of news coverage, and so on; hence, one reason for the book's title, 'the place of media power'. This simple point has wide implications. We can think of the whole media process (production, distribution, consumption) as involving the normal separation of media people from non-media people; this limits the chances of direct interaction with media institutions (cf. Debord, 1983). This separation is, in fact, one reason why the authority of media institutions seems natural: most of us simply don't go near the places where detailed knowledge of what media institutions do is available. The links between media power and geography, then, go deep, but are themselves only part of a wider pattern of how the media's symbolic power is naturalised.

By 'symbolic power', I mean the media's 'power of constructing reality' (Bourdieu, 1991: 166) in a general sense. Each programme, text or image, of course, has its particular way of maintaining your belief (that it is a true representation of the facts or a convincing fiction). But I am interested in something more general: our complex sets of beliefs about the media and the media's status as sources of social knowledge. How is belief at that general level reproduced?[4]

At the core of this book are two main claims. First, I argue that the media's symbolic power is far from automatic; in fact, it has to be continually reproduced through various practices and dispositions at every level of social life. Second, I argue that people's talk about those situations when, unusually, they get close to the media process offers important insights into the patterns of thought, language, and action by which the media's authority is reproduced. 'Media power' – by which I mean the concentration in media institutions of the symbolic power of 'constructing reality' (both factual representations and credible fictions) – is a social process, which we need to understand in all its local complexity.

Let me explain this more fully. Media power is not simply something that media institutions (or media texts) 'possess' or their audiences 'absorb'. Instead, following much recent social theoretical work on power,[5] I will analyse media power – the massive concentration of symbolic power in media institutions – as the complex outcome of practices at *every* level of social interaction. Media power is not a binary relation of domination between 'large' and 'small' 'actors', with 'large actors' (the media) having the automatic ability to dominate 'small actors' (audience members) simply because of their 'size'. Media power is reproduced through the details of what social actors (including audience members) do and say.

4

# Part 1

# A NEW THEORY OF
# MEDIA POWER

# CONTENTS

# PLATES

# ACKNOWLEDGEMENTS

First, I want to thank those without whom there would have been no research: the Economic and Social Research Council, who funded me under Research Studentship R00429534066; and all those who gave up time to be interviewed by me.

I am also grateful to Granada Studios Tour, particularly Helen Jackson, for their support of the fieldwork for Part Two; Maria Wilby of Brightlingsea Against Live Exports for her help during the fieldwork for Part Three; and the women of Yellow Gate, Greenham Common Women's Peace Camp for being most generous with their time. Thanks to the editors of *Inside Soap* and *Coronation Street* for allowing me to publish a notice in their magazines without charge. Thanks also to the following (in alphabetical order) for supplying documents or other help: Olive Allum, Wendy and Nick Bragg, Leonor Camauer, Uma Dinsmore, Helen Edwards, Darren Fitzgerald, Terry Hutt, Beth Junor, Ian Kilburn, Norma Langley, Brian Mead and Alf Wakeling.

An earlier version of some of the material in Part Two was published as 'The View from Inside the Simulacrum: Visitors' Tales from the Set of *Coronation Street*' in *Leisure Studies* volume 17(2); a longer version of material on Greenham Common from Chapter Eight was published as 'Disrupting The Media Frame at Greenham Common: A New Chapter in the History of Mediations?' in *Media, Culture and Society* volume 21(3). The permissions, respectively, of the publishers, E & FN Spon and Sage, are gratefully acknowledged.

A book such as this could never have been written without the intellectual support and friendship of many people and I want to thank a number in particular. David Morley, as the supervisor of my MA and PhD theses, has been the most supportive and subtle critic that I could have wished for, and I am very grateful to him. I also owe a great debt to the examiners of my PhD thesis, Kevin Robins and Roger Silverstone, and to James Hay and Routledge's other, anonymous, reader, for their cogent and constructive criticisms, from which the final version presented here has greatly benefited. Thanks also to Bill Schwarz at Goldsmiths and to members of Stockholm University's Department of Journalism, Media and Communications, particularly Johan Fornäs and Göran Bolin, for helpful comments on earlier versions of my work. My friends and colleagues, Dave Hesmondhalgh and Jonathan Burston, have also throughout been vital sources of encouragement and humour when most needed. Many thanks and admiration to Barbara Croucher for compiling the index so effectively.

Last, but certainly not least, I want to thank my wife, Louise Edwards, for the insight without which I would never have embarked upon this project, and for her unfailing love and support throughout its writing.

London, January 1999

# 1

# LOCATING MEDIA POWER

A television producer tells a visitor how excited his team will be to see her at the studio. 'Oh, the studio!' says the woman to her husband. 'That's where all the magic happens.' The producer smiles disdainfully: 'Oh, you've worked in television?' 'No,' replies the woman, 'but I've watched a lot of it.'

The dialogue comes from *Wayne's World*,[1] a film about how a talk programme produced by Wayne and Garth in their basement and broadcast on public access television, gets adopted by a commercial channel. The channel's sponsor proudly takes his wife one day to the studios to see the new acquisition being rehearsed. There she meets the producer's professional disdain. The short encounter crystallises in fictional form the question from which this book starts: what do non-media people's encounters with the media world (whether 'magical' or not) tell us about the symbolic power of media institutions?

More broadly, how is media power – the particular concentration of symbolic power that the media represent – reproduced as legitimate? The aim is not to criticise symbolic power as such: all aesthetic production involves boundaries and hierarchies around the fictional world it creates. Nor is it to argue that the mediation of social life is necessarily bad, requiring a return to an idealised world 'before' mediation (if one ever existed).[2] I am interested instead in questions about the particular concentration of symbolic power in contemporary media institutions: how is it legitimated and naturalised, and what is its social impact?

I approach these questions by exploring how non-media people interact with media institutions, and how they talk about those interactions. We know a lot about the media's institutional structures, and about how people interact indirectly with them through consuming media texts, but direct interactions between non-media people and media institutions remain something of a mystery. What happens, for example, when people witness media production? What are people's experiences of appearing in the media themselves? These questions remain underresearched.[3] Yet it is in such cases – when people see the media process close up – rather than in the relaxed, but distanced, context of everyday domestic consumption, that the media's

3

symbolic power is most likely to be contested. People's talk about these interactions offers insights into what is perhaps the most fundamental question for media theory: why do we place any value, or credence, in media outputs at all?

To emphasise non-media people's direct interactions with media institutions is also to focus on the *spaces* where those interactions take place: studios, filming locations, sites of news coverage, and so on; hence, one reason for the book's title, 'the place of media power'. This simple point has wide implications. We can think of the whole media process (production, distribution, consumption) as involving the normal separation of media people from non-media people; this limits the chances of direct interaction with media institutions (cf. Debord, 1983). This separation is, in fact, one reason why the authority of media institutions seems natural: most of us simply don't go near the places where detailed knowledge of what media institutions do is available. The links between media power and geography, then, go deep, but are themselves only part of a wider pattern of how the media's symbolic power is naturalised.

By 'symbolic power', I mean the media's 'power of constructing reality' (Bourdieu, 1991: 166) in a general sense. Each programme, text or image, of course, has its particular way of maintaining your belief (that it is a true representation of the facts or a convincing fiction). But I am interested in something more general: our complex sets of beliefs about the media and the media's status as sources of social knowledge. How is belief at that general level reproduced?[4]

At the core of this book are two main claims. First, I argue that the media's symbolic power is far from automatic; in fact, it has to be continually reproduced through various practices and dispositions at every level of social life. Second, I argue that people's talk about those situations when, unusually, they get close to the media process offers important insights into the patterns of thought, language, and action by which the media's authority is reproduced. 'Media power' – by which I mean the concentration in media institutions of the symbolic power of 'constructing reality' (both factual representations and credible fictions) – is a social process, which we need to understand in all its local complexity.

Let me explain this more fully. Media power is not simply something that media institutions (or media texts) 'possess' or their audiences 'absorb'. Instead, following much recent social theoretical work on power,[5] I will analyse media power – the massive concentration of symbolic power in media institutions – as the complex outcome of practices at *every* level of social interaction. Media power is not a binary relation of domination between 'large' and 'small' 'actors', with 'large actors' (the media) having the automatic ability to dominate 'small actors' (audience members) simply because of their 'size'. Media power is reproduced through the details of what social actors (including audience members) do and say.

This might seem paradoxical. Surely, what is distinctive about modern media is precisely their ability to have effects simultaneously across a large territory, transcending (and making irrelevant) the scale of local interactions? But to make that assumption elides important dimensions. Historically, as Armand Mattelart has argued, the ever-increasing scale of modern communications is closely connected with the notion of communication 'as a system of thought and power and as a mode of government' (1996: xi), an unfinished history of the social production of scale. And sociologically there are important insights to be gained from the work within Actor Network Theory (Callon and Latour, 1981) on how power and influence is achieved in scientific and technological practice. We can understand the media's ability to become 'obligatory passing points' (ibid.: 287) in the general circulation of images and discourse, not as something superimposed on social practice from the outside; instead it is endlessly reproduced through the details of social practice itself. The media, I will claim, have social effects on a large scale not only because centralised mechanisms of broadcasting are in place, but also because we believe in the authority of media discourse in countless local contexts, because we believe that most others believe the same, and because we act on the basis of these beliefs on countless specific occasions. These local patterns of belief and action have become so routine that, in practice, we run them together in a general conception of the media's 'effects' largely abstracted from those specific contexts of reproduction. As a result, the workings of the media's social authority tend to be hidden, and media power comes to seem natural.

This in itself makes analysis difficult. Media power is generally too obvious to be articulated and criticised. We need analytic tools to cut into this process of naturalisation. If we follow the logic of the argument that media power is locally reproduced, however, we must acknowledge that the media's social authority is likely to be unevenly reproduced. Media power, however broad its impacts, cannot be absolute or inescapable. At the very least, there are moments and places where it is de-naturalised, perhaps even contested. My second claim, then, is that it is precisely such situations that give us insight into the normal processes by which media power is naturalised. Just as the ethnomethodologist Harold Garfinkel argued that we can understand the '"seen but unnoticed" … background features of everyday scenes' by studying what happens when those features are suspended (1967: 36, 46), so too we can understand the processes which help naturalise media power by studying what happens when they are interrupted.[6] Such disruptive moments may be more common than normally realised: it is precisely because media power is naturalised, that we do not normally connect them up into any wider pattern.

Inevitably, however, this research strategy involves choices. For one thing, if media power is as deeply embedded in social practice as I claim, then there will be significant differences in how that process works in different places, what we might call different 'media cultures'. My argument will generally assume as its background the British context with its still quite centralised broadcasting institutions, but the invitation to international comparisons with other media cultures is clear (cf. Chapter 9).

In addition, I have been using the term 'the media' so far in a deliberately non-specific way. This is open to the objection that the authority of different media (television versus radio, the press, music, film, video, and so on) varies significantly. My basic argument, however, is that many common-sense assumptions about the media's authority operate with a sense of 'the media' which *is* highly non-specific: for example, the hierarchy I analyse in Chapter 3 between 'media' and 'ordinary' 'worlds'. Such distinctions cut across the undeniably important differences between how particular media function, or the complex differences within a particular medium's outputs. Analysis needs to reflect the vagueness, as well as the precision, of talk about 'the media' (cf. Becker, 1995: 634–5). In so far as my empirical material is specific in dealing with 'the media', it refers mainly to television, but also to radio and the press; in my theoretical chapters, I also refer occasionally to film and music. My principal focus, however, remains the media in the usual 'common-sense' definition i.e. the principal mass media: television, radio and the press (including magazines).[7] I argue that the potential differences between media are less important than how people interact with the institutional sphere of 'the media' in general, and how this, in turn, reflects the media's symbolic status in our generally mediated society.

My approach to the media differs from many others in not being concerned with the impacts of particular texts. It focuses more generally on what it means to live in a society dominated by large-scale media institutions. I want to pose these questions not abstractly, but through detailed empirical work on how members of the media audience themselves talk and act. It is true of course that particular media texts contribute to attitudes and beliefs about the media's status – I will refer to a number of examples in later chapters – but this is not the only way, or perhaps even the main way, in which the media's special status is reproduced.[8] Peter Stallybrass and Allon White argued a decade ago for the importance of analysing not just discourse (and the hierarchies it expresses) but the hierarchic relationships between 'distinct discursive domains' (1986: 60). 'The formation', they wrote, 'of new kinds of speech can be traced through the emergence of new public sites of discourse and the transformation of old ones' (ibid.: 80). We need, then, to study 'the way discursive traffic and exchange between different domains are structured and controlled' (ibid.: 195). Stallybrass and White's main concern was with literature but, by analogy, an important aspect of contemporary media is the *asymmetrical* connection they establish between different sites of discourse: between public places of media production and private sites of reception. Seen in this light, contemporary media may have important features in common with earlier discursive hierarchies such as the mediaeval Catholic church (Curran, 1982).

Moving away from specific media texts allows us to place in better focus these broad questions about the status of the media in contemporary societies. We need, as Jesus Martin-Barbero has proposed, to place the media in a wider historical 'field of *mediations*' (1993: 139, my emphasis): the history of the various forms by which social action has been mediated through the public circulation of images and text. This, in turn, opens up connections with another history: the history of people's attempts at alternative 'mediation' that challenge the authority of existing media institutions. I return to this particularly in Chapter 8.

The media are a site of profound inequality and, therefore, of potential conflict. As Stuart Hall noted in an early essay, there is:

> a fundamental a-symmetry ... between those who shape events, participate actively in them, those who have skilled and expert knowledge about events, and those who have 'privileged access' to events and participants in order to report on and communicate about them: and, on the other hand, the great majorities and minorities of the 'mass audience', who do not directly participate in events (even when they are directly affected by them), who have no expert knowledge about them, and who have no privileged right of access to information and personnel.
>
> (1973: 11)

More than one dimension of power, of course, is involved here: state and corporate power, as well as the power of media institutions. I am focusing on the latter. This is not just a technical, but a political issue, since it is an asymmetry in people's ability to constitute social reality itself. As James Carey has argued, 'reality is a scarce resource'; 'the fundamental form of power is the power to define, allocate and display this resource' (1989: 87). Or, at least, we can say that this power is *a* fundamental aspect of social power. Its unequal distribution is a central dimension of contemporary social inequality.

This point has been made recently with great force by the sociologist and political theorist Alberto Melucci (1989, 1996) in his work on new forms of social activism. Melucci has for some years argued that, in an increasingly standardised and commodified social environment, conflicts over information and symbolic resources acquire a particular importance (1989: 55). Recently he has focused on the power issues surrounding the media themselves. The increase in symbolic production through the media requires 'a new way of thinking about power and inequality' (1996: 179), a study of 'new centralities and marginalities' in relation not merely to material resources (as usually defined) but 'control over the construction of meaning' (ibid.: 182).

7

'The real domination', he has argued, 'is today the exclusion from *the power of naming*'.[9] Even if this may go a little too far – since, for example, inequalities of economic resources surely remain a central form of domination – it rightly puts centre stage, not only for media theory, but for social theory more widely, the question of how the media's privileged access to 'the power of naming' is reproduced as legitimate. That is the focus of this book.


## MEDIA POWER: BEYOND TEXTS AND AUDIENCES

My argument is a response to a crisis, or at least a turning-point, in the sociology of the media (cf. Abercrombie and Longhurst, 1998; Ang, 1996: 66; Corner, 1997: 260). More than two decades of empirical work on media audiences has analysed in detail how they interpret media texts and the uses to which the media are put in everyday life. But the suspicion remains that underlying issues of power in relation to the media have not been adequately addressed, and perhaps not even adequately posed.

Let me briefly (and quite schematically) review the different ways in which media sociology has approached issues of power. A crucial term, of course, has been not 'power' but 'ideology', which has itself provoked great debate. There is no need to enter that debate here, but we can for convenience adopt John Thompson's definition of the study of 'ideology' as the 'study [of] the ways in which meaning serves to establish and sustain relations of domination' (1990: 56). The type of connection suggested, then, between ideology, media, and power, is clear: ideology in media texts reinforces wider power imbalances (whether between the state and civil society, or between corporate interests and individuals). We need to understand the difficulties with this, since they are important background to my own approach.

Perhaps the simplest treatment of the media–power relation is to analyse ideological structures 'contained' in media texts themselves. This can sometimes be effective if combined with a sophisticated theory of how wider power imbalances and ideology are reflected in media production (Kellner, 1995). But, from the perspective of how best to study the relation between power issues and the media, such an approach offers no detailed consideration of how media texts are actually used. It is all too easy to treat media texts as symptoms of some general ideological formation, providing 'privileged access to the social realities of their era' (Kellner, 1995: 108). To this there is a simple but fundamental challenge, formulated by Justin Lewis:

> The question that should be put to textual analysis that purports to tell us how a cultural product 'works' in contemporary culture is almost embarrassingly simple: where's the evidence? Without evidence, everything is pure speculation.
>
> (1991: 49)

What, then, are the alternatives?

Audience studies or reception studies in their various forms have attempted to address the challenge Lewis poses. For example, David Morley's early work (1980) on the audience for the BBC TV current affairs programme *Nationwide* foregrounded the question of what audiences *do* in relation to media texts. This in itself was not fundamentally new (it was already part of American mass communications research), but the connections Morley made between the practice of viewing and issues of power and ideology were new and important. Morley, drawing on Stuart Hall's (1980) well-known encoding/decoding model as well as Frank Parkin's (1972) sociology of class cultures, argued that the audience's 'decoding' of the media text is connected with the wider field of communications (work, school, family, leisure) to which viewers belong (cf. Morley, 1992: 77). He aimed to relate how audience members interpret a text to their position in that wider field. Hall's model had simplified this relation through two key assumptions: first, that each media text is encoded in analysable ways, which determine a 'preferred meaning' for that text, related to dominant ideology; second, that there are basically three interpretative positions for an audience to adopt – a decoding that uses the same codes with which the programme was 'encoded' to produce the 'dominant' reading, one which adjusts the programme's codes to produce a 'negotiated' reading, and one which uses a quite different code, to produce an 'oppositional' reading. Although a text is open to more than one decoding, there remains according to Hall and Morley a more likely or 'preferred meaning', and it is this skewing of interpretations which reproduces dominant ideology. Morley then attempted to connect the likelihood of people adopting alternative decoding positions to sociological variables such as class and occupation.

In spite of its importance in emphasising audience interpretation in its own right, this approach has clear limitations, as Morley himself (1992) later recognised. The limitation most relevant here is that the term 'decoding' – basically, a literary model of textual interpretation – oversimplifies what audiences actually do with media texts. People may have multiple levels of engagement (Buckingham (1987, 1993), Corner and Richardson (1986), Liebes and Katz (1990)). What about irony, scepticism, and willing suspension of disbelief, to name just three possibilities? The complexity of what audiences do with media material matches the variety of functions fulfilled by the media beyond the purely 'textual', including a ritual, participatory function whose ideological effects completely escape the encoding/decoding model. But if what audiences do with media texts is generally more than a formal 'reading' of their contents, the text cannot be the only entry-point to issues of power in the media.

This conclusion is reinforced by other considerations. There is the argument that we are simply saturated with media contents, so that the impact of any particular media text is impossible to establish. Not only are all of us confronted with a large number of media texts every day, but there are a myriad interconnections between them.[10] As John Fiske (1987: 117) has argued, a particular media text such as a soap opera episode, does not exist in isolation: it is commented upon, anticipated, celebrated or developed in countless other media texts (press columns, news stories, celebrity magazines, and so on). Ien Ang is therefore surely right when she comments that 'it becomes more and more difficult to delineate what "the television text" is in a media-saturated world' (1996: 41). Put another way, identifying the 'effects' – for example the ideological effects – of any particular media text has become highly problematic.[11] The flow of media inputs is so dense that we receive many of them, perhaps even most of them, in a state of distraction similar to that in which we take in billboards along a highway (Grossberg, 1987). In any case, there is no single point in any text where a definite link between ideology and reality is forged (Hay, 1992: 365–6). Once we register the sheer complexity of the media environment we inhabit,[12] encoding/decoding and other text-oriented models of power and ideology seem at best like theories for special cases where reception is focused most intensely. That limits their usefulness if, as Barwise and Ehrenberg (1988) have plausibly argued, television is generally a 'low involvement' activity.[13] Not all media consumption, of course, is distracted (Caldwell, 1996: 25–7) and it can be argued that ideology may have all the greater effect for being absorbed with reduced attention (Corcoran, 1987). But there are good reasons, at least, to doubt whether the media text and/or its reception are the only, or even the best, starting-points for analysing the relations between the media and power/ideology.

There has, however, been other work within media sociology which has analysed the social impacts of the media in a different way, moving beyond texts or audience interpretations. The two writers most relevant here are Paddy Scannell and Roger Silverstone.

Paddy Scannell's work has foregrounded two previously neglected dimensions of the media: the historical and the phenomenological. Together with David Cardiff, he pioneered a historical analysis of the BBC (Scannell and Cardiff, 1991), combining institutional history with a sociologically informed account of how a particular type of public broadcasting developed, attuned to modern British society (Scannell, 1988b, 1989). This historical approach is grounded in a phenomenological analysis of how radio and television's forms are embedded in everyday life, particularly its temporality (Scannell, 1988a, 1996). Modern societies, Scannell argues, while economically and functionally integrated in innumerable ways, are spatially dispersed and so will not hold together at all without a common 'universe of discourse' (1989: 153). The electronic media are a major source of that discourse.[14] Scannell and Cardiff's historical approach shows the complexity of how the British media's social authority developed. Through a long and uneven process affecting programming, modes of presentation, speech styles of broadcasters, and so on, the audience (especially its working-class and lower middle-class members) came, so they argue, to feel that the 'world' of broadcasting was in some sense their own world. Only 'through ordinary language' could broadcasting reproduce 'the everyday life of whole populations as ordinary' (Scannell, 1988b: 2). Broadcasting became embedded in the temporal routines of everyday life through its regular programme schedules (1988a), while 'live' media events enabled a national sense of 'actuality'. Through all these developments, television and radio became routinely integrated into national and individual life.

Scannell's broadly functionalist account of broadcasting's impact on everyday life in Britain is distinctive for emphasising issues of 'system integration' rather than 'social' (or value) integration (Lockwood, 1964). This is an interesting way of neutralising the analytic problem of power/ideology in media theory. The media's most important effect, Scannell argues, is not to sustain certain specific ideologies at all, but to expand the sphere of the 'merely talkable about' (1989: 144).[15] But there are major problems with this approach. Scannell, for example, gives little space to considering how men and women, or people from different ethnic groups, might be 'integrated' into the media's 'universe of discourse' in different ways (or to different extents). He attempts to maintain a sharp line between non-ideological, systemic aspects of the media and more contentious matters of value. But even apparently neutral matters of media form may have specific, value-related connotations. An interview from Shaun Moores' ethnographic work on the impacts of satellite television in Britain illustrates this well. He quotes an Asian man who preferred watching the Sky Channel news, rather than the BBC: 'with the BBC you always feel as though the structure of society is there – the authority ... I think Sky News has more of a North American approach ... They treat you like equals' (Moores, 1993b: 635). Surely a common 'universe of discourse' may be as much a medium for audiences to grasp what they do *not* have in common as what they do? The empirical evidence for the socialising effects of radio and television is partial at best.[16] Worse, by concentrating on the unifying and integrative role of radio and television, Scannell seems to ignore how they may '*cut ... across* the geographies of power and social life which together define national or cultural space' (Rath, 1989: 89, added emphasis), or alternatively how they may reinforce the divisions already inherent within those geographies. The public world to which broadcasting connects us is not a pre-existing entity whose boundaries are consensually established, independently of what the media does. On the contrary, the public world's boundaries are the subject of continual definitional conflict in which the media play a central role (cf. Carey, 1989: 86–7). Yet Scannell gives little emphasis to the discursive hierarchies which remain integral to media production itself. When he does acknowledge them (1989: 162–5), their relation to his wider argument is undeveloped.

Scannell's work, then, avoids the difficulties of using media 'texts' or audiences to analyse questions of power and ideology, but at the cost of privileging issues of media form, as if they can be neatly separated off from matters of value. This move is problematic, since it ignores exactly those issues of power and ideology that arise in relation to the form of broadcasting itself, the concentration of symbolic power that it involves. As Baudrillard once commented, and as I will argue throughout, 'media ideology (or as I prefer to put it, the reproduction of media power) functions at the level of *form*' (1981: 169, original emphasis).

Another approach to the media/power relation has seemed more promising: what we might call an anthropology of media consumption. One strand of work[17] has developed an account of 'media-logic-in-use' (Traudt and Lont, 1987: 143), above all in the daily contexts of family life with their complex interaction between many technologies. A strength of this work has been to highlight the power relations inherent in such domestic contexts. Another strand of work has developed not so much the detailed anthropology of media consumption as an anthropological approach to the media's general symbolic significance. It is the latter that is more relevant to my argument.

Roger Silverstone's work on television, in particular, has explored the paradoxical relationship between its familiarity (its inescapable ordinariness) and its pervasive cultural and social significance. It is the former that makes the latter's effects so difficult to analyse (1981: vii, cf. above). Silverstone's work has gradually shifted away from studying the media at the level of particular texts (1981, chs 5 and 6; 1983) towards articulating the media as a social process at a broader level. Television works, he argues, not so much through specific texts, but through 'its occupation of the particular spaces and times of a basic level of social reality' (1994: 22). The same could be argued for other media: radio, the press. The media need to be understood as an overall social process, which of course involves both texts and audiences/listeners/readers, but need not only be analysed in terms of their direct interaction.

Silverstone has analysed how television operates at the most general cultural level, its 'mythic' dimension (1981, 1988). Television, he has argued, 'is the frame *par excellence* of our culture' (1981: 77). It is the institution of television that connects our 'mundane' everyday world to a wider world. This dimension of television – neglected in most other accounts – is of fundamental importance in understanding not only television but also the media in general. It is central to the model of the naturalisation of the media's authority that I develop in Chapter 3. Silverstone, in part, adapts Durkheim's (1995) [1912] theory of the social generation of the sacred/profane distinction, introduced in the next section. First, however, I want to note one issue on which my approach differs from Silverstone's: how do we conceptualise the media's *differential* symbolic power and its social consequences?

Silverstone (like Scannell) has tried to keep separate questions of television's broad cultural function from questions of how television relates to specific ideological formations. Indeed, he has characterised his work as 're-thinking the relationship between mass culture and ideology' (1988: 22). There is a good reason for this. As Silverstone (1983: 149) argues against Bourdieu, not all issues of cultural form can be reduced to questions of legitimation or the arbitrary play of power. I agree: the premature application of ideological analysis leads to misleading and overgeneralised accounts of media culture. Perhaps this is the fundamental problem with earlier attempts to approach ideology and power principally through the media text. But the difficult question remains of how media culture and power/ideology in the media interrelate and, while Silverstone frequently acknowledges it, he does not fully resolve it. His separation of the 'mythic' (the workings of all cultures at some fundamental level) from the 'ideological' (historical formations of power) is too sharp. It obscures the important point that *our* 'myths' – the most central meanings of *our* culture – function principally through a frame (the media) which is itself a historically specific social mechanism with particular power effects. To that extent, issues of culture can never be kept separate from issues of power.[18]

I need now to explain the basis of my own approach to media power. This shares with Silverstone's model a Durkheimian starting-point, but then takes a different course.

## AN ALTERNATIVE MODEL OF MEDIA POWER

John Corner has written recently that 'the conception of "power" within a notion of televisual process has now become a matter of the utmost importance and difficulty' (1997: 258). The same might be said of 'power' within the media process more generally. As we have seen, both media text and audience have proved problematic as starting-points and, even in work that tries to move beyond them, there remains a tension between preserving a sense of the complex context of daily media consumption and maintaining our grip on the issue of media power. In particular, how can we integrate into our analysis the effects of the concentration of symbolic power in media institutions?

My focus, quite deliberately, is not on how media outputs reflect specific external pressures (ideological, economic, statist, and so on), or other detailed issues of media representation. My argument works at a more general level, focusing on questions of social ontology, rather than epistemology: on how the media affect what kind of things become 'social facts' and 'social realities' at all.

## An analogy from Durkheim

Any theorisation of the media's social impacts must start from their privileged role in *framing* our experiences of the social, and thereby defining what the 'reality' of our society is. It is Silverstone (1981, 1983, 1988) who has analysed this most precisely, with particular reference to television. Television is, he argues, a ritual 'frame': a cognitive, imaginative, and practical space through which everyone can access simultaneously the things that mark off the 'social' – what is shared by everyone – from the private and particular.[19]

This analysis derives in part from Durkheim's theory (1995) [1912] of how religion's pervasive distinction between 'sacred' and 'profane' is socially generated. Crucial here is Durkheim's underlying distinction between social experience and ordinary experience, the force of which, he argues, grounds the sacred/profane distinction itself. This force derives from the individual's awe in the presence of the 'social' (1995: 208–25). Durkheim's account relates specifically to the sense of the sacred in a particular nomadic Aboriginal society, which came together only occasionally for ritual occasions focused around totemic objects. But in spite of its particularity, Durkheim's description of the totemic object's power is still highly suggestive for an analysis of television:

> Imputing the emotions [of the social: NC] to the image is all the more natural because being common to the group, they can only be related to a thing that is equally common to all. Only the totemic emblem meets this condition. *By definition, it is common to all. During the ceremony, all eyes are upon it.* Although the generations change, the image remains the same. It is the abiding element of social life.
>
> (ibid.: 222, emphasis added)

Analogously, in a society of almost universal television consumption, and largely shared patterns of programme availability,[20] the simple fact that television is 'by definition ... common to all' itself grounds its function as a frame for the social. As Silverstone puts it, television's 'authority depends on its continual presence' (1983: 150). This function has over time been reinforced by many 'media events' (Dayan and Katz, 1992) when television has performed the framing role quite explicitly (major sports events, royal ceremonial, political crises), but it is not only a dimension of exceptional media events; it is inherent to the media's permanent position as the frame through which private worlds face the social.

At this general, functional level, it is artificial to separate television from other mass media: radio and the press. The social role of radio is often underestimated (Scannell, 1996). As for the press, it is true that (with its highly segmented readership) it is not a mass medium in quite the same way as television and radio (Abercrombie, 1996: 153), but even the press are characterised by their regular and very wide availability. All media, in any case, interpenetrate in consumption. The crucial point is not the differences between media, but the framing function of 'the media' (the institutional sphere of the media) as a whole.

I develop this argument in more detail in Chapter 3. But at this stage, I want to bring out how it connects with a second argument about the categorisation, or *ordering*, of the social world. Important here, once again, is Durkheim's theory of the social origins of religion: particularly his account of the 'sacred'/'profane' distinction (1995: 33–9). I am not of course claiming that the media are literally 'sacred' (cf. Silverstone, 1981: 181). Rather, the sacred/profane distinction is a useful structural analogue for a different distinction: between 'media world' and 'ordinary world'. This distinction, I will argue, is particularly important in naturalising the media's concentration of symbolic power.

What distinguishes the division between 'sacred' and 'profane' according to Durkheim is not a question of content ('anything ... can be sacred', 1995: 35), nor the fact that it is used to rank objects and people (there are many forms of ranking whose significance is less profound), but simply the fact that the division is 'absolute': 'the sacred and the profane are always and everywhere conceived by the human intellect as separate genera, as two worlds with nothing in common' (ibid.: 36). The division divides 'the world into two domains, one containing all that is sacred and the other all that is profane' (ibid.: 34). It is for this reason that maintaining this division in practice requires a general separation of sacred and profane things (ibid.: 38): a parallel to the separation of media production from the rest of society, already noted.

We can leave aside debates about whether Durkheim's analysis of the social origins of the sacred/profane distinction is useful within the sociology of religion. What matters here is that it is a useful model of how the symbolic division between 'media world' and 'ordinary world' arises; this division is fundamental to understanding the media's social impacts. The media/ordinary division underlies, for example, the frequent contrast between 'media people' and 'ordinary people'. Like the sacred/profane distinction, it seems effectively absolute, a naturalised division of the way the world 'is'. Yet it too is socially grounded. Just as the sacred/profane distinction is (according to Durkheim) grounded in the way the social is framed in a sacred context, so too the framing of the social through the media is what grounds a pervasive distinction between 'media world' (everything associated with the media process) and 'ordinary world' (everything outside it).

It is at this point that we reach the limits of a Durkheimian model. The media/ordinary distinction, I would argue, is certainly not a 'social fact' in the Durkheimian sense: it is not beyond contestation. Although it operates *as if* absolute, it is constructed, not natural. It cuts across and reshapes social reality, reifying the vast sector of social life outside media production as a so-called 'ordinary' domain (see Chapter 3). It also masks the complexities of media production processes themselves. And above all, it disguises (and therefore helps naturalise) the inequality of symbolic power which media institutions represent. We must extend the Durkheimian model considerably, if we are to analyse the issues of power and inequality inherent to centralised institutions of representation, whether religion- or media-based (cf. Elliott, 1980). This is no reason, however, to reject the insights which Durkheim offers into the media's social significance. On the contrary, his analysis of how apparently absolute distinctions are socially generated remains essential to explaining how we have come to accept the concentration of symbolic power in media institutions as natural.

## The media as social process

The challenge is to connect these very general concerns with detailed empirical work. The connection lies in analysing how people interact with the media process, or (to use a working term which is useful here) people's 'interactions with the media frame'.

I use the term 'media frame' here purely as a working term. 'Frame' is chosen because it connects to the media's function of 'framing' the social (on which see further, Chapter 3).[21] Using 'frame' in this way contrasts with two other quite common uses of the 'framing' metaphor in media studies and sociology: first, in terms of the devices through which media texts structure or 'frame' our perception of the realities they represent (compare the idea of a 'storytelling frame'); and, second, in terms of the framework of expectations and plans which are associated with, or 'frame', an action (the notion of an 'action frame'). While occasionally I draw on these usages, the terms 'frame' and 'media frame' will normally refer to the media's role as the ritual frame which focuses our access to the 'social'. It is this much broader sense that is important to my argument.

I intend the term 'media frame' to cover here both 'objective' *and* 'subjective' aspects of the media's workings. By 'objective' aspects, I mean: the totality of media institutions, the social, economic, and regulatory frameworks that connect them together, the organisational and other constraints which affect their work, and the actual patterns of inclusion and exclusion which characterise how media institutions represent social life. By 'subjective' aspects, I mean: the various cultural and social processes through which those objective aspects are adapted culturally, that is, how they are themselves 'mediated'. By 'the media', as already mentioned, I mean, principally, the common-sense definition of the various mass media: television, radio, and the press. A related term is the 'media mechanism' (used in the singular). I use this to refer to the media's objective status as a form or mechanism of representing the social world.

'Objective' and 'subjective' aspects of the media frame are, of course, closely interwoven, so the purpose of distinguishing between them here is purely to clarify what types of research strategy we can adopt. We may concentrate on the 'objective' aspects of interactions with the media frame (who works in the media, who the media represent, who they do not, and so on) or on 'subjective' aspects (for example, how media stars become spaces for imaginative identification). A further alternative – and this will be my approach – is to focus on the naturalisation inherent to the media frame: that is, the processes through which the 'objective' features of the media frame are normally masked behind its 'subjective' aspects. The ambivalence of the term 'media frame' reflects precisely the workings of this process of naturalisation.[22] As already suggested, the key to understanding this naturalisation is to study the moments when it is disrupted. At such moments, people become wholly or partly aware of interacting with the objective aspects of the media frame: they move between its 'subjective' and 'objective' aspects.

People's accounts of such moments reveal, I suggest, something of wider significance. When we consume the media in the ordinary course of events, our primary concern is not likely to be with the objective features of the media mechanism, the actual processes it involves. In textual consumption, we interact with the media principally as 'nature', not as 'history': they function as 'habitus', 'history turned into nature' (Bourdieu, 1977: 78; see further Chapter 3). There are exceptions – for example, soap audiences' knowledge of aspects of the production process[23] – but even that knowledge is consistent with leaving the wider naturalisation of media power undisturbed. Instead, I will look at situations where that naturalisation is disrupted. As Callon and Latour have remarked, the challenge for sociology is always 'knowing where to place oneself':

> [the sociologist] sits just at the point where the contract is made, just where forces are translated, and the difference between the technical and the social is fought out, just where the irreversible becomes reversible ...
>
> (1981: 301)

Similarly, my interview material provides insights into just those points in the media process 'where forces are translated', where the naturalised authority of the media ceases to be 'nature' and becomes strange, even contestable: what we might call metaphorically the 'place' of media power.

## Structure of the book

Place (in the geographical sense) is also central to the study of media power, as I argue in Chapter 2, which also explains what I draw from recent 'postmodern' theories of space, place and the media, and where I differ from them. In Chapter 3 I develop a detailed theoretical model of the social, symbolic and spatial processes which help naturalise media power. I then explore those processes through the evidence provided by two types of 'limit situation'. Part 2 looks at visits to media tourist sites (filming sites, such as Granada Studios Tour, site of the *Coronation Street* set) where people come close to the media production process. In the main chapter of Part 3 (Chapter 7), I consider situations at news events where non-media people see at first hand the media production process applied to events that concern them. A third area, emerging from the second, is people's practices of 'alternative mediation', their attempts to contest how situations are mediated: these are analysed in Chapter 8 of Part 3.

Through analysing people's talk and actions in these various situations, I intend to trace how the media's concentration of symbolic power is normally naturalised and occasionally de-naturalised. Another way of characterising my interview material is through a series of spatial metaphors. In Part 2, I look at people's voluntary visits to places featured in the media. These journeys can, in some ways, be seen as *pilgrimages*: that is, journeys to central places of commonly agreed value. They are, of course, places of leisure: the main example studied is Granada Studio Tours in Manchester, the site of the external set of the long-standing British television soap, *Coronation Street*. In Chapter 7 of Part 3, the focus shifts to situations where people find themselves present at places where aspects of media production can be observed directly and without any entertainment packaging. These are places where people *witness* the media process (as well as aspects of the political and law enforcement process). My main example of 'witnessing' is the protest against live animal exports in the port of Brightlingsea on the British east coast in 1995. In Chapter 8 I consider more active forms of 'witnessing', which involve symbolic production: that is, experiences of witnessing orientated towards contributing to the media process itself.

Chapter 9 draws these threads together and considers how my argument is likely to be affected by coming changes in media technology. I also place the argument within wider debates about the future of media sociology, especially debates between 'political economy' and 'culturalist' approaches.

## Some parallels

No new development in media sociology, or any other subject, occurs in isolation, and the same is true of my own focus on people's encounters with the media process beyond textual consumption. It is worth briefly clarifying this book's relation to other work that might seem most relevant to its main argument.

One general precedent is Altheide and Snow's work on how the media's organisational and cognitive forms are absorbed into everyday life. Their unjustly neglected analysis raises important questions about the whole media field: for example, the impact of media formats on how information is processed and the impact of media coverage on individuals such as sports personalities (Altheide, 1985). They work, however, with rather broad notions such as 'media logic' (Altheide and Snow, 1979) and 'media culture' (Snow, 1983; cf. Real, 1996), without quite making clear how they are reproduced in practice or how they relate to issues of symbolic power. A closer parallel is studies of fandom (for example: Bacon-Smith, 1992; Harrington and Bielby, 1995; Jenkins, 1992; Lewis, 1993; Stacey, 1994; Vermorel and Vermorel, 1985) and celebrity watching (Gamson, 1994). This work has been crucial in focusing attention on the symbolic practices of media consumers and is therefore important background to my own case studies, particularly Part 2. I am, however, concerned less with the practices of fans as a separate group, than with more general frameworks of meaning and naturalisation, which affect both fans and other, less engaged consumers. I will not therefore draw in detail on the fandom literature, important though it is.

A further precedent, at least for Part 3 which deals with people's experiences of news events, is 'critical events analysis' (Kraus, Davis, Lang and Lang, 1975). This aimed to analyse how news events are produced and consumed as part of 'the full social process in which élite actions are linked to public actions and social change' (ibid.: 208) (cf. Lang and Lang, 1969; Michaels, 1994). This involved studying not just the 'direct effects' of news coverage on audiences, but the whole social process of production and consumption, including interactions at the site of the news event and the impact of coverage on participants (ibid.: 210). There is also a growing tradition of work on the media strategies of social and political activists, although (as explained in Chapter 2) its emphasis is rather different from mine.

The most important recent parallel has been investigations of non-media people's experiences of appearing on television talk shows. There have been detailed studies of US participants (Gamson, 1998; Grindstaff, 1997; Priest, 1995, 1996) and UK participants (Livingstone and Lunt, 1994).[24] Priest's account is particularly striking since it could not have been developed through any form of audience studies: many of her informants were not regular television viewers at all (1995: 194), yet they registered the social impacts of television in important ways.

I will draw insights from such work at various points. What is needed, however, is a wider theoretical framework for understanding how the media's social authority is reproduced.


## THE STORY SO FAR

This book attempts to provide just such a theory, based not on media texts or audiences' interpretations of them (reception studies), nor on the structure and economics of media institutions and media markets (political economy), but based instead on analysing the direct interactions between non-media people and media institutions, and non-media people's talk about them.

This is hardly a mainstream position. I have developed it as a way out of the impasse which critical media theory now faces: how to acknowledge the sheer complexity of the media's colonisation of everyday life (cf. Corner, 1995: 44), without losing a grip on the crucial questions of power and inequality to which the media give rise? Exclusively text-based approaches simply aren't adequate. That means shifting the focus from the usual question of how far the media help reproduce external power structures to the underlying question of the symbolic power concentrated in media institutions themselves (cf. Garnham, 1986). How is that concentration of power reproduced as legitimate and naturalised? As we have seen, my answer begins at the theoretical level from an analogy with Durkheim's work and the symbolic division between 'media' and 'ordinary' 'worlds', what in Chapter 3 I will analyse in more detail as 'the symbolic hierarchy of the media frame'. This division and the hierarchy to which it gives rise is not natural but a construction, a reification, an arbitrary division of the social world.

It might, however, be argued against my own approach that it too involves a reification: it sets things up in advance in terms of an opposition between non-media world and media world, between non-media people and media people. Ultimately, I must leave this for the reader to judge in the light of the detailed empirical analysis of Parts 2 and 3. The immediate answer, however, is that, although the hierarchy of value (between 'ordinary person' and 'media person', 'ordinary world' and 'media world') is *constructed*, the difference of symbolic resources between those outside media institutions and those within them is *real*.[25] There is a real difference in terms of ability to make yourself heard and have your account of social reality accepted. Obviously it is not only media institutions which concentrate symbolic resources, and entry-conditions into media industries are themselves shaped by many social variables; as a result, the study of media power must ultimately be linked to the study of other types of power. Far too often, however, it has been neglected entirely in social analysis, as if it could simply be reduced to other factors (state power, economic power). But it is precisely the real difference in symbolic resources between media institutions and those outside them that underlies the arbitrary symbolic division of the social into two 'worlds' ('media' and 'ordinary'). This division has an impact on social reality that is profound, even if generally hidden.

To put the emphasis so firmly on how the symbolic power of media institutions operates at a general level cuts across some usual assumptions of media sociology. First, it requires a single analysis that bridges two areas of media production which normally are considered separately: factual and fictional programming. Not only, however, is the boundary between factual and fictional programming often blurred in practice (Corner, 1995: 13–14; Dahlgren, 1995: 38–9), but it is a fallacy to believe that media power is only socially significant where factual representations are involved. As I argue more fully in Chapter 3, it is, in part, the concentration of so many functions in a limited number of media institutions – both the provision of information *and* the focusing of social imagination, both news *and* soaps – that makes media power so difficult to challenge. A unified analysis of the impacts of media power is therefore essential.

It might, also, be argued that my approach gives too little emphasis to the positive aspects of media cultures: the shared pleasures most people (myself included) derive from the media, the ways we all use media materials as resources in everyday talk and in the longer-term construction of identity. Those pleasures are hardly trivial; they are, it can be argued, essential means by which people cope with other social inequalities (see, for example, Brown, 1994; Dyer, 1992; Lipsitz, 1990; McRobbie, 1991; Riggs, 1996; Walkerdine, 1995). This is an important point and I have been conscious throughout the writing of this book of the need to keep it firmly in mind. Far from denying the positive aspects of media culture, my argument is that it is in part *through* the many processes by which the media are absorbed into everyday social life (including the pleasures they generate) that an additional level of social inequality is entrenched: the inequality between those with greater access to the media's symbolic power and those with less. Yet the more media are involved in our fantasies, our self-images, and our descriptions of reality, the more this underlying inequality matters – both sociologically and, I would argue also, politically.

It is here that my argument stands opposed to some other recent work in media sociology, particularly Abercrombie and Longhurst's interesting book *Audiences* (1998). Some of their premises are similar to mine. They emphasise media saturation, the embedding of media material in everyday life, the interaction between media in a general media environment, and the importance of studying localities of media-related interaction rather than an abstracted process of textual reception (ibid.: 87–8, 161, 170). However, their proposed 'new paradigm' for audience studies differs markedly from mine. Whereas I argue that power issues – above all, power differences between non-media people and media institutions – remain central to analysing the media's social effects, Abercrombie and Longhurst argue that they should be 'assigned a lower priority' (ibid.: 97). Both 'audiencing' and performing (whether for real or imagined audiences) have, they claim, become pervasive in a media-saturated society suffused by 'spectacle' and 'narcissism'. It is more important, therefore, to concentrate on people's uses of shared media materials in forming their own identities than on underlying power issues in the media process. In fact, they write sometimes as if underlying issues of power relating to the media had simply disappeared. So they claim that 'in contemporary society, everyone becomes an audience all the time' and that 'media institutions do not interpose between performer and audience' (ibid.: 68, 75). These statements elide a vital dimension of media-saturated

21

societies: the inequality in the power of 'naming' social reality which the media themselves constitute.

This inequality is, of course, easily missed, since it is disguised by layer upon layer of naturalisation. But it should not just be swept under the carpet. There is an interesting parallel here with the complexities of class divisions. Richard Sennett and Jonathan Cobb (1972) wrote movingly more than twenty-five years ago about 'the *hidden* injuries of class': the impact on individuals of the naturalised distinctions between people which a class system involves. If the media themselves constitute a social division (cf. Baudrillard, 1981: 167), then we need to ask: what are the hidden impacts of this division on members of contemporary mediated societies? How is that inequality lived with and adjusted to? How, perhaps by the very same process, is it reproduced? And what, finally, does it mean to contest it?

# 2

# CHARTING MEDIA TERRITORY

Much of the content of modern communications ... is a form of shared consciousness rather than merely a set of techniques. And as a form of consciousness it is not to be understood by rhetorical analogues like the 'global village'. Nothing could be less like the experience of any kind of village or settled active community. For in its main uses *it is a form of un-evenly shared consciousness of persistently external events*. It is what appears to happen, in these powerfully transmitted and mediated ways, in a world with which we have no other perceptible connections but which we feel is at once central and marginal to our lives.

(Williams, 1973: 295–6, added emphasis)

## INTRODUCTION

Having introduced my approach to issues of media power and people's inter-actions with the media as a social process, the question arises how we should understand the media process as inherently also a *spatial* process. In the first part of this chapter, I develop this theme, partly through some reflections on other work that has considered the connections between media and space, and partly through some initial reflections on the nature of 'space' and 'place' more generally. That will set the scene for the second part of the chapter, which explains the strategy behind Parts 2 and 3 with their empirical material drawn from particular media locations.

The media's impacts on territory and on social space have attracted many sweeping claims, from McLuhan's vision of the global village to Baudrillard's pronouncement that 'henceforth, it is the map that precedes the territory' (1983a: 2): in other words, the media's representations of space take precedence over the features of space itself. While there is something important in these claims, I want to develop a different emphasis, arguing not for the media's homogeneous, unidirectional impact on space, but for the *unevenness* of such impacts. The media profoundly affect the spatial organisation of social life, but they do not efface it. If they did, that would rule out in advance the possibility of any places where the de-naturalisation of the media frame might be experienced. The interviews analysed later tell a different story.

There is a tension between grand theoretical claims about the media's impact on territory (particularly within 'postmodern' perspectives) and the lack of empirical research into the lived experiences of such change (cf. Moores, 1993a: 375). I want to explore that tension, as a way of introducing in more detail the research strategy that underlies Parts 2 and 3. I will argue that 'postmodern' accounts of the 'collapse' of space and/or place through mediation, while raising important issues, are not sufficiently grounded in empirical research; in fact, they underplay the tensions within those accounts themselves. Various writers have argued for the media's 'de-differentiating' (Lash, 1990) effects, whether on the fiction/reality distinction (Baudrillard), the segregations of social space (Meyrowitz), or the places where narrative and memory cohere (Jameson, Nora, Huyssen), but, in doing so, they have tended to underestimate the unevenness with which forces of de-differentiation are played out in practice and are themselves socially and culturally mediated. Such forces of de-differentiation give rise to new forms of differentiation, and this point is central to understanding the media's social consequences.

The need for caution in this area is already clear when we consider the complexity of space itself. Space has both objective and subjective aspects, which do not simply reinforce, but may conflict with, each other. There is a duality between space's organisational and imaginary dimensions (Lefebvre, 1991b: 182–3; Sack, 1992: xiii), well formulated by Heidegger in his discussion of 'primordial spatiality': 'the Objective distances of Things present-at-hand do not coincide with the remoteness and closeness of what is ready-to-hand within-the-world ... That which is presumably "closest" is by no means that which is at the smallest distance "from us" (1962 [1927]: 141). In other words, the way we imagine space is not reducible to the way space itself is organised. The electronic media's impact on social space is therefore inevitably complex. In fact, even if we consider the material aspects of spatial organisation, they involve the co-ordination not just of presences but also of *absences*. This follows, for example, from the fundamental principle of Torsten Hagerstrand's 'time-geography' (1975, 1978), that space's 'packing' capacity is limited. As Hagerstrand put it, 'in a given area only a limited number [can be] present simultaneously' (1978: 124). As a result, co-ordinating certain people's presences means co-ordinating other people's absences. This is an important point to which I shall return.

This complexity is compounded when we think about 'place', that is, locations in space that have significance for human agents. Places too have both material and imaginative aspects. As the geographer Tim Cresswell has put it, 'places are neither totally material not completely mental; they are combinations of the material and the mental, and cannot be reduced to either' (1996: 130). The ways in which meanings become attached to place are themselves highly subtle, involving connections between many scales of action. David Sibley (1995) has argued that there is a reciprocal conditioning between personal and social territory: the symbolic practices that generate our sense of self influence, those that generate our sense of domestic and social space, and vice versa. The meanings of place, then, have a density which is irreducible.

The implications of these points were stated most clearly by Doreen Massey. As she has written, 'what has come together in this place, now, is a conjunction of many histories and many spaces' (1995: 191). All places are intersections of many dynamic relations, including some 'constructed on a far larger scale than what we happen to define for that moment as the place itself' (Massey, 1994: 154). Places therefore do not, even in principle, have univocal meanings (ibid.: 155),[26] and this is true, even without considering the impacts of the media. Why assume, then, that the media's impact on place, space, and territory would be anything other than complex and contradictory?

Surprisingly, however, the relations between media and geography remain undertheorised. There have been calls for a rapprochement between media/cultural studies and geography,[27] but they have not so far been fulfilled. There have been large-scale theories but, as we shall see in the next section, they have tended to underestimate the complexity of the processes involved. If we turn to empirical work on the media (whether political economy or audience studies), it has tended to ignore the extent to which *the media themselves are a social process organised in space*. For example, as James Hay (1996, 1997) has argued,[28] audience studies have tended to privilege the home, as principal site of media consumption, while ignoring the wider set of spatial relations that the media process involves. In relation to film – but the point applies equally to television, radio, and the press – Hay suggests that:

> what is needed ... is a way of discussing film as a social practice that begins by considering how social relations are spatially organised – through sites of production and consumption – and how film is produced from and across particular sites and always in relation to other sites.
>
> (1997: 216)

This is a point of fundamental importance, since it recalls the possibility (mentioned at the beginning of Chapter 1) that the media – once we see them not as texts, or institutions, but as an overall social process – involve the normal separation of production sites from consumption sites. The media process, in other words, involves the co-ordination not only of presences, but also of absences (cf. above). This connects with Durkheim's analysis of the necessary segregation of the 'sacred' and the 'profane' and has major implications for the naturalisation of media power. There is, then, a 'power-geometry' (Massey, 1994: 149) to the media process which is connected to the media's symbolic authority.[29]

At this point, we start to move beyond generalised connections between the media and territory (the rhetorical claims that Raymond Williams mocked in the opening quotation), and explore a detailed spatial logic of the 'media frame' (see Chapter 1). As Williams sensed, this logic is uneven. On the one hand, the geography of media consumption reinforces other patterns of segregation, enhancing the 'privatisation of social life' (Lodziak, 1987: 185–6; cf. Gitlin, 1987: 514; Williams, 1990: 26–31). On the other hand, there is the special status of places featured in media production: the studios, the locations, the sites of witnessing news events, and so on. If this is correct, the media do not simply 'cover' territory, let alone 'collapse' the boundaries between places. Instead they shape it and reorganise it, creating new distances – for example, between the studio and the home – and building new presences, new places of significance. Taking these two points together, the 'media frame' involves a complex, but quite definite division between two types of place: a dispersed mass of sites where media consumption takes place, and a much more limited number of sites where the media are produced. This is the separation of the media sphere from the rest of social life that the Situationists highlighted (see further below).

At the same time, this separation is complicated through the multiplication of sites where access to the media is becoming available. What I have in mind is not so much the saturation of the whole consumer environment with references to media products (although that is clearly an important aspect of media geography as well), but more specifically the growth of 'access-points' where non-media people can, for a limited time and under certain conditions, connect with the process of media production. These may be sites where the boundary between 'media' and 'ordinary' 'worlds' is symbolically, but playfully, confirmed (such as the media tourist location) or sites where it is emphatically and perhaps shockingly revealed (the protest sites where people get close up to the media process which represents them).

Parts 2 and 3 will chart the uneven territory of mediated space in contemporary Britain through detailed studies of (1) journeys to mediated places, (2) sites of mediated conflict, and (3) practices of alternative mediation. But first, I want to look in greater detail at the contribution of theory, particularly postmodern theory, in this area, and the directions it suggests for empirical work.

## POSTMODERNISM, SPACE AND THE MEDIA

The general claim that there is a 'postmodern' order of space (or space-time) often underlies theories about the electronic media's social impact in 'postmodernity',[30] so it is worth noting at the outset that even the concept of 'postmodern space' involves tensions and contradictions.

Take David Harvey's important and subtle work on 'time-space compression' in postmodernity (1989). Despite his occasional unguarded claims of 'the annihilation of space through time' (ibid.: 299, cf. Marx, 1973: 539), he frequently brings out the contradictions of this process. Certainly, for some purposes, the consequences of spatial distance, and any time-lag associated with crossing it, have been reduced, even removed: accelerations in transportation, information transmission, and so on. As the speed and quantity of material flows of all sorts has massively increased, so possibilities of co-ordination between activities in different places have increased exponentially. But the result is not a dissolution of space, but much greater potential for *controlling* space and, accordingly, new forms of spatial differentiation (ibid.: 233–9). Another geographer, Donald Janelle, has developed this point (1991: 49–52). Accelerated flows of information and people always involve 'nodes' through which those flows pass: what matters, economically and socially, is where you are in relation to those nodes. Such access entails costs, which many (perhaps most) cannot meet. 'Time-space convergence' therefore takes effect as '*cost*-space convergence' (ibid.), in which differences in economic resources and 'spatial' resources (where you are positioned) are mutually reinforcing. This process has been memorably formulated by Doreen Massey as 'the power-geometry of time-space compression' (1994: 149), in which the production of peripheries is as important as the formation of centres (cf. Soja, 1989). We have already seen the usefulness of this concept for understanding the media process itself. It is too simple, then, to claim that place has ceased to matter in 'postmodernity', although this has been argued by many writers on various grounds - whether the increasing speed and abstraction of travel (Auge, 1995; Schivelbusch, 1978), the increasingly commodified nature of public environments (Boorstin, 1961; Relph, 1976; Sorkin, 1992), or the almost instantaneous transmission of information and images (Virilio, 1986). As Eric Swyngedouw (1989) has argued, instead of place always mattering less, it may in some respects have come to matter more. This is an important possibility, which my case studies explore in relation to the media.

More broadly, we cannot simply read off from changes in spatial organisation to changes in people's experiences of space and place. The latter are processes of social and cultural mediation, which require separate empirical enquiry. We need people's 'reason-giving accounts', if we are to grasp 'the lived experiences of time-space compression' (Agnew, 1987: 231; Moores,

1993a: 375). It is worth briefly reviewing some well-known theories of how the media have altered social space, keeping this note of caution in mind.

Baudrillard's pronouncements on the media's social impacts are wellknown: for example, his claims that there is an 'implosion of meaning in the media' which makes non-belief in media reference-points impossible (1983b: 97–9), and that all reality is now 'simulation', 'inscribed in advance in the decoding and orchestration rituals of the media' (1983a: 41), so that the 'real' 'is no longer real at all' (ibid.: 3). Baudrillard's claims have their basis in an argument which is implicitly geographical. The crucial feature of the media, as he argued in 'Requiem for the Media' (1981) [1969], is not their role as broadcasters of content, but that 'in their form and very operation [they] induce a social relation', a 'social *division*' between media producers and media consumers (ibid.: 169).

The spatial implications of this point had already been made explicit by the Situationists (Debord, 1983 [1967]; Vaneigem, 1989 [1963]), themselves inspired by the philosopher and geographer Henri Lefebvre. The connection between media power and the separation of the media from the rest of society was summed up well by Guy Debord in his famous text 'The Society of the Spectacle':

> The images detached from every aspect of life fuse in a common stream in which the unity of this life can no longer be reestablished. Reality considered *partially* unfolds ... as a pseudo-world *apart*, an object of mere contemplation ... The spectacle presents itself simultaneously as all of society, as part of society, and as *instrument of unification*. As a part of society it is specifically the sector which concentrates all gazing and all consciousness. <u>Due to the very fact that this sector is *separate*</u>, it is the common ground of the deceived gaze ... and the unification it achieves is nothing but an official language of generalized separation.
>
> (1983, paras 2–3, original italics, underlining added)

This emphasis on the separation of media from the rest of society (explicit in the Situationists and implicit in Baudrillard) is a fundamental insight, to which we will return. Baudrillard, however, develops it further than the Situationists (1983a: 54) by arguing that everyday reality is now so saturated by media images that the underlying separation of representation and reality *itself* becomes impossible to grasp. We live in an age where we are overwhelmed with media images of 'the real', but have no reference-points left from which to judge whether they are based in truth or not. Image and 'reality' become inseparable in the 'hyperreal'. Nonetheless, Baudrillard argues, we seek to compensate for this underlying loss of reality in two ways: first, by the excessive simulation of the real (his most famous example is Disneyland: 1983a, 25); and second, through the continual search for an underlying level of social life which is still real, i.e. truly independent of representation. We

28

are caught up in what Baudrillard calls 'nostalgia' for the real (ibid.: 12). As we shall see, these points are highly suggestive for the analysis of media territory I will make in terms of 'pilgrimage' and 'witnessing'.

The relation of Baudrillard's theories to empirical work is, however, problematic, partly because of his own apparent contempt for empirical sociology (1983b), and partly because of the extreme generalisation of his statements. For example, he writes that the media are, without qualification, 'a closed system of models of signification from which no event escapes' (1981: 175). Having identified a potential crisis of representation, Baudrillard reifies it (Martin-Barbero, 1993: 59). De-naturalising the media's authority is therefore ruled out in advance.

At one point, Baudrillard takes as support for his argument the example of an early US TV verité series about the Loud family. The result of the programme was that the real family split up.[31] For Baudrillard, any contact between media consumers and the media mechanism is automatically destructive since there is no escape from the imperatives of television. As he says of the Loud family, 'it is TV which is [their] truth' (1983a: 51). Even if you want to stand outside media power, 'it is impossible to locate an instance of the model, of the power, of the gaze, of the medium itself, since *you* are always already on the other side' (ibid.: original emphasis). Here, surely, Baudrillard's theory needs to be opened up to empirical work.[32] It seems less like a sociological theory, and more like a 'theological' schema (Huyssen, 1995: 188). Is it true that the experience of being mediated *never* leads to the de-naturalisation of the media's authority and the media's framing of reality? My case studies suggest otherwise.

Joshua Meyrowitz's (1985) account of the electronic media's social effects is, arguably, more nuanced. Adapting Goffman's situational analysis, Meyrowitz articulates how the media affect behaviour by reorganising the settings of social interaction. They alter the patterns of information flow available to people between and within situations (ibid.: 36–7). By allowing us to see into distant situations and obtain information previously only available face-to-face, television collapses what were previously segregated sets of encounters (in politics and social life generally) into translocal mediated 'situations'. As a result, new information flows occur between social groups (genders, age-groups, the powerful and the powerless). Through the electronic media, both socialisation and public life have changed radically. The impacts on places are equally profound according to Meyrowitz. There is a weakening of the once strong relationship between physical place and social "place"' (ibid.: ix). It remains true that we sense the world *from* a locality, but the sense we make of it may not be 'local'. Our perceptual horizons are 'electronically extended' (1989: 325) at all levels, so that 'the locality is not simply subsumed in a national or global sphere; rather it is increasingly bypassed in both directions … Experience is unified beyond localities and fragmented within them' (ibid.: 332).

This important argument has had wide influence within contemporary spatial and social theory. John Thompson, for example, has argued that the media have created new forms of social interaction, and new ways of exercising power, no longer tied to a shared local setting (1995: 4). Thompson (more than Meyrowitz) notes the negative aspects of this transformation, including the media's involvement in the dissemination of ideological forms and people's growing dependency on media resources (ibid.: 214–15), while acknowledging the increasing importance of 'struggles of visibility' within the mediated public sphere (ibid.: 247). McKenzie Wark (1994) has developed the implications of Meyrowitz's, and also Debord's (1983) and Virilio's (1986), work for the analysis of global media events. Such events involve, he argues, conflicts between two types of spatial relation: 'the territory' (people's localised social relations) and 'the map' (the network of media-sourced images which form people's imaginary map of their lived terrain and its 'others'). Both Thompson's and Wark's work is valuable for drawing out the complex implications of Meyrowitz's argument, whether in terms of power or in terms of how we experience place and territory. They start to bring out the importance of thinking about how the structural changes in communicative flows emphasised by Meyrowitz are themselves socially mediated.

Meyrowitz's insights also need to be refined in relation to the geography of the media production process. As Paddy Scannell has pointed out (1996: 141), Meyrowitz nowhere considers how television produces its own locales (such as the studio). In fact, with the limited exception of the performance conditions of public figures, he neglects the question of how social action is affected by *being mediated*. Why not argue that media coverage massively *multiplies* the interconnections between places, rather than weakening our sense of place?[33] In that space of interconnections, instead of boundaries dissolving, new boundaries form. Our sense of place may indeed be intensified at points where the media mechanism is itself present, where we can witness, or imagine we are witnessing, the production process.

The danger of both Baudrillard's and Meyrowitz's arguments about the media's impacts on social space is that they flatten out the potential contradictions. The same can be argued for Paul Virilio's argument that, in an age of 'electronic audiencing' (both television and the computer screen), places become interchangeable in 'the atopia of a single interface' (n.d.: 16, 21), let alone McLuhan's earlier argument that through television '"time" has ceased, "space" has vanished' (McLuhan and Fiore, 1967: 63, quoted in Ferguson, 1990: 163). A similar conclusion applies when we consider arguments that the media have undermined our capacity for narrative, and therefore disturbed the very basis of social memory and personal identity. Recent work on social memory (Nora, 1984, 1989; Huyssen, 1995) has claimed that new forms of commemoration are becoming necessary because old memory-forms (based in spatially stable communities) have been lost, the media's contribution being generally assumed to be negative. Nora, for example, argues that 'we have seen the tremendous dilation of our very mode of his-torical perception which, *with the help of the media*, has substituted for a memory entwined in the intimacy of a collective heritage the ephemeral film of current events' (1989: 7–8, added emphasis; cf. Huyssen, 1995: 32, 255). Equally negative is Jameson's well-known work on postmodernism (1984), which draws on Baudrillard. Our media-saturated world, Jameson argues, is ordered by 'the logic of the simulacrum, with its transformation of older realities into television images'. As a result, we face a loss of our historical sense (ibid.: 85, 68). Arguments about the 'postmodern' dissolution of place re-emerge here as arguments about the loss of spatial contexts for storytelling and memory. But, as elsewhere, there is a danger of exaggeration. Although television is stereotypically the 'ephemeral' medium, we surely cannot neglect its role, or the role of other media, in contemporary storytelling (Lipsitz, 1990; Scannell, 1988a; Silverstone, 1981). Indeed, as Raphael Samuel argued (1994: 13–15), we must recognise television's role as an 'un-official source[] of historical knowledge' in our 'expanding historical cul-ture' (ibid.: 25), for example through historical documentaries and drama serials. As the case studies will show, forms of social memory may be chang-ing, but they persist even in relation to television itself. In fact, they are inte-gral to some of the journeys across media territory that I will describe. In all these cases, theory needs to be supplemented by empirical enquiry.

EMPIRICAL EXPLORATIONS

It is time now to link the discussion back to my specific case studies and the theory of media power introduced in Chapter One.

**Journeys to mediated places**

Baudrillard, notoriously, wrote of Disneyland that it was a place presented 'as imaginary in order to make us believe that the rest is real' (1983a: 25). It is all too easy to argue the same for the many places now attracting tourism for their associations with media production: whether Disney's own MGM stu-dios (at Disneyworld, Florida) and MCA's Universal Studios, also in Florida, or the many film and television drama locations in Britain and other coun-tries. Media tourist sites are increasingly important in the economics of the tourist industry. In the USA in 1996, Disney-MGM Studios and MCA's Universal Studios attracted 299,000 and 170,000 visitors, respectively, from the UK alone.[34] They each represent very substantial investments: Disney–MGM, for example, initially cost more than $500 million (Wasko, 1994: 56). The English Tourist Board now enthusiastically reports visitor numbers to media locations in its annual report; television locations attracted more than 4,500,000 visitors in 1997.[35]

The strong tradition of 'realism' and regionally specific settings in British television drama (Geraghty, 1991: 35) perhaps has given special impetus in Britain to such people's interest in visiting actual places of filming (American daytime soaps, for example, rarely have a specific regional location: Brown, 1994: 89–90). The largest UK media tourist location is Granada Studios Tour ('GST'), the home of the external set for the long-running television soap, *Coronation Street* and a number of other attractions. This will be the case study in Part 2. In addition, there are a number of smaller, less commercialised television sites, which also attract large numbers of visitors: for example, the locations of the soap *Emmerdale* (in the village of Farsley), the comedy series *Last of the Summer Wine* (at Holmfirth), and the popular drama *Heartbeat* (various sites in East Yorkshire). Most such television locations are situated in the North of England.[36] Also opened recently are exhibitions closely related to media production: 'The World of Coronation Street' in Blackpool (1995– ) also run by the entertainment group, Granada and 'The BBC Experience' (1997– ) in Broadcasting House.

We could see all such sites purely in terms of 'simulation' or 'fakery', and it is common for them to be dismissed in this way (see, for example, Jeffries, 1998). In Part 2, however, drawing on interviews with visitors to GST, I argue that this underestimates the complexity of such places, certainly of those where media production actually takes place (rather than pure exhibition spaces, such as 'The World of Coronation Street'). First of all, they are as much places for accessing 'the real' as for enjoying the pleasures of 'simulation' (using Baudrillard's terms): they are actual places of filming. Second, as places where people come closer than normal to the media production process, they yield insights into the processes by which media power is naturalised (cf. Chapter 1). It is precisely the symbolic hierarchy of the media frame (see Chapter 3) that makes such places special and worth visiting.

The desire to travel is, of course, not 'natural'; it is always 'socially constructed' (Urry, 1995: 213–14). What, therefore, are the social and cultural conditions in which travel to such media locations has come to seem 'natural'? There are many general factors. John Urry (1990, 1995) and Dean MacCannell (1976, 1992) have explored the complex reasons for the late twentieth-century growth in tourism: the search for the 'extraordinary' (Urry, 1990: 11–12), for authentic images of 'society and its works' (MacCannell, 1976: 55), or simply for 'the place or site which seems to bear meaning in itself' (Wright, 1985: 22). In 1980s Britain, the scale and direction of tourism has changed markedly, with a massive increase in tourism directed at 'local culture' (Urry, 1995: 152–62) and new objects now available for the 'tourist gaze', from work environments to the 'ordinary life' of distant times. Locations of television drama combine both 'local feel' and media significance, and therefore offer a double marketing opportunity. As sites from the media's own history, they connect interestingly with the wider growth of the heritage industry (on which, see Hewison, 1987; Samuel,

1994; Walsh, 1992) and 'nostalgia tourism' (Chaney, 1994: 168). Indeed, filming locations are now increasingly marketed as part of Britain's 'heritage'. The National Trust issues a guide to its sites which have been film and television locations.[37] Being used for filming can substantially increase tourist income for little-known places. This happened, for example, to the small Midlands town of Stamford, the location for BBC's historical costume drama series *Middlemarch* (Rice and Saunders, 1996). Against this background, one visitor to Granada Studios Tour I interviewed, Debbie, could plausibly tell me that 'every holiday' for her will be 'based around ( ... ) places that are shown on TV'.

Surprisingly, however, media tourist sites – both regular sites of media production and sites visited because they were once covered in the media[38] – have received little detailed academic attention, whether in tourism and leisure studies, or media sociology. Yet the significance of *places in the media* (what we might call 'media sites') is familiar to anyone who has been, for example, to a major football match. Their aura has been well described by Nick Hornby:

> there is this powerful sensation of being exactly in the right place at the
> right time; when I am at Highbury on a big night, or, of course, Wembley on an even bigger afternoon, I feel as though I am at the centre of
> the whole world ... when you look at your newspaper the next day ...
> there will be extensive space given over to an account of *your* evening.
>
> (1992: 200, original emphasis)

What Hornby captures is the sense that your experiences at the match form part of a wider narrative which everyone shares: by being at the match, your position in relation to the media frame is changed. Normally, 'your evening' is not news, and probably involves watching news about others! But when you are at the match, the position is reversed. This point – about the narratives you can tell of your experience – applies in varying degrees to all media tourist locations, and also to places featured in the news: whether the mediated protest sites discussed in Part 3, or sites of major disasters, such as the Lockerbie air disaster, which thousands visited (Rojek, 1993: 137–8). Yet, while there is a growing body of work on the ritual aspects of staged 'media events',[39] the wider significance of journeys to media locations has not been studied.

One approach to analysing such journeys is to draw on the anthropological study of 'pilgrimage'. Tourism has often been analysed in terms of 'pilgrimage' (Urry, 1990: 10–11), reflecting the popular usage of the term 'pilgrimage' for any special journey to a historical site. But there is a specific appropriateness of the pilgrimage metaphor to media locations, because of the symbolic hierarchy built into the media frame itself. Visiting a media location is a 'liminal' or at least 'liminoid' activity (Turner, 1974), involving crossing the boundary between 'media world' and 'ordinary world' (see Chapter 3): more simply, the location is a place where you can get close to the media process. Corporate marketing of media locations often exploits this (Davis, 1996: 411): for example, one Granada Studios Tour brochure spoke of visits to the 'hallowed cobbles' of *Coronation Street* (i.e. the set). The viewer is in any case drawn to the imaginary space 'behind' the screen. Television, Christopher Anderson argues, constantly 'invoke[s] a sublime, unmediated experience that is forever absent, just beyond a hand reaching for the television dial' (1994: 82–3). Hence, the initial validity of the 'pilgrimage' metaphor.[40] I discuss in Chapter 4 whether a more detailed pilgrimage model can be developed.

The experiences of visitors are obviously crucial to developing such an analysis. Yet we know little about the visitors' perspective.[41] Spaces such as the Disney theme parks have either been 'read' as 'texts' for their ideological significance or judged according to their 'real' or 'fictive' status. As David Buckingham has remarked, to ignore the complexities of the visiting experience itself is to lose any detailed sense of how ideological or other social processes work there (1997: 288). The whole point of my case study in Part 2 is to open up such perspectives by studying visitors' talk.

Journeys to media sites have a clear significance from another perspective. Trust in the media is an important dimension of dispersed, 'disembedded' social systems (Giddens, 1990: 21) in which everyone must rely on various mechanisms that provide information or advice on matters remote from everyday experience (ibid.: 83–8). Yet there are places where what Giddens calls 'reembedding' occurs: 'access-points' where our generalised trust in institutions can be redeemed (ibid.: 88). Media locations (where you *see*, and stand in, the places that have been filmed) are precisely such points of 'reembedding' where the viewer can confirm that there is something behind the images on the screen. Again, the significance of this will become clearer in the light of the theoretical model of Chapter 3.

## Sites of mediated conflict

Part 3 will analyse non-media people's experiences of the media production process at several sites of protest action. It is in such cases, more so than at the leisure sites considered in Part 2, that the de-naturalisation of the media frame is possible. It is from this highly specific perspective that I study the interactions of social activists with the media. Part 3's analyses are quite different therefore from recent work on social organisations' media strategies (for example, Camauer, forthcoming; Gamson, 1995; Gitlin, 1980; van Zoonen, 1992, 1996). My interest is in people's accounts of their interactions with the media frame in conflict situations, part of what we might call 'the phenomenology' of the media frame. What is it like for people who are normally media consumers to see the media production process at first hand and to be able then to compare it to broadcast outputs? What implications do these experiences have for their attitudes to the media? What does their talk about these experiences tell us about the normal naturalisation of media power?

Part 3's main case study analyses the experiences of protesters against live animal exports at the English east coast port of Brightlingsea in 1995. The specific background to that conflict and the others discussed in Part 3 will be given there. Here, I want to place such conflicts within the broader context of resistance to the Conservative government which ruled Britain under Margaret Thatcher and John Major from 1979 to 1997. The period since the 1960s has seen the rise of 'new social movements' across the world: operating outside formal representational structures, they have challenged conventional definitions of 'politics' and increasingly used media resources for symbolic conflict (see, for example, Melucci, 1989, 1996; Offe, 1985). More specifically, the deep unpopularity of the Conservative government fuelled the growth of a protest culture, which by the mid–1990s was attracting many participants and supporters across class and age groups (Mackay, 1996). The beginnings of this protest culture coincided with the catastrophic defeat of a major industrial dispute along conventional lines: the Miners' Strike of 1984–5. Also in 1984, the women's encampment at Greenham Common air force base, set up to protest against the delivery there of US Cruise missiles, attracted national and international media coverage. The significance of the Greenham Common protest, which on a small scale is still continuing, is discussed in Chapter 8. Since the mid–1980s, a series of 'single-issue' campaigns occurred, reaching greatest intensity in the 1990s. The most prominent issues covered were, first, the rejection of the so-called 'Poll Tax' (1990). Second, there was a series of protests against the building of new roads at the expense of destroying housing or the countryside. The best-known were protests against the M11 extension in east London (1993–4), the Newbury by-pass in southern England (1995–6), the M67 in Pollok near Glasgow (1995) and the A30 extension in Fairmile, south-west England (1997). Third, and most relevant to the Brightlingsea case study, there were the protests during 1994 and 1995 at British ports and airports (including Shoreham and Dover) against live animal exports to continental Europe. Alongside these campaigns (which all attracted major media coverage and government resistance), the same period saw a mass of smaller, less prominent protests. Some of them had the potential to reach a larger scale, but did not do so for various reasons: for example, the 'Pure Genius' occupation of land by the Thames near central London (1996) to protest against its redevelopment (discussed in Chapter 8). Others were always designed on a smaller scale, but were none the less important as part of the rising tide of anti-government action, which has by no means been silenced by the election of a Labour government under Tony Blair in May 1997: for example, protests over Old Age Pensioner rights, disability issues, hospital closures.

Interviews with such activists are discussed in Chapter 8 (Louise and 'The Umbrella Man').

Although there was a shared political context for these actions (a widely unpopular government), it would be wrong to suggest that they were all part of a common social or political movement. The anti-road protests had as their main participants young people and others with a long-term commitment to protest action. This was inevitable since, like the Greenham Camp, such protests involved living at an unsheltered protest site in difficult conditions that often required physical courage (the Newbury tree protests, or the Fairmile tunnel protests). By contrast, the protests against live animal exports were mainly conventional actions, blocking roads in towns and so on; they were thus open to a wider range of people to participate, including many retired people. They were billed by the media as protests by 'ordinary people'.[42] Even so, there were more overlaps and connections between the two types of protests than was usually recognised.

The case of Brightlingsea was chosen for detailed analysis because it illustrated well the 'ordinary person' protest. It promised insights into the de-naturalisation of the media frame, since almost all those involved had no previous experience of being represented in the media. But all the protest events discussed, whatever their wider resonances, had an important point in common: that they were mounted away from the centres of state power (Parliament, the capital)[43] and away from the centres of media production (the television studio). As discussed in Chapter 8 in relation to Greenham Common, they were actions which challenged the media's implicit geography (its 'geography of normality': Cresswell, 1996: 95), which patterns who speaks about what and from where. They were moments of transgression when non-media people, perhaps for the first time, witnessed the process of mediation itself: a temporary and limited reversal of the 'a-symmetry' of cultural power which Stuart Hall (1973) analysed. Although some earlier studies[44] have touched upon that theme, none has focused on it in detail.

## Alternative forms of mediation

An important further theme that emerged out of my study of mediated conflict was alternative forms of mediation: this is the subject of Chapter 8. Melucci's (1989, 1996) work on social and symbolic conflict is helpful here. It analyses how people can resist what he has called their exclusion from 'the power of naming': first, through complete 'silence and retreat' from the mediated world (1996: 183); and, second, through symbolic action which, whatever its direct practical effects, may alter how social experience is perceived, how it is 'named' (ibid.: 185). It is the second with which I am more concerned.

Chapter 8 explores examples of such alternative mediations not only from Brightlingsea but from various other protests already mentioned (Greenham

Common, Pure Genius, and some individual campaigns). It considers them as various forms of 'tactic' in de Certeau's (1984) sense, cutting across the 'strategic' spaces produced by political and media institutions. Such actions, and participants' accounts of them, reflect in various ways the unevenness of media territory and the symbolic hierarchies that are at play. Through such forms of 'active witnessing', alternative narratives emerge, reminding us that 'media are not mere conveyors of messages but meeting-points of often contradictory ways of remembering and interpreting' (Rowe and Schelling, 1991: 9).

## Other research possibilities and wider perspectives

There remain, of course, many other types of interaction with the media process which it would be interesting to research. One topic is people's experience of participating in studio-based programmes, such as talk shows, on which important research, particularly in the US, is starting to emerge (see Chapter 1). Some of those I interviewed discussed their experiences of appearing on talk shows. Talk shows are a complex case, since, depending on their subject-matter, they can easily combine 'pilgrimage', 'witnessing', and 'active witnessing'. They are places where you get close, perhaps, to a famous talk show host, where you witness a significant revelation by someone else, and where you may even tell your own story in a public context. At the same time, the studio audience and the main participants are constructed in particular ways by the programme's discourse. An interesting contrast could also be developed with people's experience of involuntary revelations of the media process, for example, where they suddenly become the focus of unsought media attention: the case of 'media victim' (for initial work in this area, see Lull and Hinerman, 1998). At this point, empirical work on people's interactions with the media process opens out into ethical considerations.

My own case studies are organised around a division which is somewhat artificial: between media-related locations that are organised leisure sites, and locations that only become media locations by virtue of news coverage. Part 2 deals with voluntary trips, and Part 3 deals with (partly) involuntary witnessing, that at the same time may offer the opportunity to participate in public debate. But these categories are not mutually exclusive. The events following the death of Princess Diana in September 1997 were a vivid example of a media location that was a site of both pilgrimage *and* witnessing, both passive viewing and significant participation (I have discussed them in more detail elsewhere: Couldry, 1999a). What struck so many people, myself included, was those events' puzzling combination: the inseparability of powerful, ritualised collective emotion and media distortions of the same process. In Britain at least, the media, without significant exception, insisted that the whole country was in mourning, but this was far from the case, as emerged publicly some time after the events (Jack, 1997). The mourning for

Diana was very close to being 'hyperreal' in Baudrillard's sense. While reference points to a reality outside media representations still existed (many people knew that they and their friends were *not* mourning), their authority was devalued almost to zero. They were not part of the public story to be told.

Paradoxically the Diana events, while offering compelling evidence of the massive concentration of symbolic power in media institutions, also offered unprecedented, if temporary, opportunities for non-media people to participate in symbolic production with a public significance: to write a message to Diana that would be read by unknown others, to be interviewed by a journalist, and so on. And, because of the claims that Diana died because she was being chased by press photographers, public discussion of media power reached an unusual intensity. Events such as those after Diana's death are among the most puzzling with which media sociology has had to deal. It should by now be clear, however, that we cannot begin to grasp their full complexity, unless we are committed to empirical work (not just theoretical pronouncements) about the media's impacts on territory and unless, also, our empirical work is free to operate *beyond* the limited analytic framework of media institutions/texts/audiences. The thousands of journeys to the Diana sites simply did not fit into that outdated paradigm, yet they constitute one of the most striking moments in the recent history of the vast social process we call 'the media'.

The argument of this chapter, then, suggests two things. First, that general theories about the media's impacts on social space (for example, Baudrillard's or Meyrowitz's) raise important questions, but are inadequate by themselves. If we seriously want to think about media territory, we have to acknowledge its complexity and unevenness, and this requires detailed empirical work; hence the case studies of Parts 2 and 3. Second, although media sociology has tended to sit like a ghost at the feast of contemporary social thought – looking on as major positions about the media's impacts are staked out – there is no reason why this unsatisfactory situation should continue. Large-scale theories (from Jameson's and Harvey's theories of postmodernism, to Lash and Urry's (1994) work on 'reflexivity' and the 'resubjectivizing of place') have tended to talk across the debates of media sociology, without taking detailed account of them. This book, I hope, will encourage the necessary connections between media sociology and those wider debates.

# 3

# MEDIA POWER: SOME
# HIDDEN DIMENSIONS

## INTRODUCTION

As explained in Chapter 1, I approach media power not as a property which media institutions simply possess, but as a broad social process that operates at many levels. It is of course a fact that broadcasting mechanisms exist and that their control is centralised, but it is only because what is broadcast has some legitimacy that it is worth discussing broadcasting's social impacts at all. That legitimacy, however, is far from being a simple 'fact'. It is the overall result of countless processes of reproduction in talk, belief, and action, both by media producers and by media consumers. We must recognise this local complexity, but also not forget the large-scale arbitrariness that results: the legitimation of the concentration of symbolic power in a limited sector of society. The concept of 'naturalisation' is central here, and to this extent my approach continues in the tradition of early, Marxist-influenced media sociology (see for example Dahlgren, 1981; Garnham, 1986; Golding, 1981; Hall, 1973, 1977). Where it differs from some of that work is in how 'power' is conceived.

Media power can be understood as part of the 'habitus' in the more general sense that Pierre Bourdieu uses the term: 'history turned into nature' (1977: 78). Through seeming natural, media power is normally inaccessible to criticism; it is legitimated automatically. In this book, I attempt to explain how this happens, and how difficult it is to disrupt. An abstract theorisation is given in this chapter, followed by more concrete details in Parts 2 and 3. This, however, is only the first stage, potentially, of a much larger argument about the reproduction of social formations. It is in that context that Bourdieu uses 'habitus' in the more specific sense of the pattern of dispositions associated with particular 'positions' in social space (based on class, education, material wealth, cultural capital, and so on). It would, however, require another empirical study, and another book, to establish whether the beliefs and practices through which media power is naturalised are *themselves* unevenly distributed across society, and whether that has an impact on the reproduction of wider forms of inequality.[45]

It is already a large enough task to explore how the legitimacy of media power and media institutions are reproduced through talk, belief, and action. A problem here is that the media have been neglected in large-scale social theory. Neither Foucault nor (until recently) Bourdieu attempted to integrate the impacts of modern media into his analysis of social power.[46] While John Thompson's work has begun to remedy this, his account of the 'social organization of symbolic power' (1995: 3) gives only limited scope to issues of differential power. We need, then, to explain how a large-scale effect (the legitimation of a society-wide process, such as media power) is produced, or rather continually reproduced, through countless actions on many different scales, including the local. This opens up the importance of space and place in the media process, raising questions about the organisation of media territories themselves: the unevenness and the 'distances' they involve. It also raises questions about those moments when media power is *not* reproduced as legitimate, when it is contested.

Before discussing various dimensions of media power in detail, I want to bring out some preliminary points to clarify the types of claim I will be making:

1. What follows in this chapter is deliberately quite abstract. This is necessary to highlight the complexity of the naturalisation process itself. It is the media's multidimensionality which makes underlying issues of power so difficult to articulate. The media are both a principal focus of imagination, creativity and identification *and* a principal source of information and representation; they help define both the facts of our social reality *and* our individual desires. The fact that these conflicting functions are performed by, and entangled with, the same nexus of symbolic power is itself of crucial importance. The implications of this need careful unpacking.

This inevitably involves some artificiality. I am abstracting from patterns of discourse and action, and, as Bourdieu (1977) pointed out, the very process of abstract formulation introduces a distortion, a reification. Actual practice is, inevitably, more open-ended. The claims which follow must therefore be understood as coming with a qualification of the form: 'everything takes place as if … ' (cf. Bourdieu, 1977: 203 n49). I am trying to formulate general tendencies and patterns, but fully acknowledge that the details of particular cases may be less neatly patterned. Some element of abstraction is, however, necessary if we are to grasp at all the processes of reification and naturalisation which underlie media power itself.

2. Following on from the last point, I will be simplifying at times the relations that apply in practice between different media: not just television, radio and the press (my main concerns), but other media (film, music, video, computer games, the Internet, and so on). There are complex overlaps between how we interact with these different media, and, of course, differences

between how each of them is embedded in everyday practice. In Chapter 9, I ask how recent changes in the constellation of everyday media might affect my argument here, which is developed principally with the broadcast media in mind. I will argue there that even the age of 'narrowcasting' may not bring a dispersal of symbolic power.

3. In terms of theoretical orientation, this chapter combines the influences of Durkheim and Bourdieu, with perspectives from geography (see below under 'Spacing'), discourse analysis and actor network theory (see under 'Ordering'), and Melucci's political sociology (see under 'Naming'). It also draws on much work within media sociology (especially Silverstone, Scannell, and Hall). Even so, it leaves some avenues open for further development.

For one thing, I concentrate on those 'hidden dimensions' of media power, which are intrinsic to media-related discourse and people's interactions with the media. My argument could, of course, be supplemented by other dimensions: the relations between media institutions and the state (Hall, 1982: 86–7; Sparks, 1998: 182), the media's relation to economic and corporate power (Robins and Webster, 1986), or the media's embedding in structures of domestic life (Silverstone, 1994). Clearly those other dimensions are important and, if combined with my own argument, could open up a fascinating area for international comparison between, say, media in 'liberal' societies and state-controlled media:[47] see also Chapter 1.

My model also does not attempt to deal in detail with issues of individual psychology. Even where the case studies discuss individuals' talk and actions in detail, my approach draws more from discourse analysis than from models of individual psychology, such as psychoanalysis. I would not rule out a development of my argument along those lines, but it would entail resolving how psychoanalytic and sociological frameworks are to be theoretically integrated, an issue beyond the scope of this book. Where I do refer below to the work of Lacan and Zizek on misrecognition, it is in terms of general analogies only.

4. Finally, a definitional note. In my account of the symbolic hierarchy of the media frame, I will speak of the distinction between 'media world' and 'ordinary world'. 'Media world' (used in inverted commas) here denotes a *constructed* term within this binary opposition, which may variously be mapped onto media institutions, the 'worlds' implied by media fictions, and so on. 'Ordinary world' denotes the other term within that binary opposition. There is no 'ordinary world', and no 'media world', only one social world of which the division between 'media' and 'ordinary' 'worlds' is a product. By contrast, where I mention 'the media sphere', I mean the institutional component of the media frame, the institutions on which the media mechanism is based (cf. Chapter 1).

I will discuss five dimensions of media power in turn. These dimensions are: framing, ordering, naming, spacing, and imagining. The principles underlying most of these have already been suggested in Chapter 1.


## FRAMING

... when we appear on the tube [television], in front of all those people, that's when we live. That's life ...

(producer interviewed in Worth and Adair, 1972: 245)

Television, and the media generally, function as a frame for the social (cf. Chapter 1). They are a space through which everyone can access simultaneously what marks off the 'social' from the private and particular. This point has its basis in an analogy from Durkheim's sociology of religion: in particular, the social generation of the sacred/profane distinction. However, as we saw, the Durkheimian model in itself is insufficient. This is for two reasons: first, because it underplays issues of power – if we take the media case, we need to ask what are the social consequences of the framing function being *concentrated* in a historically specific institutional sphere (the media); second, because it underplays the complexity of the social processes through which the authority of media institutions is in fact reproduced.

Even so, the media's framing function remains the best place to start the analysis. The media's symbolic authority depends, in part, on their framing function, and this in turn depends on the fact that they can address an audience formed across the whole social range. This is still true even in media cultures with multiple channels. In the United States, which has for a long time had multiple channels, the notion of 'prime time' continues (Cantor and Cantor, 1992). Its reference-point is precisely social: 'the conventional expectation – among viewers as much as producers and advertisers – that prime time addresses a full cross section of ... society' (Saenz, 1994: 576). This is connected to television's 'ideology of liveness' (Feuer, 1983), a feature attaching not just to programmes that actually go out 'live', but also to the fact that this programme you are watching is, more or less simultaneously, on offer to a cross-section of society.[48] 'Liveness' involves a 'sense of collective immediacy and participation', absent when you hire a videotape or go to the cinema. Henri Lefebvre made a similar point:

*Radio and, even more so, television,* the sudden violent intrusion of the whole world into family and 'private' life, 'presentified' in a way which directly captures the immediate moment, which offers truth and participation, or at least appears to do so ...

(1991a: 41, original italics and ellipsis)

'Live' television or radio in this broad sense contributes to the media's framing function, since it implicitly demarcates a unique audience: those who have access to the broadcast material solely because they are watching or listening *now*. At the same time, live production features prominently in how media producers conceive their social role (Swallow, 1966: 44; Tunstall, 1993: 78; Tusa, 1993).

It is important to see that 'framing' in this broad sense is central to the authority which the media more generally have. Obviously, because of their timing and distribution patterns, some media such as television and radio can offer 'live' coverage in a more detailed and consistent way than other media (such as the press). That does not, however, mean that the concepts of 'liveness' and 'framing' have no relevance to the press, only that the time-scale on which they operate is different. The idea of the press 'exclusive' is only a variant on the idea of 'liveness': shared, but privileged, access to current events. The same principle may now apply to the Internet, at least in the USA: important documentary revelations (such as the Starr Report) have been posted on the World Wide Web before being broadcast on television and radio, and it was the Matt Drudge Web site which broke news of the Monica Lewinsky affair.

This expansion of the media involved in framing does not, however, make the concept any less relevant. In any case, the sense of 'simultaneity' essential to framing even by television is produced not simply by live television coverage itself, but by many media sources acting together. Think of the mass of 'secondary' material (Fiske, 1987: 117) about soaps – in the press and magazines, anticipating the plot, reviewing the programme, discussing the cast's private lives – which confirms the importance of watching *this* episode *tonight*. Press, radio, and television are similarly crucial in anticipating and then amplifying revelations on the Internet. To understand the process of framing, we need to look at the media taken together.

The media are not of course the only 'frame' for experiencing the social, and Maffesoli (1996) has emphasised the importance of temporary sites of dispersed 'sociality' where we feel part of the wider whole (from raves to sport). There is no reason, however, to suppose that the broadcast media have lost their universal framing function as Maffesoli sometimes suggests (ibid.: 138). There are endless examples: from soaps and sports coverage to comedy, news, and popular DJs' radio programmes. In fact, it could be argued that the media's framing function is being progressively globalised. Take, for example, the Gulf War television coverage, the verdict in the OJ Simpson trial, or the funeral of Princess Diana. The media's framing of the social is, however, distinctive because it works *without actual co-presence*. We access the social simply on the basis of an assumption of being-together, a 'conventional expectation' (Saenz). This has important consequences. Compared with the direct experience of 'the social' that Durkheim envisaged underlying the 'sacred', the media provide an 'abstract' form of togetherness which operates without altering the actual segregations in society. The media offer 'mediated quasi-interaction' (Thompson, 1990: 228). This necessarily raises questions about the mechanism of representation through which the sense of simultaneity or togetherness is achieved, issues which Durkheim's original model does not explore: questions about 'which categories of social agent get to write, speak and be seen – and which do not' (Fairclough, 1995: 40). Herman Gray's (1995) work on the racial dimensions of US prime time has pursued this powerfully. However, specific inequalities of representation are not my main concern here, but rather a general and naturalised form of inequality, connected to the media's symbolic authority, which I consider next.

## ORDERING

> These women who went round speaking at meetings ... I thought it was terrific. I think it's good that ordinary people should tell other ordinary people about the strike. The way it was put over on the television and in the papers, we was all irresponsible people.
>
> (miner's wife Pauline Street, quoted in Parker, 1986: 119)

This quotation (from an interview about the 1984–5 UK Miners' Strike) implies a major difference between, first, 'ordinary people' talking to 'other ordinary people' and, second, television and newspapers. The media, it suggests, do not constitute *ordinary* people' communicating. The term 'ordinary people' needs careful unravelling, but there is already a paradox: that the communications of 'ordinary people' and those of media people might seem different in kind. This difference, and the hierarchy it suggests, is of fundamental importance to understanding how the media's differential symbolic power is naturalised. My discussion will necessarily be schematic, but the points made here will be revisited often in the case studies.

### 'Media world' versus 'ordinary world'

I introduced in Chapter One the distinction between 'media world' versus 'ordinary world' and explained, by analogy with Durkheim's theory of the social origins of religion, that this distinction is closely linked to the media's framing function. It is the basis of what I will call 'the symbolic hierarchy of the media frame'. Like the sacred/profane distinction, the media/ordinary distinction divides the social world into two domains which are normally separate. Meetings between the two worlds must, therefore, be ritually controlled (cf. Durkheim, 1995: 38).

Since contemporary media institutions are in reality only a historically contingent mechanism for framing the social, the media/ordinary hierarchy involves a misrecognition (misrecognising the contingent as absolute). By speaking of 'misrecognition' here, I am not claiming that we are all deceived by media contents. Particular forms of scepticism about the media abound, just as scepticism about particular 'sacred' objects abounds among religious believers. There is proverbial scepticism about the press ('I never believe what I read in the paper') and also perhaps a cultural shift that Andrew Tolson (1991: 198) claims has characterised British television since the early 1980s: the ironising of earlier concepts, such as the 'celebrity', the 'authentic' real person. Various empirical studies also have emphasised viewers' awareness of programmes' constructedness and of television's commercialism (Buckingham, 1987: 160, 165, 172; cf. Livingstone and Lunt, 1994: 78–81). But, as Buckingham points out (1987: 180), such scepticism is compatible with believing in the general realism of television. Scepticism at one level is compatible with the reproduction of belief at another. As Slavoj Zizek elegantly put it when discussing ideology from a Lacanian perspective: 'the illusion is not on the side of knowledge, *it is already on the side of reality itself, of what the people are doing* … Even if we do not take things seriously, even if we keep an ironical distance, we are still doing them' (1989: 32–3, emphasis altered). Stuart Hall made a similar point when he analysed ideology in terms of 'what is most open, apparent, manifest', the 'unconsciousness' of 'common sense' (1977: 325). Applying this point to the media/ordinary distinction, we can say that, regardless of our localised scepticism about the media, the hierarchy between 'ordinary' and 'media' 'worlds' may go on being reproduced all the same.

It is 'common sense' that the 'media world' is somehow better, more intense, than 'ordinary life', and that 'media people' are somehow special. This is not based either on fact or on a cultural universal, but rather is a form of unconsciousness ultimately derived from a particular concentration of symbolic power. The media sphere itself is *not* different in kind from the world in which viewers live; it is a part of the same world dedicated to mediating it. Yet, through the naturalised hierarchy between the constructed terms 'media world' and 'ordinary world', this division of the social world is generally reproduced as legitimate.

Before developing this point further, a note of caution is necessary. Many forms of social distinction overlap in the single term 'ordinary', which makes analysing actual examples of the media/ordinary distinction particularly complex. The word 'ordinary' is, as Raymond Williams (1983: 225–7) noted, ambiguous, covering both what is shared by everyone ('the regular, the customary') and what is ranked lower in a hierarchy. Affirming 'the ordinary' (as shared) can have remarkable resonances, not least in Williams' own work (1989), but the term's usage also crosses many hierarchical divisions. In any particular case ('ordinary life', 'ordinary world', 'ordinary people'), more than one distinction may overlap: the basic distinction of (1) 'ordinary' versus 'out of the ordinary', but also (2) 'ordinary' versus 'abnormal' (in a pejorative sense), (3) 'ordinary person' versus any 'important' or powerful person (in relation to politics, royalty, the police, and so on), and (4) 'ordinary' (domestic) life versus the (implicitly more important) world of the public sphere.

I will argue that an additional distinction can be isolated: that between 'ordinary' and 'media' 'worlds'/people. This may be difficult to isolate in the context of actual talk, because it will overlap with other distinctions involving the term 'ordinary'. The media themselves often draw a distinction between types of non-media people (i.e. 'ordinary people' in my sense): some may be classed as 'ordinary' (i.e. normal), others may be classed as abnormal (cf. Chapter 2 on 'ordinary people' protests). Even so, the media/ordinary distinction is important in its own right, because it operates over and above any other hierarchies reproduced through media coverage. Indeed it helps further naturalise those hierarchies (based on class, gender, race, and so on) by suggesting that *the media's* reproduction of them is natural; at the same time, it reproduces a hierarchy based on appearance in the media itself.

## The symbolic division of the world

What does the media/ordinary division involve in practice? First, it symbolically categorises *people*. It implies that the type of person who is 'in the media' is different in kind from the person who is not (Snow, 1983: 151–2; Altheide and Snow, 1979: 43–4). Put the other way round, 'ordinary people' are not expected to be the same as 'media people': certainly they are not expected to have the skills or characteristics which being in the media is assumed to involve. Indeed, 'ordinary people' are not expected to be 'in' the media at all, but only to appear 'on' the media in certain limited circumstances. When 'real people' (non-media people) do appear on television, they are often '"employed" to be ordinary' (Root, 1986: 97). A game-show producer quoted by Root precisely reproduced the media/ordinary hierarchy: 'I wouldn't pick someone to be a contestant who would attempt to be a star. I want nice ordinary people who just come along for a bit of fun: some of them are so ordinary they are surprised to be chosen' (ibid.: 98). Alternatively, in news coverage, 'ordinary people' appear as agents only if they have done something 'especially remarkable' (Langer, 1998: 48).[49] When they do so, they indirectly confirm the usual distance of 'ordinary people' from media attention, even as they appear to challenge it. Importantly, it is not only the language of media texts themselves that confirms this division. Applying Foucauldian terminology, the whole 'discourse' of television, for example – not merely its texts, but its institutional arrangements and hierarchies, and the way both television people and their audiences talk – produces the regular 'subject-position' (cf. Fairclough, 1989: 39) of the viewer (*not* a media producer) who is 'ordinary'. Here, for example, is an excerpt from Granada Television's bid document to run a major new current affairs programme, leaked to the *Guardian*'s Media Section. It describes the options for human interest stories as follows:

> profiles could involve a celebrity ... alternatively, it could be a politician ... Or we could even focus on an ordinary person in an extraordinary situation, e.g. a day in the life of a Lottery jackpot winner, or the parents caring for a teenage daughter with CJD ...
>
> (*Guardian*, 18 January 1999, Media Section)

From this highly arbitrary perspective, viewers are simply 'ordinary people who watch television'.[50]

I am not, of course, claiming here that broadcasting discourse in Britain has remained unchanged since its original, explicitly hierarchical form (represented by Lord Reith's BBC in the 1920s). There have been significant changes, and changes are still continuing. But I am claiming that hierarchy remains in media discourse in various forms. There are, incidentally, overlaps with other areas of cultural production, for example music. As two fans said about meeting the pop stars they followed: 'you think of them as being wonderful people ... everything that everybody ordinary isn't' (quoted, Vermorel and Vermorel, 1985: 175). The difference between 'fans' and 'stars' here also is registered as a difference in kind.

Second, the media/ordinary distinction implies a difference in kind between *worlds*: between the 'world' of the media (everything involved in it: stories, studios, work practices) and the 'world' of 'ordinary life'. The 'media world' is 'larger-than-life' (Altheide and Snow, 1979: 20–21; Snow, 1983: 21–2), the 'ordinary world' is automatically mundane. As with Durkheim's sacred/profane distinction, this is not so much a distinction based on detailed comparison, but an absolute distinction that divides the world up in advance. As Cecelia Tichi has put it: 'to be transposed onto television *is* to be elevated out of the banal realm of the off-screen and repositioned in the privileged on-screen world' (1991: 140, added emphasis). Yet paradoxically media institutions, as an essential part of their function, must also seek to represent the world of the everyday. The paradox does not undermine the symbolic division; they run alongside each other. As one man said, when I asked him what type of place *Coronation Street* was: 'just everyday sort of living, well larger than life type of thing'. Alternatively, media coverage may make everyday life seem strange. As one participant in MTV's 'living soap' called *The Real World* put it: 'you feel everything you do is imbued with significance because there is a camera crew there pointing a lens in your face'.[51]

Third, following on directly from the second point, the media/ordinary distinction involves a *boundary* between separate 'worlds', which it is automatically significant to cross or approach. Patricia Priest's important work on US talk show participants (1995, 1996) vividly brings out the sense that to appear on television is 'to "step[] in" to a valued place' (1996: 81). Any entry to the 'media world' can be similarly described, as in the marketing of tourist locations: 'Step Inside the World of Television', 'Break into the World of Broadcasting'.[52] There may also be wider resonances of crossing such a significant boundary: thus one game show participant quoted by Root (1986: 112) said appearing on television made her feel 'almost like royalty'. It follows, more generally, that appearing in the media normally comprises a form of prestige or cultural capital (see below).

## Banal practices of ordering

The division between worlds, because absolute, can be adequately marked by the most banal language. Thus, when in 1963 two people watching the Kennedy lying-in-state on television decided that they had to go there in person, they recalled later: ' ... the more we watched the more we felt we just had to be there ourselves. It's so awful we felt we had to do something'.[53] One way of analysing this is that their action seemed so obviously significant to the speakers that it did not need to be explicated, only marked ('to be there', 'to do something'). Barry Schwartz, who quotes this passage, interprets it in terms of presence at a 'sacred center', but another aspect, I suggest, of these actions' automatic significance was that they involved crossing the normal boundary between 'media' and 'ordinary' 'worlds'. The banal language of cases such as this is, however, particularly resistant to rhetorical challenge (Billig, 1997: 225): as a result, perhaps, it reproduces boundaries and hierarchies all the more effectively.

This leads on to an important general point about how the symbolic hierarchy of the media frame is reproduced. I began by using a Durkheimian model, arguing that the division between 'ordinary' and 'media' 'worlds' is grounded in the special role the media have in framing the social. That remains important. However, what also makes this division so effective and pervasive is the way it is reproduced in countless local forms: through language, as just analysed, and through actions. Whereas a Durkheimian model focuses purely on the foundational importance of the ritual dimension through which the media contribute to social life, we need also to consider how the media/ordinary hierarchy is continually naturalised through what the social psychologist Michael Billig has called 'banal practices' (1995: 95). The two analyses are quite compatible, and in fact reinforce each other, as elements of a wider picture of how media authority is legitimated.

These banal practices can be traced in three areas. First, the language of people who are not part of media institutions, as just noted: the case studies will give many more examples. Second, in the language of media people, for example in media texts. Programmes' mode of address may, as Brunsdon and Morley observed of BBC's *Nationwide,* 'construct [ ] "ordinary people" as the subject of [their] particular kind of speech' (1978: 8). Television presenters may present themselves as 'ordinary', speaking up for the 'ordinary person'.[54]

The media's rhetoric of inclusiveness is of course driven by the need to maintain audiences. But, at the same time, 'ordinary people's' actual appearances in the media may be structured (by contrast with those of 'experts', for instance) so as to reinforce the media/ordinary hierarchy.[55] Indeed 'ordinary people's' structured *absences* from media texts – they are rarely seen as agents in news events,[56] they are rarely media presenters – only confirm the hierarchy. This hierarchy casts a shadow. Just as appearing in the media usually carries prestige, so too never appearing in the media may imply a lack: 'individuals may feel … unworthy if never allowed to represent themselves' (Priest, 1995: 167).

Third, the media/ordinary boundary is reproduced, more generally, in the everyday practices through which knowledge and information are produced. There is an analogy here with work done in the sociology of science, particularly John Law's work (1994) within 'actor network theory' on how information flows and decision-making in scientific organisations are ordered. Law writes of various 'modes of ordering', which contribute towards the creation of experts and objects of knowledge (1994: 110–11). For example, practices may involve 'relatively consistent patterns of deletion', in other words, asymmetrical relations which result in some people or things being deprived of the ability to act in certain ways, and others being specifically empowered. Alternatively, practices may favour 'characteristic forms of representation', which also imply a silent position for other people or things, what Law calls a mode of 'silence'.

This analysis of knowledge-generation in science can be applied to the media. There are myriad patterns of 'deletion' whereby people who lack an accredited relation to the media sphere are passed over when speaking or acting for the media is necessary. The other side of 'deletion' is that those 'appropriate' for media performance have an enhanced role: they become 'obligatory passing points' (Callon and Latour, 1981: 287). Or, as Stuart Hall (1973) once put it, particular social agents (politicians, experts, and so on) are 'systematically overaccessed'. Crucially this includes the systematic overaccessing of media people themselves: this is so obvious as to be barely worth stating, yet fundamental to the naturalised status of those who work in the media. There are also many contexts where a form of representation appropriate for the media is favoured over other forms of representation (crucial in a mediated 'promotional culture': Wernick, 1991). As a result, actions or statements not suitable for media representation may exist in a 'mode of silence'. Media consumers themselves generally occupy a place of 'silence' within the media's 'mode of ordering', since their status to intervene in the media's flow is strictly limited.

There are, in sum, many ways in which a hierarchical relation between 'media' and 'ordinary' 'worlds' is reproduced. In the course of this section, I have moved from a purely symbolic hierarchy along Durkheimian lines to an organisational hierarchy reproduced continually through people's words and actions. The two are linked, however, since each makes the other seem natural. Matters of 'value' and 'fact' are closely interwoven. I pursue this theme in the next section.


## NAMING

'What makes the world beyond direct experience look natural is a media *frame.*'

(Gitlin, 1980: 6, original emphasis)

There is another important way in which the media's differential symbolic power is naturalised. This derives from the media's role in generating most of the 'facts' about the social world. Following Melucci (1996), I call this process 'naming'.

This raises the question of our trust in the media. Silverstone (1994: ch. 1) has developed a complex argument about our trust in television as a domestic technology. This is based, in part, on the work of Giddens (1984) who has argued that all daily life is based on trust (cf. Fukuyama, 1995). Trust relates to our fundamental need for 'ontological security' (Giddens, 1984: 64) based on bodily control and predictable patterns of interaction with the physical and social world. Silverstone argues that we 'trust' television since it fulfils a similar need through its continual availability and regular cycles of contents. Elsewhere, Giddens has analysed another aspect of trust: the role which 'expert systems' play in mediating between us and matters about which we have no direct knowledge, but which none the less affect our lives (1990: 88, 92). Analogously, television news, Silverstone argues, acts as 'a key institution in the mediation of threat, risk and danger' from the outside world (Silverstone, 1994: 17).

A similar argument could be made in relation to radio (cf. Scannell, 1996). As for the press, the position is more complicated. There are probably differences in the levels of trust people have for individual newspapers (this is true also to some extent with television and radio channels), and there is certainly evidence that people generally trust the press less than television as a source of news (see Gunter and Winstone, 1993: 45–6).[57] Television's power as a visual medium gives it a special advantage over all non-visual media: in detailed and complex ways it can convince us that it helps us to 'see for ourselves' (Corner, 1995: 13–14). The position of particular media is clearly not, therefore, identical in this respect.

My point, however, is a more general one. I am concerned with how the media, taken together as an institutional sector, perform an essential role within modern societies whose members and organisations are massively interdependent, yet highly dispersed. They provide an essential flow of information and meanings, that enable the generation of new discursive resources at a societal level, both through factual information and through media fictions, such as soaps, which may focus important social debates. But this function depends, of course, on our trust which is a two-way process: trust on the part of information-producers that they can rely on being represented by the media; trust on the part of information-receivers that they can rely on the accuracy and representativeness of the media as information source. This two-sided trust in the media is a deeply entrenched disposition of major functional importance in our lives. Trust in the media, at this very general level, is reinforced in various ways. We are ready, in principle, to trust the media because of their status as 'frames' onto social reality and the symbolic power which flows from that. Hence, the media's information-flows about the social world are readily naturalised as not just facts, but as 'the' facts about society: as 'actuality', even 'history', in the making.[58] It is the sense of being close to 'actuality' that supports news journalists' sense of the value of their own judgements about newsworthiness (Schlesinger, 1978: 108–9, 128–9). Materials which the media themselves originate (for example, fictional dramas) are readily integrated into factual information-flows and so themselves become part of 'actuality' (Gripsrud, 1995: 251).

A number of factors, then, ensure a basic trust in the media. This trust has not only an ethical aspect ('the media ought to be telling the truth'), but also an ontological aspect ('the media reveal reality'). As a form of 'thinking-as-usual' (Schutz, 1973b: 96), our trust in the media is generally reproduced automatically without reference to those factors which, if made explicit, might undermine it: the role of the media's own practices in systematically reproducing certain definitions of 'news' and key news-related terms (the 'political', the 'deviant', the 'criminal', the 'strike'),[59] or certain versions of geography or history,[60] rather than others; the media's role in 'agenda-setting' (McCombs and Shaw, 1972), and so on. This general trust is likely to be reproduced even if there are large areas of social reality regularly obscured from us: shadows, as it were, cast by the media frame. Without specific knowledge and resources, we are unlikely to suspect them. As Todd Gitlin put it in the quotation opening this section, it is representation *within* the media frame that makes the wider social world 'look natural'. As we see in Parts 2 and 3, however, people's trust in the media can be disrupted with dramatic effects. They may experience a conflict between their knowledge that 'this is what happened' (something that happened to them) and their assumption that a different version of it (the mediated one) must also somehow be 'reality'. Without an explicit recognition that the media are merely a mechanism for constructing reality, the conflict must remain unresolved, a paradox. Resolving it means questioning the media's naturalised authority. Once again (as in 'Ordering') it might be argued that I underestimate people's mistrust of the media; as just mentioned, one form this might take is different levels of belief in different media. What I am arguing, however, is that specific scepticism at one level is compatible with belief at another;

'belief' must be understood not only in terms of what is explicitly articulated, but also in terms of unarticulated patterns in how we think and speak, and in how we act.

The three dimensions of naturalisation considered so far are interrelated: they work together to help naturalise the media's concentration of symbolic power. The media's status as reporter of 'the facts' about social reality (Naming) helps naturalise their status more generally as the 'frame' through which we obtain access to social reality (Framing). This helps reinforce the symbolic hierarchy between 'media' and 'ordinary' 'worlds' (Ordering), which in turn helps reinforce the status of media material (whether fact or fiction) as social 'reality' or 'actuality' (Naming again). A largely closed cycle of reproduction whose overall result constitutes what I call the *'symbolic hierarchy of the media frame'*. These are not, however, the only dimensions along which the media's differential symbolic power is naturalised.

## SPACING

> All production and consumption as well as social interaction can be viewed as a steering by humans of their own *and other* trajectories according to certain ordering principles.
>
> (Hagerstrand, 1975: 7, added emphasis)

Media representations may reinforce spatial patternings already inherent in social organisation. For instance, the marked 'metropolitan' focus of social, economic, and cultural activity in Britain is probably reinforced in media discourse. The reason is not wilful media distortion but those systemic constraints built into media production, which are spatial in nature: news coverage's highly selective 'map' of the nation reproduces an uneven spatial distribution in the sources on which the media generally rely (Brooker-Gross, 1983; Brunsdon and Morley, 1978; Golding, 1981; cf. globally, Wark, 1994: 8–9). In this section, however, I am interested in the relations between media and space in a more general way. What are the implications of considering the media as a spatial process? While my analysis will not draw on the details of Hagerstrand's 'time geography', it is inspired by his insistence that social practice always involves the hidden coordination of presences *and* absences. What is the structure of presences and absences that comprises the 'spatial order' or 'geography' of the media frame?

The starting-point has already been suggested in Chapter 1: the regular separation of media production from media consumption. The material resources necessary for media production are, and usually have been, spatially concentrated (I will focus here on broadcasting institutions for simplicity). A principal site where such resources are concentrated is, of course, the television or radio studio. Studios are limited in number, unevenly distributed, and access to them for those outside media institutions, or their major sources, is highly restricted. In television and radio's early history, such restrictions had clear practical justifications. Television and radio equipment was expensive and scarce. In addition, cameras and sound-recording equipment were cumbersome and outside broadcasts difficult to mount, although this itself need not have prevented audiences being encouraged to visit studio buildings.[61] These restrictions, however, were never merely technical matters. For, as Webster and Robins have argued for communications generally (1989: 325), 'the appropriation of ... resources has always been a constitutive aspect of capitalist societies quite outside of any technological context'. Certainly, 'technological' constraints in broadcasting have in recent decades been greatly reduced, first through portable cameras and less cumbersome sound-recording and editing techniques in the 1950s, and then (since the 1960s) through the development of portable video cameras. Yet access to media production resources remains largely under the control of media institutions, and highly restricted.

'Professional' values (which, for example, determine the technical quality of what can be broadcast) still reinforce and legitimate these divisions. In fact, those values themselves are influenced by media people's lack of contact with their audiences. As has often been noted, the media generally work from an image, rather than real knowledge, of their audience:[62]

> ... mass communicators' reliance upon their milieux as sources of meaning and orientation brings with it a concomitant *distancing from, and even devaluation of*, the views held by members of the mass audience.
> (Schlesinger, 1978: 107, added emphasis)

The association of distancing with devaluation is not accidental. It is one aspect of the wider process I want to analyse: the naturalisation of the symbolic hierarchy of the media frame through the 'spacing' of the media process. Surprisingly, although Nigel Thrift called more than a decade ago for a 'geography of social knowing and unknowing' (1985: 381), the implications of the media frame's spatial organisation for the knowledge imbalance between media producers and media consumers remain largely unexplored.

Some consequences, however, can be stated quite readily. First, and most obviously, most of the media audience lack media production skills: those skills, and the resources necessary to acquire them, remain concentrated elsewhere. Second, people with no involvement in media production (people who are 'only' viewers) have no direct control over whether production resources are used to represent *them*. Being represented in the media is something which 'happens' to them (or, more likely, does not). As a result, when non-media people have the opportunity to represent themselves, their descriptions may seize on the materiality of this unaccustomed situation.

Here is an activist I interviewed at the Pure Genius land occupation (see Chapter 8) who had never been on camera before:

> … I'm holding a big mike and this camera's right there. And it was a bit unnatural to start with, but I all of a sudden started getting into it, I really enjoyed it ( … ) and Julie [a friend] was here and I said, 'This is Julie!' And introduced Julie and held the mike over so she had a little go, so she's on it as well.

A further consequence flows from the fact that the locales of media consumption generally lack resources for media production, so that media production and media consumption are mutually exclusive in spatial terms.[63] There is little basis for people to develop practices which connect media consumption with the limited knowledge they may have of media production. Factors encouraging a more reflexive attitude towards media consumption (regularly seeing the process of media production, practice in media production techniques) are therefore largely absent. Some knowledge about media production is circulated by the media themselves (for example, 'backstage' material about the production of soap operas), but this does not, I suggest, fundamentally alter the overall pattern of knowledge distribution.

There is, as noted in Chapter 2, a 'power-geometry' (Massey, 1994: 149) implicit in the time-space compression of broadcast communications; access to the means of media production is a carefully managed and unequally distributed resource. This, in turn, makes such limited access opportunities as are available all the more marketable: hence, the growth of media tourist locations such as Granada Studios Tour. What distinguishes the segregation of the media sector, however, is its *symbolic* consequences. Most economic, political, and cultural production in contemporary societies is segregated: it has its own spaces and arenas, to which access is restricted. Such segregation makes it easier for the legitimacy of 'professional' bodies of knowledge to be protected. But, as Guy Debord (1983) pointed out, the media sector is distinctive in that it has as its responsibility *the representation* of society as a whole. The media process does not merely interact with the rest of society; it has a major impact on how the rest of society understands and imagines itself. As already argued, the media's framing and other functions result in the symbolic hierarchy between 'media' and 'ordinary' 'worlds'. But the actual segregation of the media production process helps reinforce that symbolic division.

Just as Durkheim (1995: 38) argued that the separation of the sacred and the profane is necessary to the reproduction of that symbolic hierarchy, so too the separation of the spaces of media production and media reception helps reinforce the symbolic hierarchy between the 'media' and 'ordinary' 'worlds', simply because potentially de-naturalising aspects of production are never seen by most people. In fact, this separation itself is normally disguised. A basic feature of broadcasting is that it gives us 'de-spatialized' access (Thompson, 1993: 187) to other places. The media frame's actual spatial organisation, by contrast – its rigid separation of producers from consumers – normally goes unremarked. To visit a filming location, then, may be to experience the media frame's spatiality directly for the first time, as well as to register the symbolic boundary which divides 'ordinary' and 'media' 'worlds'. In the case of locations from media fictions, it is also to cross over imaginatively into the 'world' projected by that fiction. That is why it makes sense to describe such journeys as pilgrimages. In a similar way, getting onto television can evoke the ritually resonant metaphor of 'touching'. As one commentator put it, studio audiences 'don't come to hear the visiting guest, perhaps not even to be near the star, but *to touch the medium*, to have their faces on the screen in that instant when the camera pans the audience, *to be on'* (Schrag, 1978: 54 , quoted Gamson, 1994: 137, my emphasis). To be 'on' is to experience life 'on the other side of the cameras' (Granada Studios Tour brochure,1992–3). In media locations, spatial, symbolic, and imaginative boundaries overlap. In fact, as we see in Part 2, those boundaries may be played with and ritually dramatised. The overall effect, then, of visiting such locations may be not to undermine those boundaries, but to confirm them as natural, and thereby reinforce their legitimacy.

At sites of mediated conflict, by contrast, people (without necessarily choosing it) find themselves in a situation where the mechanisms of media production are concentrated. There they may witness the spatiality of the media frame in a way that is not ritually effective but shocking: for example, when people who want to be represented realise that it is not they, but only 'media people', who control where the camera goes (see Chapter 7). In such cases, the 'ideological' function of the media frame's 'spacing' (cf. Lefebvre, 1991b: 363–5) – its disguising of potential conflicts over media practice through segregation – may break down. These moments are, however, rare and for that reason difficult to articulate. The 'spacing' of the media frame generally continues to be latent and the media's differential symbolic power remains naturalised.

## IMAGING

'Where the people meet *the* people'
(Madame Tussauds marketing slogan, 1997)

Probably everyone has some imaginative investment in the worlds that the media portray. Our pleasure in those worlds helps legitimate media power in an obvious way. Here, however, I am interested in a different point: is the symbolic hierarchy of the media frame reproduced through imaginative processes as well as the social, symbolic and spatial processes already discussed?

Two processes are of particular interest: fantasies about media people and, less familiar, what we might call 'imaginative play with the media frame'.

The 'media world' (and its celebrities) appear extraordinary, in part because we misrecognise the fact that they are only mediated versions of the social world (and its people). We regard as somehow special those who, but for appearing within the media, would be interchangeable with ourselves: this is the basis of the 'magic' of the 'media world' (cf. Chapter 6). The other side of this is to regard ourselves as '*merely* ordinary', by comparison with the 'media person'. (The 'media person' too, perhaps, may feel that in reality they are 'merely ordinary', experiencing a conflict with their public self: 'celebrity', John Updike once wrote, 'is the mask that corrodes the face'.) There is potentially here a similarity with Lacan's (1977) argument that all self-identity is formed through misrecognition, a misrecognition fixed at the 'mirror stage' when the infant mistakes the idealised version of itself in the mirror for the uncompleted process that is its actual self. There are also, however, important differences. In Lacan's analysis, the misrecognition is inevitable and foundational. In my analysis, the misrecognition is only contingent, since it derives from the social processes which reproduce the symbolic hierarchy of the media frame; however, the misrecognition is naturalised, so that it seems necessary. The ordinary is misrecognised as the 'merely' ordinary; it is this misrecognition that the Madame Tussauds advertisement plays with. Here, above all, we see the 'hidden injuries' of the media frame.

One form of misrecognition emerges in fantasies about media people (cf. MacCannell, 1992: 248–50). There are of course many sources of celebrity-focused fantasy (music, film, sport) and many different types of fantasy (fantasies of physical and mental power, wealth, sexual desire). I am definitely not saying that there is something necessarily damaging about such fantasies: they arguably fulfil a social function (Alberoni, 1972; Dyer, 1979; Reeves, 1988). My point, rather, is that, to understand them, we need to grasp the misrecognition on which they are based. The playing out of such fantasies necessarily reproduces that misrecognition, and thereby reinforces the naturalisation of media power. This is true, in spite of the differences in how the status of 'media people' is marked in different media. It has often been remarked, for example, that television and radio, as everyday media, produce 'personalities' or 'celebrities' whose status is rather different from the 'stars' produced by film or music.[64] While important, this does not mean that no misrecognition arises in relation to such 'personalities'. On the contrary, broadcasting's rhetoric of 'ordinariness' makes the status of such personalities all the more paradoxical. They are presented, at one level, as 'just' 'ordinary people' and in soaps, of course, they play 'ordinary people' as well. Yet they remain 'extraordinary' because they appear in the media.

Another object of imaginative identification may simply be the medium itself. I mentioned in the last section how people in a studio audience may be interested, not so much in the 'personalities', as in 'touching the medium'. As we see in Chapter 5, Granada Studios Tour visitors want to see *Coronation Street* stars, but *who* in particular they see may not matter much: the star is a token for the programme and, indirectly, the medium. Such imaginative play with the medium has many forms: being on the set, seeing the studios, following the crew on location, and so on. This play can be understood more generally as a form of 'symbolic reversal' (Babcock, 1978), reversing the hierarchy of the media frame. Also interesting are cases where media texts themselves *represent* such forms of play. A historical example comes from the successful wartime BBC radio show, *Band Wagon*, where the comedian Arthur Askey was presented as doing what audiences could never do: he interrupted the broadcasting process, by barracking the radio announcer, and lived 'ordinarily' in the 'media world', in an imaginary flat in Broadcasting House (Scannell and Cardiff, 1991: 270–2).

In these various ways, the reality of media power is socially negotiated, but not in reality reversed. Such play, like many symbolic reversals, 'keeps to the mould of the phenomenon ... inverted' (Handelman, 1990: 52; cf. Bourdieu, 1991: 89–91), thereby reproducing, not subverting, its boundaries. Sometimes, however, the play becomes more serious, as when people try to become 'extras' on television (Chapter 6). It is here that the fantasy of entering the media world risks confronting the misrecognition upon which it is based. Just as stars are paradoxical – they are both ordinary, and not ordinary (Dyer, 1979: 49) – so too the media process itself is paradoxical. On the one hand, it is imagined as special and magical because by entering it the 'ordinary person' is transposed to the 'media world'. On the other hand, as those who fail to become extras discover, the media process is a real, and far from magical, process of exclusion. This painful discovery can, even so, be rationalised as reflecting the inevitable,[65] or can simply become the basis of a joke (the comic figure of the person who is merely 'famous for being famous'). But in some cases, as we see in Part 2, the tensions, which imaginative identification with the media frame involves, come close to being made explicit.


## FURTHER IMPLICATIONS

I have argued that the media's differential symbolic power is naturalised through the media's role in framing, ordering, and naming social reality. Together, these dimensions reinforce each other to produce what I have called the 'symbolic hierarchy of the media frame'. This hierarchy is further naturalised through a spatial order (in which media operations are segregated from other spheres) and through imaginative play and fantasy. It is of course, as I noted earlier, somewhat artificial to isolate five 'dimensions' of naturalisation in this way. My purpose is simply to clarify some important connections and show that media power is legitimated through a network of processes which cross the whole media terrain: from the production of news, to fantasies about stars, to journeys to media locations.

Because the legitimation and naturalisation process is society-wide, it is impossible to describe exhaustively. Another contributory process is *competition* for access to the symbolic power of which the media sphere is the focus. Everyone knows the 'importance' of the media, and how difficult it is to 'get into' them. Most of us enjoy competing for media-related symbolic 'capital' at a low level: exchanging knowledge about 'media people' we have been acquainted with, spottings of a 'media person', and so on. Visits to media locations can be seen as structured moments when acquiring low-level symbolic capital of this sort is guaranteed. At the same time, as Pierre Bourdieu (1993) argues more generally for the cultural sphere,[66] such competition is itself consistently misrecognised, or *masked*. Consider the victors in this competition: they do more than win the game on its own terms (winning access to the media's symbolic power). They also win the right to cease being recognised as competitors for symbolic power: they enter the media's 'actuality', so that their self-directed competition for symbolic power retrospectively appears legitimate. They earn what Bourdieu and Passeron called (in relation to the education system) 'the supreme privilege of not seeing themselves as privileged' (1977: 210), and, of course, not being seen that way by others.

Alternatively, instead of being masked, criticisms of the unequal competition for symbolic power may be condensed in proverbial expressions, whose full implications are never unpacked. One example from my interviews with visitors to Granada Studios Tour is the comment that television people only become famous because of the support of audiences:

'It's the public that have put them where they are.' (Julie)

'It's us, the public, that are keeping them in work.' (Debbie)

'We make them what they are by watching the programme.' (Susan)

The implication – that the very division between 'media' and 'ordinary' people is a construction – was not drawn. In fact, each of these interviewees valued meeting *Coronation Street* cast members highly. Occasionally, however the reality of competition for symbolic power becomes fully unmasked. 'Living soaps', where 'ordinary people' are filmed living their 'real lives', are perhaps a good example. They involve an abrupt transition from 'ordinary person' to 'media person'. Perhaps this is why one performer on BBC2's *The Living Soap* reported hostility from other non-media people: 'We get a lot of abuse for being on the telly.'[67]

Another very different way in which the naturalisation of media power is reinforced is through the *pathologisation* of those who threaten to de-naturalise the boundaries between 'media' and 'ordinary' 'worlds'. This, I suggest, is one reason for the well-known phenomenon of the pathologisation of media fans (H. Jenkins, 1992: 9–24, Vermorel and Vermorel, 1985: 248–9). Pathologising is a common process for reinforcing various types of social and symbolic boundaries (Foucault, 1979; Said, 1978; Sibley, 1995): the boundary between 'media' and 'ordinary' 'worlds' is no different. As the case studies show, people are pathologised simply for getting 'too close' to the media's operations. Both 'crazed' television fans who take their interest in the media production 'too far' and 'silly' people who participate in mediated protests may be pathologised. They are, in effect, 'polluting' in Mary Douglas's sense: 'matter out of place' (1984: 35). As Douglas argued, 'dirt is never a unique, isolated event. Where there is dirt, there is system', and the common systemic feature here is that non-media people who get close to the process of mediation disrupt the media frame's implicit hierarchy. Thus, both *Star Trek* fans and protesters at Brightlingsea may be told to 'get a life',[68] that is, to return to the place of action allotted to them.

If my analysis is right, media institutions have a particular interest in protecting the boundaries around their own symbolic power through pathologisation. Media fans are standardly mocked in journalistic accounts for this reason.[69] Here is the beginning of a typical article:

### ADDICTED TO TELLY
**How an obsession with TV turned four lives upside down**
For some people, watching their favourite TV shows just isn't enough. Mary Keenan meets four fanatics who admit they put their quest for telly trivia before friends and even their family …
(*Daily Mirror*, The Look [Supplement], 18 April 1998)

Equally, it has often been noted how media producers pathologise audience members who contact them directly (Elliott, 1972: 140; Gans, 1980: 231; Schlesinger, 1978: 107–8). At one protest I analysed, a woman challenged the local media for failing to cover the protests sufficiently. The hostile response from the institution concerned, and her difficulties in dealing with that, provide a vivid example of such pathologisation from the receiving end:

… he gave me a right bollocking. [He said] that ( … ) I should never have done it ( … ) I was ever so upset ( … ) I felt like a very naughty schoolgirl, who was severely reprimanded and I never contacted [name deleted] again because I was terrified they'd recognise my name ( … ) I was more frightened of him than I was of the 300 policemen walking at me and stepping over me.

(interview with the author)

Pathologisation is more than just fun; it is a powerful weapon for protecting the boundaries around media institutions' symbolic power.

## CONCLUSION

As explained earlier, my aim has been to develop a model of the different processes by which media power is naturalised, and how those processes interconnect and reinforce each other. Without some degree of abstractness, it would be difficult to make clear the complex interrelations that are involved.

Like any model, however, my account runs the risk of exaggerating the orderliness of what it models. Certainly I am not claiming that media power is always reproduced evenly and without any possibility of contestation: that would be to repeat the error for which in Chapter 2 I criticised Baudrillard. There are inevitably disruptions. My interviews provided evidence of this, such as the following comment from a Brightlingsea protester who had visited television studios in London to protest at the coverage provided by a particular programme:

> Yeah, it was great. So it can be done ( … ) and I think, as times goes on, if people think there's a programme on the television that is not right … they can get people together and say, right, we're going to go up there and stop it ourselves.

The fact, however, that this simple act felt like a discovery is itself eloquent evidence of the naturalised separation of media producers and their audience. But the impact of such disruptions should not be exaggerated. They will only have a wider impact if connected up into a larger pattern. But what would that pattern be? A society-wide challenge to the legitimacy of media institutions, presumably. We would hardly expect the media themselves to amplify that process; on the contrary, as the events after Princess Diana's death made clear, the media may try hard to prevent that outcome (Couldry, 1999a). It is, then, neither correct nor necessary for my argument to say that the naturalisation of media power is a completely even process; my argument is only that it is generally effective, and that such disruptions as occur generally have a limited impact.

The same point applies to the differences between how particular media are regarded. Clearly, it is not the case that all media are given the same value or respect in every circumstance (cf. above under 'Naming'). Recent developments illustrate this well. First, in the aftermath of Princess Diana's death, in Britain there were considerable recriminations within the media as to which had caused Diana's death (television blaming the press, the broadsheet press blaming the tabloids, UK tabloids blaming 'foreign' paparazzi).

More recently, there have been various cases in the UK when television production companies have been accused by the press of fabricating documentary programmes (the most prominent involving Carlton TV and a documentary on drug smuggling).[70] In the USA too, both press and television have recently been forced to retract stories through pressure from other media reports (most prominently, CNN and *Time*'s allegation in 1998 that US military used a nerve agent in the Vietnam War). These battles reflect increased competition within the media sector, but they may also have long-term influence on attitudes towards particular media. There is no reason, however, to believe that such disputes and scandals will significantly affect the overall authority of 'the media'. They are, after all, allegations and disputes made largely within the media sphere; if remembered at all, they may simply reinforce the authority of some media institutions at the expense of their competitors.

My concern is much more general; it is with what Pierre Bourdieu (1992: 118) has called a '*de facto* division of labour of social production with regard to major varieties of experience', the massive concentration of symbolic power in the media sphere itself. The media's status is, as I have argued, legitimated through many things other than specific 'beliefs' in specific media. Nor is it a matter of some sort of 'dominant ideology' that supports media power.[71] Media power is reproduced through the spatial order of the media frame, 'common-sense' patterns of thought and language about the media, barely articulated assumptions about what is likely to be true or not, who is of value and who is not. Above all, media power is reproduced because it has come to seem natural.[72] The forms and extent of this naturalisation are certainly not immune from change; Chapter 9 looks at the impacts of new media technologies in this area. Real change, however, will require something more fundamental than a series of intra-media disputes. But there is a limit to how much theory can achieve on its own. It is time now to look at some detailed examples.

# Part 2

# MEDIA PILGRIMS: ON THE SET OF *CORONATION STREET*

# GENERAL INTRODUCTION

The 1980s and 1990s have seen a massive proliferation of tourist and heritage sites in Britain and many other countries (cf. Chapter 2). An important, but little-studied, aspect of that expansion has been media tourist sites. At one end of the spectrum are the highly commercialised, organised sites with museum-like displays and theme park entertainment. Best known are Disney–MGM and MCA's Universal Studios in the USA. Disney–MGM alone receives in the order of 25,000 visitors daily (Fjellman, 1992: 445). At the time of writing, there are unconfirmed reports that both Disney and Warner Brothers are exploring the possibility of taking over the British Government's huge and controversial 'Millennium Dome' on the Thames in south-east London, to convert it into a leisure site with film studio tours similar to those in the USA (*Independent on Sunday*, 29 November 1998). At the other end of the spectrum are the many locations in Britain and elsewhere, which are not fully commercial leisure sites (entry is free), but are visited simply because they have been sites of media production, especially filming. In the past ten years in Britain, it is these smaller, less commercial sites which have expanded fastest. This is connected to British film and television drama's particular emphasis on 'realism' (Higson, 1984), which of course implies real locations: whether the stately home setting for a heritage film, or the real-life street and landscape for a television drama serial. As a result, there are many sites to visit, and tourist authorities have begun to market them as a way of attracting people to their regions. (Yorkshire Tourist Board, for example, in collaboration with local media companies now issues a guide to sites in its region which are media locations; you can go on a 'Yorkshire Television Official Holiday' to the part of Yorkshire where the popular television drama *Heartbeat* is filmed.)

Granada Studios Tour ('GST'), which opened in July 1988 on a site next to Granada Television's Manchester studios, falls somewhere between these two extremes. On the one hand, it is now a fully developed commercial theme park, but on a much smaller scale than the main US sites. Operated by a separate subsidiary of Granada Group PLC, it represents an investment of approximately £25 million (Disney–MGM by contrast cost more than $500 million); GST has received over four million visitors since it opened, with up to 4,500 visitors a day during the peak summer season (source: interview with Helen Jackson, Operations Manager of GST, September 1996). It markets itself as 'Europe's Biggest Film and Television Day Out'. It is a significant site, but still small compared with Disney–MGM's turnover. On the other hand, a major part of GST's attraction has always been one particular location: the external set (built in 1982) currently used in filming *Coronation Street*, Britain's longest-running television soap. This programme is produced by Granada Television.

GST's original focus was exclusively television, and certain television attractions have remained since 1988: (1) the external *Coronation Street* set; (2) 'Telestars' (where you can 'appear' in a *Coronation Street* episode via Chromakey superimposition techniques); (3) a tour of television 'backstage' areas (mock-up dressing-rooms, make-up rooms, special effects demonstrations, a set of 10 Downing Street, and so on); and (4) two other large-scale sets ('Sherlock Holmes' Baker Street' and 'The House of Commons', both from Granada television series). As the marketing emphasis has switched to more general media themes, other attractions have been added: a sound effects show, the 'Motionmaster' show with moving seats, and various film-related rides. Originally the whole site was covered in one tour of fixed duration, but now visitors can choose whether to concentrate on rides and general entertainment or spend longer on the attractions related to television.

Although relatively small on an international scale, GST is none the less a complex site with many associations. This emerged when I asked visitors if they had been anywhere similar; their answers ranged from filming locations, to general theme parks, to pure heritage sites such as Beamish (an open-air museum of regional life and history in north-east England: see Bennett, 1995: 110–21). I won't attempt to give a general picture of all GST's visitors. I will focus on visits by private individuals (not GST's extensive corporate entertaining), and particularly responses to the television-related aspects of GST, above all the set of *Coronation Street,* or 'the Street' as both set and programme are known. Most of my interviews were conducted near there.

To complete the context for Part 2, I must say something about the programme *Coronation Street* itself. As Britain's longest-running television soap (it opened in 1960), it has acquired an iconic status, at least in Britain; it is exported also to countries with large expatriate British communities, such as Canada and New Zealand. It was the first British television soap to establish itself as representing an image of 'ordinary' British working-class life in north-west England. It was not until the 1980s that other British soaps emerged with comparable influence and close regional associations, such as the BBC's *Eastenders* (based on working-class east London), and Channel Four's *Brookside* (based on working-class Liverpool). *Coronation Street* is a classic representative of the 'realist' tradition Higson analysed, with all its faults:

> Place becomes a 'sign of reality': the implication is that it speaks a history, a memory. But always access to this history seems blocked … The fascination is with a moral landscape, hence the resistance to a historical reading of the landscape.
>
> (1984: 9)

The programme has long been criticised for its regional and class stereotypes and these continue, even as in the late 1990s it responds in various ways to fierce competition from other soaps, through more high-profile treatment of controversial social issues (sexuality, race) and through more plots and stars attractive to young people. *Coronation Street*, then, has something of a ritual status, because of its longevity, and because of the relatively constant and stereotypical image that it has projected for four decades. At the same time, GST is the largest, best-known and most established media location in the UK. Given all this, GST seemed a good place to start exploring the issues about media power discussed in Part 1.

Part 2 is based on the following sources: eighty-four short interviews conducted at GST during August–September 1996 (lasting generally around 10–15 minutes, sometimes longer); nine longer interviews, lasting between one and three hours, conducted mainly in people's homes during the period November 1996 to February 1997; letters received from twenty-one people in response to advertisements placed in two soap magazines; and my own fieldnotes from visiting GST. I will be drawing on the full range of this material to trace patterns of language and thought which bring out my wider themes of media power and its naturalisation. I will look in most detail at the longer interviews conducted off-site. I did not ask the names of people interviewed on-site; gender and other details are indicated, where it seems important; those interviewed off-site are referred to by pseudonyms, and introduced here.

The people interviewed off-site were: Julie, a 52-year-old carpenter's wife from the Midlands; Peter, a 24-year-old catering worker from the Midlands; Sarah, a 21-year-old professionally qualified health worker also from the Midlands; Barbara, the 17-year-old daughter of an electrical engineer, who was still at school and lived in Greater Manchester; Beth and Chris, a 40-year-old nurse and a 36-year-old catering manager, married and living in Manchester; Kim, the 14-year-old daughter of a care-home proprietor from the Midlands; John, a 49-year-old clerical worker from Dorset, who had grown up in the North; Debbie, a 27-year-old printing worker from Kent; and Susan and Glenys, aged respectively 55 and 41, who worked together as teaching assistants in Sussex, and visited GST together. I also discuss in detail

Michael, a 28-year-old teacher from the Republic of Ireland, who wrote to me, but whom I could not interview: he gave extensive answers to written questions I sent him.

More detail about the construction of the samples and my methods of analysis is given in the Appendix.

# 4

# ON THE ACTUAL STREET

## INTRODUCTION

The external set of *Coronation Street* is GST's principal attraction for many, perhaps most, of its visitors, and there is something paradoxical about it. People pay to visit a location they have already watched free on television for years; part of the pleasure is not seeing something different, but confirming that the set is the same as something already seen.

As we will see, the set undoubtedly has the 'power of place' in Dolores Hayden's (1995) phrase,[73] and yet it seems poorly qualified to satisfy her definition of the term (ibid.: 9): 'the power of ordinary urban landscapes to nurture citizens' public memory, to encompass shared time in the form of shared territory.' The Street set is only an image of an 'ordinary urban landscape' (no one has ever lived or died there); at most it is a focus of British television's dispersed 'electronic network' (Rath, 1985: 200). The Street set's 'power of place' rests not on public history in the usual sense, but on shared fiction. It is a place which condenses memory, a place with 'aura', a 'ritual place', even a place of 'pilgrimage'. It embodies a connection between visitors' history of watching the programme and their brief 'time on the Street'.[74] The meaningfulness of this connection derives, I will argue, from the symbolic hierarchy of the media frame. It is this shared interpretative framework, rather than detailed issues of economics or marketing, that is the subject of this chapter. Questions of meaning, however, go a long way to explaining why GST should be a tourist site at all (see also Couldry, 1998a and 1998b).

What do people do on the set of *Coronation Street*? They walk down it: people sometimes summed up their visit in this phrase. But, since many spend an hour or more on the set, there must be more to the visit than that. People take photographs and are photographed at points of interest – outside the Rovers Return pub, the shops, the houses – but that too is over quickly. Almost everyone spends time testing the boundaries of the set's illusion: looking through the houses' letter boxes or windows, pressing doorbells and knocking on doors; looking round the houses' backs (the 'old' houses have paved yards backing onto an alley, the 'new' houses have gardens). People compare the details of the set with their previous image of the Street. Some of the set's details, in fact, are aimed at visitors, not the television audience: for example, the 'for sale' notices in the newsagent's window. There is a lot of laughter, especially when the set is crowded. It's enjoyable to pretend, for a moment, that you live on the Street, posing with door knocker in hand or calling up to one of the characters. The visit is an elaborate form of performance[75] and exploration.

Many visitors will already have visited GST before. Of the twenty-one people who wrote to me, six had visited more than once and another seven said they wanted to return. Of the site sample, 21 per cent had visited before, some more than once. Taking the site sample, returnees were three times as likely to be women as men; they also (as one would expect, given the entry costs)[76] were more likely to live in GST's own region (76 per cent from the North of England). Even if returnees are a distinct subset of visitors, the fact that people return to GST *at all* needs to be explained. Chris Rojek has written of 'the sense of anticlimax that often accompanies the visit' to contemporary tourist sites: 'we see it; but have we not seen it before in countless artifacts, images, dramatic treatments, and other reproductions?' (1993: 196). That risk is all the greater at GST: everyone has seen the Street countless times on television. As one young couple put it: '[Woman:] You see it every night on TV, so there's not all that much difference apart from size. [Man] To say you've actually been there, that's probably part of it.' Not only, however, were such comments rare, but, even for this couple, 'to say you've actually been there' was not trivial; it had significance, even if not a personal one. Indeed the routine nature of the visit may depend precisely on the Street set's taken-for-granted symbolic significance: 'it's something everyone does and that's it. It's like ( ... ) the Tower of London ( ... ) I mean, you wouldn't sit down and discuss your visit to the Tower of London with people' (Beth). Perhaps visiting the Street set is significant precisely *because* it is the place you routinely watch. As one man put it: '[CS] is the part [of GST] that we seem to enjoy most because it's something you see every week on television.' We need to unravel the implications of this apparently simple statement.

Most people I interviewed were positive about their visit to GST. There was, of course, a wide spectrum of engagement. People may visit out of interest: to see 'what goes on', 'how it all works', finding it 'educational'. There is the pleasure of participating in the fiction, seeing '*Coronation Street* come to life'. But the visit may also involve considerable emotional investment for both men and women: 'for years, I've always wanted to come' (woman); 'I've just been desperate to see it for years now' (woman); it may be 'a dream come true' (Michael), 'a lifelong dream' (woman). For John, the intensity of going to the Street was 'like being on a drug'. Peter spoke of the 'adrenalin' rush when he visited the Street:

*Plate 1* The set of *Coronation Street*, Granada Studios Tour, June 1996

*Plate 2* The set of *Coronation Street*, Granada Studios Tour, June 1996

> Just feel so excited when you go on to the actual Street ( ... ) don't know what it was ( ... ) it was a bit of adrenalin I think, it seems strange, I know, but that's what happened every time I went.

Some people said they found it difficult to believe that they were actually there, on the set (six cases). Underlying all these reactions is the sense that it is significant to 'be there': it is an 'experience' marked off from the 'ordinary' (a defining feature of the 'tourist gaze': Urry, 1990). As one man put it: 'I want to see the place ( ... ) where this thing is, you know. It's an absolute experience, isn't it, a magnificent experience, isn't it, to come to this place.' Being on the Street set, then, is intrinsically significant.

It is the *shared* framework of significance underlying people's visits to the Street that I want to explore: this framework may be shared by those bored and those fascinated with the set. I will draw on as wide a range of my material as possible, but later in the chapter will look closely at the words of those most intensely engaged with the set. I do not claim their detailed reactions are typical of my wider sample but rather that, because they put so much weight upon that framework of significance, they reveal its structure most clearly (cf. Appendix).

## QUESTIONS OF IDENTITY

Before discussing the detailed meaning of visiting the set for individuals, I want to consider visits, more generally, as public expressions of identity. One obvious significance is as an affirmation of Northern, working-class identity, for which the programme *Coronation Street* has provided a widely-recognised stereotype for almost forty years (Dyer *et al.*, 1981; Geraghty, 1991; Shields, 1991: 222–9). The dangers and constraints of this stereotype were occasionally remarked upon by Northerners who had been to the South or reproduced by interviewees from the South. Glenys spoke as if *Coronation Street*'s image of Victorian terraced streets was the North's only reality, a reality set permanently in the past: 'they seem to be like a beat behind us up there, don't they?' The stereotype is, of course, only partly negative; the associations of a 'Northern' sense of 'community' are positive. A connection with their own living conditions was acknowledged by visitors who were themselves Northern and/or working class. They talked of *Coronation Street* as just 'ordinary', 'everyday living'; 'showing how people live', 'showing working people's lives'. However *Coronation Street*'s image of (Northern) working-class life has been rejected as outdated by other British soaps, whether representing the 'South' (*Eastenders*) or the 'North' (*Brookside*) (Geraghty, 1991: 34).

The question of what *Coronation Street* 'represents' – and therefore what visiting the Street set might represent – is complex. For some, the visit no doubt affirms Northern and/or working class identity. This was explicit in some interviews: Barbara (middle-class, from Greater Manchester), John (lower middle-class, living now in the South, but with a working-class upbringing in the North East), Beth (lower middle-class, from Manchester). For Beth, who had lived abroad for some years, *Coronation Street* 'is our heritage ( … ) our culture', a sign of not just Northernness but also of Englishness, like 'the smell of green grass'. Issues of identity connect with the rhetoric of GST and Granada Television (companies with a mission to 'represent' the region), as this comment of an HGV driver from Lancashire made clear:

> Being in the North-West, it's on your doorstep, I've watched it for years ( … ) I've been brought up watching it ( … ) and here we are [laughs]. You know, it comes up on telly and you think, Ah, it's only round the corner that, bit like your local ( … ) Like the tour rep said, it's put us on the map sort of thing ( … )

On the face of it, visiting GST seems just like a 'pilgrimage' in Victor Turner's sense of a value-affirming journey to a central site (Turner and Turner, 1978: 241; cf. Turner, 1974). However, the more useful precedent may be not Turner's work (which emphasises the affirmation of universally shared values), but Michael Sallnow's work (1981, 1987) on pilgrimage by Peruvian Indians to contemporary Christian sites already sacred before the Conquest. Sallnow analyses these pilgrimages as affirmations of *difference*, 'project[ing] one's local ethnic status … onto a wider translocal landscape, where it begins to acquire a more categorical meaning' (1987: 204). Transposed to regional and class differences, we can say that part of what visiting the Street set represents is an affirmation of class and regional difference at a central site. At the end of the chapter, I return to whether we can apply the concept of pilgrimage in a different way.

The overall position is, however, even more complex. Not only does *Coronation Street* represent only one in a whole field of competing representations of Northern and/or working-class identity on British television; for many it is also strongly associated, not with social reality now, but with the past: whether a personal past ('a breath of home'), or, more starkly, a social past that is lost. As one woman pensioner from Derby put it:

> I'd say [CS] was a happy place really. I was born in a place like this, you know, the little houses … We got the companionship you don't get today, I mean in a house like that you wouldn't lay dead for four days and nobody find you, would you?

Or a middle-aged couple from Warrington:

| | |
|---|---|
| *Man* | [sighs] I think [CS] is a place that no longer exists in reality really ( … ) |
| *Woman* | They have tried to update it but comparing it to where we live that neighbourly spirit has disappeared, you know. |
| *Man* | Yeah, and mainly due to television ( … ) people come home from work or wherever and they shut the front door and they switch on the telly and that's the end of it. |

The irony that the community which *Coronation Street* projects has been destroyed in part by television itself is powerful. But, if many people are conscious of the programme's lack of realism, we cannot claim that visiting GST is a simple affirmation of class or regional identity. Indeed any affirmation of identity at GST is complicated by the fact that the programme is, as everyone knows, a fiction and at GST you see how that fiction is constructed. The potential disappointments that flow from this are quite separate from any wider sense of social identity affirmed by being there. For Beth, as mentioned, the programme's connection with her life (particularly her childhood) was intense. But, reflecting on her visit, she felt disappointment: 'It's like when you were a child, you imagine something, then you go back to it as an adult and it's totally different ( … ) it was exactly like that. Everything just seemed very small and flat.' Here issues of identity are cut across by issues of fiction.

Indeed, it is striking how little people spoke to me explicitly about class or regional identity. Perhaps it was too obvious to mention. Certainly the dynamics of the interview situation (with me being a middle-class Southerner) may have encouraged some reticence, although many visitors to GST are neither working-class nor from the North of England. But another important feature of GST is that there is no place where class and regional identity are explicitly focused as such. There is an economic reason for this (maximising the attraction to the whole British television audience), but in any case it is narratives about media production, not specific forms of social identity, that are GST's focus. There is, however, another sense of identity affirmed at GST which cuts across regional and class divides: the 'community' of the programme's fans. A number of people mentioned their pleasure in the 'camaraderie' this generates (five cases). It was expressed by Susan and Glenys (both lower middle-class Southerners):

| | |
|---|---|
| *Susan* | … as you're looking over there, you say something, and then somebody behind you will say, Oh, so-and-so and so-and-so. And you tend to get … into another crowd then ( … 10 pages) |
| *Glenys* | So we were all there … with a common … thought, that we wanted to see Corrie ( … ) so you could talk to people and know that you had something in common even if it was only the fact that we were all *Coronation Street* fans. |

Others had a sense of 'everyone together the way it should be', of 'one big happy family'. The community of fans connects people who do not know each other and may come from different regions and classes. It is an emergent 'proto-community' in Paul Willis's phrase (1990: 141). People's experience of discovering fellow-fans at GST is similar to what Maffesoli (1996: 11, 13) has called the 'empathetic "sociality"' we feel when we find '"those who think and feel as we do"'. This sociality clearly also has an important gender dimension. But, again, however, this sociality (and the affirmation of gender difference it implies) is not necessarily the experience of all women fans. Debbie, for example, was pleased that the set was largely empty when she was there. Indeed, from my observations, most people went round the set on their own or with the small groups in which they came. There was certainly a sense of sociality on the set – expressed most outwardly in laughter – but visitors generally experienced this *in parallel to*, rather than with, each other (cf. The Project on Disney, 1995: 62–3).

To understand better the significance of visiting the set we need to look more closely at its meanings for individuals, rather than as a social or group act. First, however, I want to examine an area which bridges social and individual meanings: memory.

## MEMORY

Since *Coronation Street* is Britain's longest-running television soap, GST is an obvious example of television-related nostalgia. It can easily be fitted into the general growth of 'heritage' and 'nostalgia' tourism and Baudrillard's and Jameson's vision of real history being overlaid with a media-driven postmodernity (cf. Chapter 2). But GST can also, and perhaps surprisingly, tell us interesting things about the construction of social memory. The issue of how the media themselves are remembered has been largely neglected in wider social theory. My argument, however, is that GST (in particular, the Street set) functions as a material form for commemorating the practice of viewing television.

Following Maurice Halbwachs' (1992) [1924] fundamental insight that memory (both individual and social) requires a framework or *cadre* – a shared material and social context – in which to be reproduced, and following Paul Connerton's (1989) analysis of how rituals actually produce social memory through acts of repetition, we can see the Street set as a 'mnemonic system' (ibid.: 87), that takes effect through visitors' actions on the set. What does this mnemonic system commemorate? Obviously not the existence of the programme (this is 'commemorated' every time people watch) but rather the programme's past history and visitors' own past practice of viewing. The set, I suggest, provides an ordered space – a 'framework' (in Halbwachs' term) – in which memories of viewing can be organised, shared and thereby reproduced. Because of GST's commercialism, this commemorative function is easily overlooked. This feature of the Street set parallels a distinctive feature of the programme itself. For nearly forty years, *Coronation Street* has offered a continuous fictional reality, operating in parallel to viewers' lives. For some, it may serve as a mnemonic system for events in their own life. John, for example, expressed this powerfully:

> … for 36 years it has survived and that is incredible ( … ) And the thing about it is, and this sounds really silly, but I've grown up with it, I've actually experienced things in my life, and when I think back ( … ) to certain episodes, I can relate them to things in my life, and I think, well, oh yes, when Patricia Phoenix was in it, I was working at such and such a place and we went on such a trip, or when Ena Sharples [did] whatever, I can remember I was living in such and such. And I can relate it ( … ) to my family and what they were doing at the time … so that nostalgia is fantastic, and you can't change that.

For such visitors at least, visiting the set has a temporal depth connected not just with the programme's history, but with their own lives.

But how specifically does the set work as a memory-frame? First, visiting the Street involves mapping your sense of the Street's geography from years of watching onto the set's actual geography. Some found this easy, others wanted a map or name plates to confirm who 'lived' where. Either way, the process of working things out has a commemorative function. It takes many forms: for example, people's comments or jokes about details of houses and props ('Vera said she didn't want the stone cladding', 'I didn't know Gary had a satellite dish', and so on), or their questions to guides or each other about the set's history. Second, visiting the Street set can remind people of specific episodes from the programme's past. Such memories are stimulated by many aspects of GST: the show of video clips from old episodes called 'The Coronation Street Experience'; the photographs of past scenes dotted around the site;[77] the costumes and props from the programme shown on the Backstage Tour ('costumes held since Annie Walker's days', as one woman put it); and the shops full of souvenirs branded with Street characters. In recent years, the commercial exploitation of nostalgia for *Coronation Street* has increased markedly (through videos of old episodes, the recycling of old episodes on cable and satellite channels). But there can be a more personal aspect as well. Some people supply their own vivid memories of past episodes as they walk on the Street. Barbara, for example:

> I couldn't believe that I was actually on the spot of the 1983 showdown that rocked the nation, between Ken, Mike and Deirdre ( … ) I then carried on walking and approached the spot where Ena and Elsie bickered

for all those years and even nearly came to blows in one episode that I now enjoy watching on video.

For Barbara, the Street set was a place with a precise history. It might seem paradoxical to consider television, let alone the set of a television programme, from the point of view of commemoration: television is, after all, stereotypically the ephemeral medium. But a programme comprising nearly forty years of storytelling involving a large proportion of the British population surely requires some mechanism of commemoration. As Christine Geraghty (1981: 18) pointed out, programmes such as soaps are constrained in how much of their 'accumulated past' they can 'remember' in their storylines. Against this background of generalised forgetting, the act of visiting the Street set is hardly trivial.

Being on the set, however, does not only reproduce memories of the programme. Being there is itself inherently memorable, transforming future watching of the programme. Take, for example, the apparently banal things people do on the Street set to connect up with the outside, non-fictional world: posting cards in the Street pillar-box or using the telephone box (both of them functioning!). When people described these acts, they often referred to an *anticipated* act of commemoration, to occur when they watched the programme again or when the card was received:

> I even rang my mum from the phonebox on the end of the Street *just so that I could say* I'd been in it *every time it came on the TV.*
>
> (Barbara) [added emphasis]

> I sent [a card] to my mother-in-law and my sister-in-law ( … ) and one to my daughter-in-law and one to my daughter ( … ) *so they all said,* You really were there!
>
> (Susan) [added emphasis]

Writing or making a call is something you do on the Street which others can later vouch for as evidence that you were once there. Indeed *anything* you do in relation to the set is something you will be able to recall when you watch the programme:

> The first thing I saw was the telephone box from which I phoned home to say, I was on *Coronation Street*. Now every time the Street comes on I say [to myself] you made a call from that box.
>
> (Michael)

> Mother speaking to her son as they go up the Street set: 'when you watch *Coronation Street*, you'll be able to say to your Dad, you've looked in every letter box'.
>
> (Fieldnotes)

Doing something on the set of *Coronation Street* is 'inherently memorable' in precisely the sense that Michael Billig (1992) has analysed in relation to people's meetings with British royalty. Such meetings are memorable not simply because of their content, but because they are guaranteed to be retellable: they are joined to a frame of reference (royalty) whose continuity is itself assumed to be guaranteed (ibid.: 220–23). Similarly, the programme's continuous frame of reference makes everything you do on its set inherently memorable, and this is reinforced by each subsequent viewing:

> For us [the visit to GST] was just a wonderful experience, something we will remember for the rest of our lives. Every time we see the titles come up on the program we live it all again.
>
> (Susan, letter)

Such 'inherent memorability' is a feature of situations where the normal hierarchy between sites of discourse (Stallybrass and White, 1986) is suspended. The link with a place or person whose significance everyone knows is automatically retellable, and that fact creates a connection significant in itself. Establishing such a link can be seen, adapting de Certeau, as a 'tactical' use of the programme's 'strategic' storytelling frame which ensures that your own actions in relation to the programme are memorable (de Certeau in fact does not consider the possibility of interacting, as here, with the space of television production itself). For once, that frame yields a story that you can report in the *first* person. As Debbie put it: 'It's not just somewhere on telly now, it's actually somewhere I've been, I've actually stood there.'

The discussion of memory therefore raises issues of narrative and connection: in particular, the connection with the storytelling frame of the programme which visiting the set involves. I develop this theme in later sections.

## BEING ON THE STREET

The basis for the Street set's significance seems very simple: it is the place where the programme's filming goes on, the actual place you have watched from your home over the years. There is, of course, also an important fantasy element to being on the Street, the feeling that you are in the place where the cast are filmed: it was 'quite magical really, to actually believe that you're there on the spot where ... the stars walk along' (a comment by Barbara echoed in other interviews). But this imaginative connection with the programme's fictional frame depends on fact: the fact that the set *is* the place of external filming. What are the implications of this?

The Street's significance as the place where filming in fact goes on was marked routinely in people's language. To be on the Street set was to be on the 'actual Street', to 'be there' at the place where 'programmes are actually made'. Its houses are the 'real' places of filming, not mere 'studio sets' or 'mock-ups'. This was a principal reason why people went to the Street set: 'I just wanted to see where it was done' (Julie); 'good to see the actual street where the show is filmed' (letter). The fact that the set is the actual place of filming was not something most people quickly registered before moving on. I often heard people testing it out, wanting it confirmed:

Woman (20s), in large group of women, asks guide: 'Do they really film here?'

Man (middle-aged) asks the guide: 'Is this the original *Coronation Street*?' 'No', he's told, 'this was built in 1982'. 'Where was the original one?' 'It's where the New York Street is' is the answer. 'But it was all done here [i.e. on this site]?' 'Yes', says the guide.

(Extracts from fieldnotes)

Not everyone is convinced of this fact, a point to which I return when considering how the authenticity of the Street set is staged (Chapter 5). Some people reject the idea that the Street set is significant just because it is a place of filming. Such counter-opinions emerged occasionally when I interviewed a couple or larger group: for example, the view that historical sites are more authentic. These, however, remained minority voices among those I met – not surprisingly, since my sample was weighted towards those interested in the Street set.

Visiting the Street set may even involve an element of dislocation. If television 'constantly invokes … an unmediated experience that is forever absent, just beyond a hand reaching for the television dial' (Anderson, 1994: 82–3), then collapsing this distance may be puzzling: 'it's really weird though walking on it, because you watch it on TV and then you're thinking, well, people actually walk down this Street filming' (as one woman put it). Debbie recalled this sense of strangeness, when she reflected back on the visit much later: 'I don't know, it's sort of like being in a dream really, thinking I'm actually walking down *Coronation Street*. I just couldn't believe it ( … ) it just doesn't seem real sometimes'. For some people, the significance of 'being there' – on the Street set – goes beyond what they can rationally explain. For John, there was a sense, almost, of privilege: 'I know that's silly because literally millions of people go a year now, and millions of people have seen it, but I felt that I was the only one, I felt I was there and I'd seen it for so long, and … it was like a dream come true, really.' A Canadian woman, originally from India, visiting during a holiday in Europe, put it this way:

It's hard to express what I felt when I walked up to the Street to actually feel I was there, I mean I think that's going to stay with me for ever. Because it was such a wonderful feeling, it just left me speechless, you know, I just wanted to stand there.

Glenys talked about the photograph she and Susan put up at work after their visit:

We've got a photograph ... on our wall in our room at work, of the two of us outside the Rovers [Susan laughs] ... and that's us [laughs]. And we've got lines all round it, so everyone can see it. We've been there [laughs].

Why does it matter so much 'just to stand there', to be able to show others you have been there?

## AURA

We saw how important it is for most visitors to know that the Street set is the actual place of filming. This relates, in part, to a distinctive feature of British soaps: the way they represent a place with a distinct regional identity (cf. Chapter 2). An extension of this notion of authenticity is the assumption that the soaps are filmed in real places (cf. Buckingham, 1993: 226), or at least produced in a place situated in the narrative's region. Here is how one man from Lancashire, who had emigrated to Canada, put it:

Anybody watching any show in the States, if they went to Miami, I mean they may not see people from *Miami Vice* because it may be filmed somewhere else entirely, but we know this [CS] is filmed here, you see.

We also have seen that, for some visitors, the Street is a place with a precise history, associated with specific episodes. Another woman wanted to enter the set of the Rovers Return because 'there's a lot things happened there over the years'. In each case, the Street set is regarded as a place with a history which is 'fictional' only in a general sense (the sense in which *Coronation Street* as a whole is a fiction). If we regard the Street set as a place of filming (the perspective most people adopted), then the set has a real history – of *filming* – but one tied to the development of the programme's narrative. It is the real, not fictional, place where fictional events were actually filmed.

That sense of history was at issue when John rejected going to Blackpool to see Granada's 'World of Coronation Street' exhibition.

I've no desire to go, I would hate it, because it's not the real one. [short laugh] All right, so people could say, 'But that [CS] isn't the real one'. But it is, it's where they film the outdoor scene, it's the one where the actors are, where the studios are, where it all originated. Where did Blackpool come into it?

This comment was not unusual. One woman who was visiting Manchester during a holiday in Blackpool put it: 'no, we thought we'd come to the original.' Others rejected the Blackpool 'Experience' as 'not the real Street'; only the Street set itself was 'the real thing', 'the real place'. Why? Because 'you know it's all done here'.[78] Note that John's sense that the Street set, and only the Street set, is worth visiting exists *despite* his knowing that it is 'only' a set and that others regard it as such ('all right, so people could say, "But that isn't the real one"'). There is a knowingness here, which fits uneasily with the apparent 'postmodern' truth, wittily expressed by Umberto Eco, that we live in a world in which the 'completely real' is *identified* with the 'completely fake' (Eco, 1986: 7, quoted in Rojek, 1993: 160, my emphasis). I come back to these cognitive questions in Chapter 5. People's preferences for seeing the 'real Street' (the 'original') are also interestingly at odds with Walter Benjamin's famous thesis (1968) on the loss of aura in the age of mechanical reproduction. What people who reject the Blackpool 'Experience' hope to obtain at GST is precisely an 'aura' – not the aura of something outside the mechanical reproduction of filming, but *the aura of the place and process of filming itself*: using Benjamin's phrase, 'its unique existence at the place where it happens to be' (ibid.: 220). As Debbie put it in relation to the Street set, 'people never appreciate it, unless they're there'.

John's language suggests that this aura, for him, is more than some general notion of 'being there' inherent in any media site, but rather a quality precisely tied to the set's material history. Benjamin defined 'authenticity' in just this way: 'the essence of all that is transmissible from [the object's] beginning, ranging from its substantive duration to its testimony to the history which it has experienced' (ibid.: 221). Compare that with John's explanation of why the Street set is better than a mere studio set:

> I have seen studios ( ... ) but nothing to compare with the Street ( ... ) When you're sitting in the studio, you do see ( ... ) the unreality, but on the Street ( ... ) it's a real street, albeit there's nothing behind the door as such. But you're still there, it's still real ( ... ) There was a funny thought that went through my mind, that it had been raining ( ... ) And I actually looked down and thought, this is real because there's real rain, it sounded so stupid. And I stood in a puddle and I thought, Oh Crikey! Yeah, this is real, it's not covered over, it's always outdoors ... the actors go out in all weather ( ... ) it's real rain and it's real cobbles and it's real dirt [laughs] ( ... ) You don't expect a set to be that real.

John was not the only visitor to regard the rain on the set as significant (I came across two other cases), so his comments cannot simply be dismissed as eccentric. Why is the rain so special? Hardly just because it confirms the physicality of the set: a studio set is equally physical. The rain is significant in part, I suggest, because in a small way it is 'a testimony to the history' which the set 'has experienced' (Benjamin); it is a token of the set's authenticity and John's authentic experience of it, his definitive access to its 'aura'. The rain which has fallen, and will remain, on the set after John has gone allows him to project into both past and future the connection – between viewer and Street – that 'being there' involves. From a different perspective, the reality of the rain on the set may serve for John as a 're-embedding' (Giddens, 1990: 88) of the media mechanism itself: a re-embedding of his trust at a distance in media 'reality'. The set, although 'only' a set ('you don't expect a set to be that real'), stands in for something broader, a dimension of mediated social reality itself.

## THE STREET SET AS RITUAL PLACE

Here is how Michael described being on the Street set:

> From the moment I put my foot on the Street I feel like a star. I start my walk down the Street starting from the 'Rovers Return' to the 'corner shop'. I look through _all_ the windows and through _all_ the letter boxes. I touch the stone cladding of number 9. I feel so so very happy and trouble free when I walk down the Street ( … ) I just can't believe it. Every time I walk down the Street I get that same wonderful happy feeling ( … ) It [GST] is the best thing and most wonderful thing I have ever done. [original emphasis]

There is a palpable sense of ritual here. Again, rather than dismiss it as eccentric, I want to contextualise it in terms of what is perhaps the Street set's most fundamental attraction: its status as 'ritual place'. This will take my analysis of the set's significance one stage further, linking it explicitly to the symbolic hierarchy of the media frame, a concept which until now in this chapter I have avoided using explicitly.

We return here to the basic question: what (for all visitors, not just devoted fans) does being on the Street set involve? Being on the Street involves a comparison between what you have watched over the years and the set itself. This is, on the face of it, a banal comparison (seeing if the Street 'is actually like it is on telly', as one visitor put it), but its dimensions are worth considering. First, you are linking things in two different _time-frames_, the years during which you have watched the Street and the time now when you walk onto the set: 'for me, it was amazing because I've seen it on the TV for so many years now ( ... ) For me it was brilliant to finally see everything' (woman); 'it was weird to walk down the road that I had seen on television since I was about three as it was really familiar and unfamiliar at the same time' (Sarah, letter). It is the bringing together of two separate time-frames (the time of your regular watching over the years, the time of your visit now) that allows a sense of completion: 'to finally see everything'. This sense of completion is so vivid in John's account that it is worth quoting at greater length. Immediately before he went on the Street set he had seen the video selection called 'The Coronation Street Experience'. Afterwards, a curtain was pulled, revealing a wall which is partly transparent, and the Street behind:

> I shall never forget the first time that I saw the 'Street'. At the end of the tour the public is guided to a 'Coronation Street Experience' which consists of a slowly revolving platform which moves around and shows the sights and sounds of past events in the Street. As the last one fades and the revolving stage stops, you are faced with a brick wall. This slowly moves away to reveal, for the first time, the actual set of the Street outside. (letter)

Here the transition between the time-frames of long-term watching and present visit is reproduced exactly in the transition from the final video image of the Street to the sight of the Street set itself. Barbara's account was similar:

> You went in a room where they showed you a video of sort of past episodes, and then they drew the curtain back. You'd watched it on the telly and then it was actually there. And then you set off and then you walked along it.

The feeling of walking into the space of the screen is vivid, and this 'freedom' is clearly a designed effect of sites such as GST (Rojek, 1993; Davis, 1996). It works, however, partly because it reproduces in miniature the transition between time-frames that being on the Street itself involves. That is why, for Barbara, there was 'no point of actually going on the Street and then doing the video'.[79]

Second, being on the Street involves comparing the results of two different *activities*, two ways of looking, for which sometimes people used different words. 'Watching' the Street on television – at least without new developments in interactive television – you are constrained in how you can look at the set: you are limited by camera-angles, and so on. 'Seeing' the Street set allows you to look at its details in your own time and from any angle, and then put the whole thing back together:

> I wanted ( ... ) really to try and put the whole thing together myself. You

know, from not just watching it on the square box at home, but to actually see it. (woman)

I spent quite a bit of time there [on the set] and then after lunch I went
back there and took a small turn [ … ] you know standing back and seeing it and picturing it in my mind as to how it appears on TV. (woman)

Seeing what the set is actually like is an active process of finding out, qualita-
tively different from watching television.

There is also a third, *spatial* dimension to the comparison. 'Watching' the
Street is something we do in the home, whereas 'seeing' the Street set can
only be done in GST's public space. Being on the set therefore connects two
normally separate sites of discourse: the home and the site of media production. All these dimensions (time, activity, and space) are combined in Julie's
comment:

It was nice to see. An experience that you ( … ) actually sit in your living
room and you're actually watching that place, but now you're actually
standing in that place, and you can say ( … ) I've actually been there, and
it felt good.

'Being there' involves connecting your everyday practice of private viewing
with the public place where the programme is actually filmed.

This connection of different times, places, and activities is neither neutral
nor trivial:

It's magic, it's a great feeling, sitting at home when you watch telly and
say *I was there!* To think you could do that. (woman)

Just nice to know that you've seen [it], when you watch telly, that
you've actually been and seen it for yourself. (woman)

As we saw earlier, this connection is revived when you watch the programme
in future:

I mean, we were *unbearable* when we first came home, because as soon as
it came on, [we said] We were there! [Glenys laughing]. And that's
where we stood! ( … 4 pages) Every time we see it, we think, [whispers]
Oh we've been there! [Glenys laughs] And it's still, it's still there, Oh,
we've been there. It's really good, you know. (Susan)

Because the connection made by 'being there' is intrinsically significant in
this way, the most basic acts of occupying space on the Street are significant
in themselves: 'to actually stand in the Street is lovely' (woman); 'just

walking up and down something you see regularly in front of your eyes' (man). It is enough that you are 'there'.

I want to suggest that what underlies the Street set's 'power of place' – the force of the connection it embodies – is the way it formalises and spatialises the symbolic hierarchy of the media frame. The work of the anthropologist Jonathan Smith (1987) is helpful in making precise this apparently abstract point. Smith has drawn on Durkheim and Levi-Strauss's theories of symbolic classification to develop an original account of ritual place. The key points of his argument for my purpose are as follows. 'Ritual' is 'a mode of paying attention … a process for marking interest' (ibid.: 103) rather than a particular type of content. 'Place', in turn, is 'a fundamental component of ritual: place directs attention' (ibid.), and it performs this function, again not because of any particular content, but 'rather as *social position* within a hierarchical system' (ibid.: 45, added emphasis). 'Ritual' he argues:

> relies for its power on the fact that it is concerned with quite ordinary activities placed within an extraordinary setting … Ritual is a relationship of difference between 'nows' – the now of everyday life and the now of ritual place; the simultaneity, but not the coexistence, of 'here' and 'there'. Here (in the world) blood is a major source of impurity; there (in ritual space) blood removes impurity. Here (in the world) water is the central agent by which impurity is transmitted; there (in ritual space) washing with water carries away impurity. Neither the blood nor the water has changed; what has changed is their location. This absolute discrepancy invites thought, but cannot be thought away.
>
> (ibid.: 109–10)

On the Street set, analogously, people do ordinary things: walking up and down, looking in shop windows, and so on. But they do them in an extraordinary setting: the frame of the Street set. Indeed, the whole process of being on the Street, as just argued, brings out connections – and differences – between the 'ordinary' process of television viewing (the 'now' of everyday viewing) and the 'extraordinary' moment of the visit (the 'now' of being on the 'actual Street'). The two situations remain of course separate, and the difference 'cannot be thought away': it is a difference within a symbolic hierarchy. The set is not any space, any street, but the 'actual Street' that you and everyone else have been watching all those years from your home. It is, in this precise sense, a ritual place, where two 'worlds' are connected.

It is time to return to John's discussion, quoted earlier, of the rain on the set. If we apply to it the notion of the street set as ritual place – as a ritual 'frame' (in Mary Douglas' (1984) sense) that symbolically connects two hierarchically ordered places and temporalities – its meaning becomes still clearer. There is a parallelism between John's 'world' (the viewer who is temporarily a visitor) and the media's 'world': 'you're still there, it's still real', 'actors go out ... you can walk'. For a moment the two 'worlds' intersect. There is rain in both 'worlds' (the rain which fell on the set before John came, the rain still there when he is there) and of course it is the same rain. The rain, in other words, is what *articulates* these two 'worlds', normally segregated from each other. The rain embodies the connection, and the difference, that makes the Street set a ritual place.[80]

Once we understand the Street set as a ritual place, then otherwise puzzling aspects of people's accounts become clearer. First, the importance some people attached to the set being clean: they doubted whether it was the real place of filming because parts of it were dirty. I asked Barbara about the graffiti around the backs of the set which I knew annoyed some guides. She quoted her friend's reaction: "'I don't know how they can do it ( ... ) this is the *Coronation Street*, how can they write on the fences?".' Second, there is some people's sense that entering the Street set is like crossing a boundary: a 'limen' or threshold in van Gennep's (1960) sense. We saw earlier how John and Barbara described their entry onto the set. Susan mentioned how she and Glenys deferred walking onto the set until the last moment:

> We delayed going down the Street, we really did [Glenys laughs] ( ... one page) I stepped out of the [souvenir] shop, actually onto the Street ... I was clutching on [to Glenys] ... [Glenys laughs] I went, Ooh! [highpitched] We're here. We're here. I went, Ooh God! It's a mad woman.

Also interesting are remarks on the small differences between people's image of the Street from television and the physical space of the set. One difference people recounted to me months after their visits was the small gap between the Rovers Return and the start of the terraced houses. Here is Julie:

> I tell you one thing that I have never noticed, that I did notice, that there's an alleyway. You've got the Rovers Return and then there's the alleyway and *then* there's the houses. Now I never noticed that before until I went to the Street ( ... ) that was another thing that amazed me. (cf. John)

The importance given to this apparently trivial difference exemplifies the 'parcelling out' which Levi-Strauss regards as typical of all ritual: a process which 'makes infinite distinctions and ascribes discriminatory values to the slightest shade of difference' (1981: 672–5, quoted in Smith, 1987: 111). At GST the 'ritual' lies in elaborating the differences between Street set and television image of the Street, which condense the underlying difference between the 'media world' and the 'ordinary world' of watching.

This reinforces the sense that journeys to GST are, effectively, 'pilgrimages'. GST is a pilgrimage point in the sense that it is a central, symbolically significant place which focuses the attention of a whole territory, the dispersed 'territory' of the 'electronic network' (Rath, 1985: 200). It is a place where 'special' time can be spent apart from the time of 'ordinary' life (cf. Turner, 1974), time that is special simply because spent within 'media space': 'your time on the Street'. What is affirmed by going there is not necessarily values associated with *Coronation Street* the programme, or even with the act of watching it. What is affirmed, more fundamentally, are the values condensed in the symbolic hierarchy of the media frame itself: its symbolic division of the social world into two.

# 5

# THE REALITY OF THE FICTION

You see the bus [on the programme] coming up here and you realise the
reality of the illusion.

(teenage boy, heard on the *Coronation Street* set: Fieldnotes)

That's the thing that I can't seem to get over ( ... ) the fact that they like
fox you completely. So it makes you realise that television is all false
[laughs] really.

(Sarah, interview with the author)

## INTRODUCTION

Analysing a media tourist site as a ritual place, as I have done in Chapter 4, is a
little unusual. Where attention has been paid to them at all, it has been more
normal to class such sites as *fictive* sites, which have little academic significance beyond that.[81] GST is seemingly a perfect example of Baudrillard's
hyperreality thesis. But this, I am arguing, is only the start of its interest. People's talk about visiting GST shows a complexity of attitudes, which is far
from unsophisticated, yet at the same time reveals much about the naturalisation of media power. Just as Chapter 4 brought in anthropological perspectives, so too here I will develop my argument by importing insights from
wider social theory: Dean MacCannell's work on the significance of tourist
sites, and Michael Billig's work on people's accounts of meeting royalty. At
various points also, I will bring out what makes GST distinctive, compared,
say, with the better-known Disney sites.

We cannot, of course, discuss the Street set without considering the question of illusion. The set is the set of a fictional television programme. As the
first quote above brings out, visiting the set puts into question one level of
naturalisation inherent within the media frame: television's make-believe,
the narrative 'verisimilitude' (Wilson, 1993) of the media text. But that does
not mean that the set is mere fiction. On the contrary, the basis of people's

pleasure in the illusion is that GST contains the actual place where *Coronation Street* is filmed. This is fact, not fiction. Appreciating it is quite consistent with knowing both that the programme itself is a fiction and that its set involves visual illusion. People's balancing of fact and fiction with regard to the set is complex, as we shall see. Underlying this, however, is another level of naturalisation inherent in the media process: the wider naturalisation of the media's concentration of symbolic power. It is the media's 'make-believe' in this broader sense that is at issue in the second quote. That issue takes us back to the wider question of media power, and is addressed later in the chapter.

## FEELING THE SET IS REAL

On the Street set, external shots of the Street are filmed. It is a 'real place' of filming, a phrase used by several interviewees. So, when Sarah suspected that the Street set might only be a construction for visitors, it was the backs of the Street that convinced her, because they 'actually have the props and stuff' used in filming. (The converse applies in relation to the filming of indoor scenes, filmed in a separate (closed) studio building, with 'mock-up' indoor sets included on the Backstage Tour. For indoor shots, it is the inaccessible studio building that is the 'real studio'.) The fact that the Street set is 'real' in this sense is central to the pleasure of visiting it: 'it's a working set, and yet we're still allowed to ( ... ) be there, which is brilliant' (Beth). This implied 'symbolic reversal' is considered further in Chapter 6.

If the key issue for visitors in relation to both external and internal sets is whether they are used in filming, then the truth in neither case is automatically obvious,[82] which means people spend time puzzling over it. In the case of the outdoor set, a confusing factor (noted by almost everyone) is the Street's size: it is slightly smaller than an actual row of houses. Some discount this (knowing the effects of wide-angle lenses), some are disappointed. Either way, this has to be explained away, if you are to believe this is the 'real set'. In the case of the mock-up indoor sets, guides' comments about whether they are used for filming are inconsistent. The result is some confusion, as with this woman student:

> I don't think that they actually film on there, I'm a bit sceptical about it, it's a bit ... how close can you get kind of thing. And it didn't really look all that authentic ( ... ) it just didn't seem real to me.

Here not just the 'reality' of the sets is at issue, but their 'authenticity'. The two are, of course, connected. The set's authenticity (the sense of its reality *as* a set) is what people come to experience at GST: 'to see it all in reality', as one visitor put it. Some people experience this without further prompting: they just know that the Street set is the 'real set'. Others either lack this certainty or simply want the 'authenticity' of the set 'staged'. The phenomenon of 'staged authenticity' was first analysed by Dean MacCannell (1976) in his pioneering study of contemporary tourism. Leaving aside MacCannell's wider theory (that tourist sites stage authentic contact with central, yet normally distant, aspects of social life), his specific concept is useful here where the Street set's 'authenticity' is both obviously important and partly staged.

How might this staging be achieved (or not, as the case may be)? One way people imagined it happening was through seeing action from the programme. That, Sarah said, would 'make me feel like I'd really seen [the Street]'. Alternatively, by seeing the cast. Here is one elderly woman's comment:

> It's like *Coronation Street* but ( … ) not like you see it on telly ( … ) it hasn't got the atmosphere ( … 1 page) it's like it, but you've nothing to ( … ) compare to say it is *Coronation Street* like … you've ( … ) nobody from the cast and shops not open.

Although she clearly knew it was the Street set, she wanted confirmation. 'Cognitive' and 'imaginative' aspects are interconnected. It is the *reality* of the set as set (once factually confirmed) that makes possible the fantasy that you are, temporarily, part of the programme (cf. Gamson, 1994: 171 for a parallel in the case of celebrity watching). It also helps to feel immersed in the imaginary space of the Street. As one woman said, sitting with her husband on a bench put for visitors on the Street: 'It's just really nice sitting here, just sort of cutting out everything and being sort of part of it.' This is difficult when the Street is crowded with visitors who are not part of the programme. Entering the buildings on the Street is one way people imagined cutting out distractions. Many said they wanted to do this (seventeen examples), perhaps even to buy something in one of the Street shops (three examples). But this is impossible, since the insides of Street houses are just 'backstage' areas filled with props. Not surprisingly, this was another reason some people found the Street set inauthentic. One woman suggested it would be more authentic to have waxworks of the cast inside the houses on the Street. Others expected furniture inside, or remarked that the houses were only 'shells', not 'lived in'.

When people said they expected the set to be 'lived in', there is no reason to believe they meant this literally. Rather they expected it to look 'as if' lived in: in other words, as a *set* of *Coronation Street* should 'authentically' look. The reference-point here in establishing whether the set is/feels 'real'/'authentic' is not social reality in general (is *Coronation Street* 'real'? is it a 'realistic' fiction?) but the reality of the representation, the reality of the set's 'as if'. As one man put it: 'this is the real stuff. I know it's not filmed here [i.e. not at this moment] but … it's *as if* it's being filmed here.' There is nothing deceived or confused about this. Artificiality and reality – imaginative and cognitive dimensions – necessarily go together. The reality of the Street as set both grounds its potential as a place for imaginative play and entails its artificiality (from another perspective). Some mentioned this artificiality without prompting from me (five cases). Susan's comment suggested that she and Glenys had been challenged on this point by friends and family:

> You see … *we know it's not real*. I mean we're not obsessed by it, so much as we live the characters. We know it's a programme on telly, and we love it so much that we've been there. [added emphasis]

This complex state of belief and disbelief is only surprising, if we assume all visitors to GST are either disbelievers or 'dupes'. A similar complexity has been analysed, for example, in Hollywood celebrity watchers' relationships to the celebrity industry (Gamson, 1994: 175) and among young people viewing soaps (Buckingham, 1993: 224–7). It is part of engaging with any form of fiction.

## MEETING STARS

Meeting the *Coronation Street* cast is, as we saw, one way the Street set's authenticity is staged. Such meetings, therefore, have an 'evidential' role, as well as offering participation in the fictional space of the programme. They can also be understood as real negotiations of the power relations between 'media people' and non-media people.

Stars are essential to the economics of soap production and most other areas of cultural production. Soap stars are promoted not only through the storylines themselves but through a host of secondary productions: newspaper reports about plot developments and the cast's lives, television magazines (such as *Inside Soap* and the 'official' magazines for particular soaps, *Coronation Street* and *Brookside*), celebrity magazines (*Hello* and *OK*), star autobiographies. Soap stars make promotional appearances all over Britain (opening shops, playing in charity football matches). *Coronation Street* stars, once established, are central also to the economy of GST itself. Its shops sell countless souvenirs tied to characters. The possibility of meeting or seeing a Street star has been part of what GST markets. While the scheduled star 'walkabouts' ended in 1995 (as the cast's workload increased), special appearances are often guaranteed for coach tours, the cost included in the tour price (source: informal discussions with guides). Some holiday breaks include 'Nights with the Stars': special evenings of entertainment by Street stars outside GST's normal opening hours. In any case, since GST is situated next to the Granada Television Studios, people hope to see the cast as they walk to or from the filming studios. Coach operators tell their passengers good times to spot them. Every weekday lunchtime people gather at the railings behind the

Street set, waiting for stars to appear. Occasionally, promotional events involving Street stars occur on the set: the handing over of a cheque to a charity (Fieldnotes), even a photo-opportunity involving the Labour Party leader (not yet Prime Minister) Tony Blair, drinking beer with the cast outside the Rovers Return in August 1996, which I witnessed! The 'stars' theme is repeated frequently around the site: on the Backstage Tour, you walk up the 'Stairway to the Stars' and visit astrologer Russell Grant's 'Reach for the Stars' (pun intended). The possibility that you might see a star is, in any case, implicit in the idea of any 'Studios' tour. Many people mentioned contact with stars as important (fourteen cases) or expected (six cases).

How are we to understand people's talk about meeting members of the cast? It is too easy to dismiss them simply as forms of 'para-social' involvement: (Horton and Wohl, 1956). I found only two cases where people referred to media stars as 'friends', although perhaps people were reluctant to admit such emotional investment to me face to face. It is more productive to understand these meetings as negotiations of power.

## 'We're worse than them fans'

Meetings with Street stars generally do not involve an intense emotional investment with the *star* (judging by the interview and letter material); instead they have a generic, abstract quality. I asked some people on site, who had said they wanted to meet a cast member, if it mattered who they met. Of those who gave a definite answer (N=38), a majority (twenty-four) had no particular preference. Those who did, generally referred to a character or character type, not an actor or actress. As Glenys put it, 'You don't go to see the actress Helen Worth, you go to see [the character] Gail Platt'. Even Michael, who came closest to regarding the Street cast as individual celebrities, spoke of them in character: 'I was delighted to meet Vera [the fictional name] ( ... ) I think she is the [most] famous landlady [i.e. pub licensee] in the world.' As often noted, television 'celebrities' are less likely than film stars to have detailed star profiles outside of the programmes in which they perform (Ellis, 1982: 106–7; Marshall, 1997: 122–31; Reeves, 1988: 155–9).

Some people were defensive about being seen as a fan who mistook fiction for reality: 'I wouldn't be so daft ... as if anybody died to send them a wreath.' There is a much wider question here about whether such confused people exist; even if they do, are their actions evidence of individual pathology, or of people playing with a social and symbolic framework more explicitly than usual? Such stories tend to be about *others*. While there are no doubt pathological forms of living in a mediated society, the more interesting general question is how particular positions and actions within the media frame get constructed as pathological (cf. Chapter 3).

This process of pathologisation was certainly reflected in visitors' comments. They generally avoided presenting themselves to me as a fan of the

*Plate 3*  The set of *Coronation Street*, Granada Studios Tour, June 1996

*Plate 4*  Telestars booth, Granada Studios Tour, June 1996

cast rather than of the programme. More interestingly, while some people gathered to see cast members, many others quite deliberately did not and walked past. This was not simply lack of interest. Some of the keenest fans I interviewed said they never waited in the crowd (Barbara, John, Peter). Perhaps those with the most active interest in the programme felt this 'passive' activity beneath them. However, the low status of acknowledging the cast's status so explicitly was reflected in others' language as well:

| | |
|---|---|
| *NC* | Would you like to meet a member of the cast … ? |
| *Woman* | … we're not that *way-out minded* are we? No. |
| *Man* | ( … ) No, I don't think I'd be all that bothered one way or the other ( … ) I don't think I'd *scurry off to skawp* at them or something like that [laughs]. [added emphasis] |
| | |
| *Man* | I mean when you go round there to the railings, where everybody's looking over as they come in, you know, what it reminds you of really, they're a load of *monkeys at the zoo* [wife laughs], and we're all paying our money to stand there and *gawk* at them [laughs]. [added emphasis] |

Even those who did wait for the stars might distance themselves from the others standing there:

> A woman in her 60s says to another elderly woman who she is with: 'What are you waiting for? For the stars?' The other replies: 'We could wait all day. We're worse than them fans.'

> (Fieldnotes)

The same pathologisation could be imagined from the point of view of the stars themselves: 'if you're pestered by people, it can be a real bind', 'they'd get mobbed', 'they'd be robbed'. I return at the end of this chapter to consider why people should distance themselves from the appearance of being 'fans' of the cast.

## 'Actually meeting them'

When people talked about an actual or imagined meeting with a member of the *Coronation Street* cast, they described themselves or others as 'freezing', standing with mouth wide open, eyes staring, not knowing what to say.[83] In other words, they acknowledged the extraordinary nature of the contact being made. The extraordinariness lies not in the detailed content of the meeting, but simply the *fact* of it. Just as what matters most about being on the Street is simply 'being there', so meeting a star above all means making contact with the world in which stars move. So, when people talked about their meeting, instead of mentioning details about what the star said, or how (s)he looked or dressed, most comments revolved around whether the star was or was not willing to talk. Positively, stars could be 'lovely to talk to', have 'all the time in the world', be 'friendly', 'a gentleman', 'approachable', 'natural', 'patient with fans'. Negatively, they might be 'grumpy', not like to be touched, avoid people, not acknowledge them, or be rude. In each case, it is the quality of contact that is emphasised; it is through such contact that the symbolic boundary between 'ordinary' and 'media' 'worlds' is, temporarily, crossed.

The specialness of such a contact was reflected in another way. Since not all stars might be approachable, or people anticipated being tongue-tied when they met them, some preferred to make contact at a distance. Standing in the crowd and waiting for the stars was one way of doing this, provided it involved being seen by the stars (at least collectively), as Debbie's comment makes clear:

> Seeing the stars coming over for their lunch, that was brilliant! ( ... ) But I mean they didn't ... bother ... well, not coming over, but sort of like acknowledging us or anything like that ( ... ) one of them was really grumpy ( ... ) and that's really put me off him now.

Even a look from the star would be an acknowledgement of contact and therefore significant (cf. Gamson, 1994: 132). The most common form of distant 'contact' imagined was seeing the stars as they walked among the crowd on site (there were scheduled 'walkabouts' most days until 1996 and, when I interviewed people, many still thought this practice continued). This way, risks of embarrassment from direct engagement were minimised (cf. Goffman, 1972 on minimising risks), yet the contact seemed natural. The importance of 'natural' contact is worth exploring further.

When stars appeared, or were imagined to appear, they are usually doing something not staged, but routine and natural: 'walking amongst us', 'walking around', 'knocking about', 'floating', 'strolling', 'ambling', 'wandering around', 'we may see them around' (Fieldnotes).[84] The star should be behaving in an ordinary, relaxed way but, crucially, *in the same space* that the visitors themselves occupy. In fact, since 'walking around' is precisely what visitors do most of the time at GST, the star is simply imagined doing what everyone else does. But it is precisely this 'ordinariness' that is a sign of the extraordinary. As Michael Billig comments on people's accounts of meeting royalty, if royalty are encountered doing 'ordinary' things, this is treated as a 'discovery' that they are 'ordinary *"after all"*' (Billig, 1992: 78, added emphasis). But it is precisely the fact that their ordinariness is a 'discovery', which confirms that royalty, in reality, is not ordinary at all.[85] So too with the stars. A related point about stars' presence is that meetings with them should be spontaneous: this is another way of saying that these meetings' authenticity should be successfully 'staged' in MacCannell's sense. Their staging should not be too obvious. No one suggested meeting a star in an artificial setting, even though in earlier years stars had made staged appearances on the Back-stage Tour. That, one woman suggested, was not a real meeting. John is explicit on the importance of spontaneity:

> I've never actually looked for them [the stars] ... And again I don't think I'd want to because the spontaneity of seeing ( ... ) [Seeing] Chloe Newsome [a CS actress in 1996], it was so unexpected and because no one else had seen her and because she was going into the studio and I ac-tually saw her doing it.

An appearance of spontaneity is important, even if you know that a star appearance has been planned: 'we knew we were going to meet two, but we didn't know who and we didn't know how, when or what you see. So she just turned up' (Julie). As Billig comments on meetings with royalty: 'the prefer-ence was for the informal, chance meeting' (1992: 75). Such 'natural', appar-ently spontaneous contact, even if indirect, is special because it confirms that the space you are in (doing nothing special) *is* the space where the Street stars themselves 'ordinarily' are. What matters is making real contact with the media world. A spontaneous, chance meeting allows you to feel the contact is real. A meeting too obviously staged does not.

In all this, as suggested earlier, it is the generic quality of the 'contact', rather than any personal relationship with a particular star, that is important. Yet it would be wrong to overlook the powerful personal significance that this generic contact can have. Here John describes meeting Bill Roache (who has played 'Ken Barlow', since the series' first episode):

> I was just wandering around and the door opened ( ... ) and William Roache came out. And nobody had noticed at all ( ... ) it was on a Sunday and he'd been doing the outdoor shots, and Tracey [his daugh-ter in CS] was in hospital, it was that time. And he walked, and I looked at him, and I said, 'Hello', and he said, 'Hello there', and I said, 'Can I take a photograph?' 'Of course you can, take as many as you want.' And still as I was speaking to him, nobody'd noticed, and there was nobody with him, and he wandered around, and I'd taken three photographs, and nobody's looking ( ... ) [and then] everyone just made a beeline for him. And he stood there for an hour, not an exaggeration, because I was there the whole time.

This moment, as he tells it, has a strange intimacy: John and the star at first seem abstracted from the public space and yet, in spite of the extraordinary situation, John is 'still speaking', still making contact. For a moment which (by watching others as they came up) he prolonged into an hour, John remained in the same space as the star ('I was there the whole time').

Consider also this extract from an interview with a middle-aged woman and her elderly mother (I was silent during this dialogue):

| | |
|---|---|
| *Mother* | … I just wish I could have met a star ( … ) Or if I'd have gone round a studio. |
| *Daughter* | It'd be nice if somebody came up the Street and wandered around, one an hour, one an hour, a different one every hour. |
| *Mother* | Oh, it would've been lovely. |
| *Daughter* | Just to see different people, probably not to talk to them, just to see them, walking up the Street, or around wherever we've been, yeah. |
| *Mother* | Yeah, it would've been lovely. |
| *Daughter* | Just to see one. |

All the themes of this section are condensed here: the generic nature of the contact ('just to see them', 'just to see one'), the preference for keeping a distance ('probably not to talk to them'), the importance of spontaneity and ordinariness ('wandered around'), and above all the intrinsic importance of connecting two spaces, two 'worlds': the importance of feeling that 'they' have been 'around wherever we've been'.

The significance of meeting stars, then, as with being on the set, is explained by the overall framework I have been developing: both are contacts across the differential implicit in the symbolic hierarchy of the media frame. Next, I want to consider more generally people's encounters with the television production process, returning later to the possibly disruptive aspects of meeting the cast.

## SEEING THE FICTION IN 'REAL LIFE'

### 'Amazing what they can do'

Part of the pleasure of visiting GST and the Street set is that they show how programmes such as *Coronation Street* are produced: they reveal, on one level, the reality of the fiction. The limited access to the production process provided at GST takes on significance because more extensive access to the 'media world' is normally so strictly controlled (cf. Chapter 3). It is interesting to see how television works:

> It was good to see how the camera can trick you into thinking that things are realistic. And they've got to be clever to do it and not to show that the top of the stairs doesn't exist. And I suppose the actors, you've got to give them credit as well, because they've got to do it as if it's a real thing.
>
> (Julie, cf. Kim)

Discovering the visual deception involved in the programme is a pleasure in itself:

*Woman*      Well it's the whole thing ( ... ) just seeing the sizes of the things is phenomenal ( ... ) I mean ( ... ) I still wonder how they get the vans going at a decent speed up and down the top of the Street.

*Man*      It's the deception I think they've had over the years, it's the realisation of this, you know, that you've been conned really [both laugh] and it's amusing to see that ( ... ) It's almost a model, you know, it's such a tiny scale.

This woman (like others: four examples) noted the humour of realising that the cars and buses you think drive at normal speed along the end of the Street have to stop the moment they go off camera because the space in reality is only a few yards long. There are other surprises too: the size of the set which virtually everyone mentioned, discovering that internal and external scenes are shot in different places, and so on.

Since knowledge about media production is relatively scarce, but at the same time valued, GST is an opportunity for visitors to increase their cultural capital (cf. Chapter 3). This notion, deriving from Bourdieu, has been applied principally to 'high' forms of cultural capital such as art museums (Bourdieu, 1973; Hooper-Greenhill, 1988) and heritage sites (Merriman, 1989), even historical sites filmed on television (Rice and Saunders, 1996: 92–3). But in this case the 'capital' involved is knowledge of television's mechanism itself.[86] The value of such knowledge was reflected at GST in a range of talk about how a realistic illusion is actually created. For example, I overheard two men as they walked around the set. They were looking intently into the windows of Fiona's Salon, touching the window frames. One said to the other: 'amazing what they can do ( ... ) with superimposing ( ... ) But it's properly built ( ... ) Wide angles trick you but in fact it's tiny, you can't swing a cat in it'. Such technical talk took many less detailed forms: from a general appreciation ('they've done a really good job', woman; 'they make it look so good', Debbie) to comments on the 'trickery of the camera' (man) and 'cleverness of the deception' (Susan). People's pleasure in seeing television's workings also exemplifies what Dean MacCannell analysed in contemporary tourism generally: 'the museumization of work and work relations' (1976: 36): cf., on Disney–MGM, Fjellman (1992: 283–4). But it is a rather special case, since seeing how television works does not just inform you about other people's work processes; it reveals the visual deceptions practised upon you as a viewer. As just noted, this may increase your 'cultural capital' as a viewer. Some knowledge about media production has in recent years been disseminated by the media themselves: for example, 'behind the scenes' television programmes and videos about *Coronation Street* and *Brookside* and magazine articles about location-shooting or scripting.

The impact of the access available at GST is not significantly to de-naturalise the media frame as a whole. On the contrary, I would argue, it reproduces its symbolic significance. This knowledge is easily absorbed back into the normal practice of viewing itself: as one woman put it, 'we shall fall back into it [the programme]'. Occasionally, however, discovering the 'reality of the fiction' emerges as disruptive, rather than pleasurable. One elderly couple were disappointed by the 'falseness' of the Street set, partly because they knew they were excluded from the building where most filming goes on: '[Man:] ... that's the studio there [pointing to Granada Television building]; [Woman:] That's where I would have loved to have gone.' Whereas so far in this chapter we have concentrated on the insights people gave into the realism of the television image, its 'verisimilitude', and how it is produced, in this last quotation we approach another level of disruption: disruption of the naturalisation of media power itself.

## 'Seeing them for actually who they are'

I want now to look more closely at three interviews (Debbie, John, and Sarah) where this wider disruptiveness of getting 'too close' to the media frame was recognised in some way and negotiated. Actual or imagined contact with 'soap stars' is again important because of the contradiction they embody: on the one hand, they are 'ordinary people' who portray 'ordinary people', on the other, as 'media people' they are to some degree marked off from the 'ordinary' (cf. Chapter 3). It is often through the details of people's language that these contradictions are worked out.

John had reflected a lot about television. He had some experience of the theatre and had tried unsuccessfully to be a *Coronation Street* extra. He greatly enjoyed the artifice of the Street set and had an acute sense of its ritual power. He mentioned to me a wider concern about GST a number of times, developed through an analogy with changes in the public perception of British royalty:

> When I was young, you didn't see the Royal Family ( ... ) you never saw Buckingham Palace, you never saw the inside, you didn't hear about them. Last few years, you practically know everything about the Queen ( ... ) documentaries on the television showing everything inside the palace, showing all the rooms you've never seen before, totally destroys the mystique ( ... ) and that's one of the reasons the Royal Family has gone down in my opinion. The Street is very similar and I've got very mixed feelings because as a great fan, it's *wonderful* to see the stars ( ... ) How far do you go? ( ... ) It's destroying the mystique ( ... ) Last time I was there, I thought how far are they going to go next? You know, am I

going to wander into the café and have tea, with a sticky bun with three of the stars? ( … ) I don't know how to cope with that, because it's wonderful to see everything. But having seen it, what's left?

Too much contact, John believed, would destroy the 'mystique' in which he had considerable emotional investment. We can interpret this, in part, by reference to the more basic level of naturalisation within television: the maintenance of visual and dramatic illusion. Indeed, all forms of fictional world must maintain separate 'backstage' and 'frontstage' stage areas: confusion between them undermines the credibility of the illusion. Perhaps this was all John meant. I would argue, however, that it was not the programme's verisimilitude about which John was concerned: having had some experience of acting, he knew well the interplay between appearance and backstage reality. His analogy with the decline in respect for the Royal Family suggests that his concerns related to wider processes of social power. What he feared most, I suggest, was the undermining of the symbolic status of stars and the programme, their 'mystique'. This was a question not of television's 'veridical' illusion (already de-mystified for him) but of the media's symbolic hierarchy itself.

In order to maintain television's 'mystique' in this wider sense, John saw the necessity of maintaining the television world's segregation: there had to be a limit on the situations where, as a fan, he could feel close to the stars. He connected this with television's professionalism, its maintenance as a separate professional sphere: 'I think you've always got to have that bit of mystique … and I think that keeps it more professional as well.' This reflects what in Chapter Three I argued theoretically: that the media's symbolic authority is, in part, reproduced through the systematic segregation of 'media' and 'ordinary' 'worlds'. Yet, as John realised, there are commercial forces which appear to be working in a different direction. Television's 'backstage' is now, to a limited degree, revealed; this is precisely the point of GST and other places which market access to media 'pilgrimage' points (Davis, 1996: 411). Note that the most disruptive contact with the media world John imagined is precisely *ordinary* contact: having a sticky bun with a star in a café. It is ordinary contact with the stars that disrupts, since it destabilises the hierarchy between 'worlds': regular, 'ordinary' contact with the stars reduces 'their' world to the viewers' 'ordinary' world, undermining the symbolic boundary between them. Significantly (although John feared it), this type of contact is never on offer at GST.

Debbie also felt the need to maintain the segregation of 'media' and 'ordinary' 'worlds'. Like John, she also had a strong sense of the Street set as a 'ritual place'. But she did not want to be an extra in *Coronation Street*:

Debbie     ( … ) I don't think I'd want to be in *Coronation Street* somehow. I don't think I'd want to be there when they're all acting and … see them, I think I like just watching it on telly.

| | |
|---|---|
| *NC* | Why is that? |
| *Debbie* | ( … ) I think I just like to keep them as … that's how they live, rather than me sitting in the Rovers while they're [saying], Right go on Vera, say your words, or whatever. No. I think that would spoil it a bit. So, yeah, maybe something that I didn't watch. |
| *NC* | What seeing them behind the scenes might sort of … ? |
| *Debbie* | Yeah, seeing them for actually who they are … |

Again, on one level, we can interpret Debbie as simply wanting to preserve the dramatic illusion ('that's how they live'). But more, I suggest, was involved. She seemed to realise that the stars, if she saw them in the wrong context, would be revealed as merely ordinary people who work like she does, receiving orders like any other employee ('Right go on Vera, say your words'). Her sense of the 'glamour' of television (mentioned by her elsewhere) could only be maintained if she kept apart from the 'media world'. Again, what is imagined as disruptive is not contact as such but *ordinary* contact: sitting in the studio and seeing the cast in their ordinary state, working. Then 'media' and 'ordinary' 'worlds' would be reduced to the same, social world. Knowing this would undermine the symbolic division that the media frame involves; it would, for Debbie, undermine her subject-position as viewer, as an 'ordinary person who [merely] watches television' (cf. Chapter 3). It would be to see 'them' 'for actually who they are'.

There is a paradox here. Debbie was saying (imagining) that she wanted to avoid ordinary contact with the cast, but elsewhere (see Chapter 6) it was clear she wanted to be a television extra. She wanted to participate in the world of television – to cross the boundary between 'ordinary' and 'media' 'worlds' – yet, on the other hand, her desire to do so involved an identification with the 'media world' which could only be preserved if she maintained her position *outside* it (the position of viewer). If the boundary between 'media' and 'ordinary' 'worlds' were removed, then the whole basis of her desire to cross would disappear. Her desire was connected to a prior 'lack': the lack built into the position of 'ordinary viewer', someone who is *not* a media person. As discussed in Chapter 3, this 'lack' is not absolute in a Lacanian sense, but a social construction, deriving from the media's particular concentration of symbolic power. As a social construction, it must continually be reproduced by social and spatial means. It requires the normal spatial segregation of 'media' and 'ordinary' 'worlds'. As both Debbie and John's words suggest, that segregation is reinforced, in part, through the very formulation of the desire to transcend it.

The only way out of this paradox is to acknowledge the real nature of the media as a socially specific mechanism of representation. This, in effect, is what Sarah did. Sarah was more self-reflexive than other interviewees about the status of her visit to GST (note that she had more formal education than the other full interviewees, being the only university graduate. In her

101

interview, she reflected on her visit to GST and related it to a more general disillusionment with television:

> You expect it all to be real, you know, it's like you're being foxed every week [laughs], like they're very crafty, it makes you realise, you know, that what you're watching is, you know, just all make-believe really ( ... ) It makes you realise how powerful television is really ( ... 4 pages) That's the thing I can't seem to get over is the fact they like fox you completely. And it makes you realise that television is all false [laughs] really.

Her awareness of deception (compare other people's comments on the camera's 'trickery') was generalised into a wider reflection about television as a medium and its power. She talked of the oddity of seeing the sets, distinguishing between her 'rational mind' (for which they were just sets) and her 'other mind, the bit that wants it all to be real'. Her reflections on meeting the actor Bill Roache expressed the paradox of media celebrity in a clear form:

> It's quite odd because they seem like, when you meet them outside, they seem like real people, but you know, when they're on television they also seem like real people but they seem like different real people, if you see what I mean [ ... ] So it's quite a shock to think that that is their job and that's what they do and ... you know, you get involved in something that's completely made up as it were.

The soap star was a 'real person', who did a job like everyone else, and yet his job was to deceive other people that he is a *different* 'real person'. At the same time, meeting a star was the highlight of her trip. Part of the problem for Sarah was a failure in how the set's authenticity was staged: 'it was like ( ... ) you were searching for some piece of evidence that it actually did all happen there.' She expected to see the Street characters on the set, 'but it's not like that at all [laughs], it's just like people like yourself drifting around'. Instead of a place where she could imagine herself in the fiction, the set 'just seemed like an everyday sort of place and not a special place'. It was just an 'ordinary' place with 'ordinary people' in it. Even Bill Roache was just 'ordinary': 'quite ordinary really [laughs] ( ... ) there's not a lot you can say about him really, he sort of came and did his, like, star bit, and came and went off again.'

Instead of her achieving ritual contact with the 'media world' from the 'ordinary world', everything Sarah saw convinced her that the media sphere was just another part of the social world: a part of it dedicated to deceiving you into thinking it was somehow different, precisely a mechanism of representation. When she watched the programme after her visit, her puzzlement came back to her (the quotation at the head of this chapter): 'that's the thing I can't seem to get over ... the fact that they fox you completely. So ... it makes you realise that television is all false [laughs] really.' Sarah, then, appeared to resolve the paradox she encountered in the only way it can be resolved: by acknowledging the real nature of the media as a mechanism of representation, not 'reality' at all.

## CONCLUDING COMMENT

Meetings with soap stars focus particularly clearly the paradoxes inherent in the media frame. Soap stars are not known as people of extraordinary achievements, although they are generally recognised as skilful actresses or actors. In most ways, they are like everyone else, not special. That is why some people did not want to meet the Street cast: '[Man:] No, I don't think I'd be all that bothered one way or the other to be quite honest, I mean they're just working artists.' Meeting stars away from GST (in completely 'ordinary' situations, not ritually managed) could be embarrassing, as a number of people recounted. In soap stars, the underlying naturalisation of the media's symbolic authority becomes vulnerable, as television's rhetoric of 'ordinariness' conflicts with its symbolic hierarchy. The soap star is necessarily presented as both 'ordinary' (as character and, to some degree, as person as well) and more than 'ordinary' (as 'media person'). This contradiction risks becoming explicit when the star is met, not in character but in person. To do so is to get too close to the paradoxes of the media frame, to realise that the soap star is, in reality, no more than ordinary. This is another reason, perhaps, why people often wished to distance themselves from being fans of the stars, rather than fans of the programme.

Soap stars are, however, a special case. This chapter has considered people's encounters at GST with the reality of television's fiction. A number of themes have been held in tension: first, visitors' awareness of the fictive status of GST and the Street set, which is quite compatible with insisting upon the fact that the Street is the real place of filming (cf. Chapter 4); second, people's participatory pleasure in discovering how *Coronation Street* is constructed as a visual illusion; third, and more speculatively, the connections between people's imaginative involvement in the programme, and the (indirect) preservation of the spatial segregation which helps naturalise media power. Overall, however, at a commercial site such as GST, we would not expect the potential de-naturalisation of the media frame to be significantly reinforced. On the contrary, GST is a place where, by and large, the media/ordinary hierarchy is confirmed. The next chapter explores this further.

# 6

# PLAYING WITH BOUNDARIES

How do visitors to GST encounter and negotiate the boundaries (spatial, social, and symbolic) between 'ordinary' and 'media' 'worlds'? As already suggested, the result of visiting GST is not generally the de-naturalisation of these boundaries, but their reproduction. I analyse, first, how the media/ordinary boundary is registered at GST in various ways, including visitors' dispositions to accept those boundaries. Then, I discuss how that boundary is reproduced in talk of the 'media world', and also in talk about its symbolic obverse, the 'ordinary world'. Finally, I consider visitors who want more than a symbolic transgression of the boundary between these two 'worlds'; they want to be television 'extras' and actually enter the 'media world'. At this point, we start to locate GST in the wider 'landscape' (Hay, Grossberg, and Wartella, 1996) of audience practice.

## BOUNDARIES AND LIMITS

If Chapter 3's argument – for the multidimensionality of the processes through which media power is naturalised – is correct, then we would expect the 'boundaries' which mark that power to take a number of forms: linguistic, spatial, social, symbolic, and (more broadly) the habitual dispositions through which those boundaries are reproduced as natural. I consider each in turn.

### Linguistic traces

The boundary between 'media' and 'ordinary' 'worlds' was regularly registered in people's language. This was true across the whole sample, not just the most engaged fans. Such evidence is important since, as Michael Billig has argued (1997: 225), it is the 'small words which seem beyond rhetorical challenge and which are routinely and widely repeated' that may reveal ideology or, equally, power (cf. Appendix on method).

Some features of the interview language may by now be obvious. Again and again, people used the words '*actual*' and '*actually*',[87] marking off things in the 'media world' as unusual, out of the ordinary, and therefore of automatic significance. This was particularly clear from the off-site interviews where people spoke at greater length, but occurred in a significant number (twenty) of the site interviews, across the whole age and class range and equally between men and women. This marking occurred, first, in terms of place: being 'actually' on the 'actual' Street (nine cases); being 'actually' on the 'actual' set, the set they 'actually' use, the 'actual' pub, the 'actual studios', and so on (thirteen cases). Or more simply: 'actually' being 'there', 'actually on the spot where … ' (six examples). Second, these words may mark out particular actions: 'actually seeing [the Street, the sets, filming, and so on] … ' (thirteen cases); 'actually walking [on the Street] … ' (four cases); 'actually standing [on the Street, the sets] … ' (two cases). Filming or media production were, in particular, marked off as significant: 'actual filming', 'programmes actually being made', being where they 'actually film', and so on (fourteen examples). To be in, or close to, media production matters automatically; this is registered by which the words 'actual' and 'actually'. This significance derives from the symbolic boundary between 'media' and 'ordinary' 'worlds' being disrupted, breached, or played with.

This boundary is registered, less emphatically, by the word 'just'. Because acts which approach the boundary surrounding the 'media world' are automatically significant, 'just' to do them is significant, without further elaboration: 'just to see them [the stars]', 'just to see it [the Street]', 'just walking up and down [the Street]', 'just to stand there'. Or by extension: 'just nice to know you've seen it', 'just wanted to see where it was done', and so on. This automatic significance was registered in another elliptical, and clichéd, expression: 'being there'. 'Being there' is sufficient in itself to express the significance of visiting the Street set ('I've already been there', Julie; 'it's just like knowing you've been there', Kim) or other media sites ('we were actually there when he did the weather', Debbie; 'you're just there and you're on TV there and then', Peter). The examples could be multiplied. The phrase 'being there' (and all its variations) can be both banal and eloquent, for example in John's interview: 'I felt that I was there and I'd seen it for so long', 'you're still there, it's still real'. This banal expression can bear such emphasis, I suggest, precisely because it is the *transposition* of the 'ordinary' into an extraordinary, 'media' context that is being marked in language. 'Just' 'being there' is itself extraordinary.

## Physical boundaries

GST, like any corporate entertainment space, has rules about where you can and can't go. My interest is not in GST's spatial regime as such, but, first, in how boundaries at GST relate to the spatial order of the media frame – physical and invisible boundaries frequently overlap here – and, second, in how those boundaries (both visible and invisible) are symbolically reversed. These details show vividly the workings of media power's reproduction. As the geographer Robert Sack has argued, one major function of 'territoriality' is to establish 'different degrees of access to people, things, and relationships' (1986: 20). It is differential access to the means of media production that helps naturalise media power (see Chapter 3).

There are signs on the Street set, making clear where the public cannot go. The gardens of the new houses are out of bounds: 'DO NOT ENTER – THIS IS A DRESSED SET, NOT A LEISURE AREA.' The importance of spatial restrictions was reflected also on the Backstage Tour. I heard one guide explain the status of the indoor sets as mock-ups by acknowledging that the real sets were elsewhere ('can't let the public in there'); a guide introduced the mock-up programme control room as 'a room you'll never see', that is, not in reality.

Not surprisingly people played with these boundaries, thereby indirectly confirming them. In the case of the Street houses, the boundaries beyond which you cannot go also protect the set's illusion (inside, the 'houses' are not sets, but storage areas). Almost everyone looks into the old houses, which front directly onto the Street. Their words sometimes registered the boundary at stake: 'you can see *right in*', 'can I look through the letter box, is that *allowed?*' (Fieldnotes). The significance of these boundaries was registered also in people's laughter as they tried to negotiate them: for instance, when taking a photo of the new houses' gardens through a hole in a fence. None the less, in my experience, people generally respected these spatial restrictions. The same applied to the temporary boundaries set up when Tony Blair did a photo-opportunity on the Street in August 1996. People had to stand behind red velvet ropes away from both the actors in the event and the photographers who were there to frame it. No one objected. Indeed a spatial boundary (for onlookers) is implicit in the very idea of a photo-opportunity.

Compared with the spatial restrictions they expected at media locations, people sometimes spoke of a sense of freedom at GST: the fact that you can 'spend as much time as you wanted', 'walk up and down it as many times as you want'. But others experienced physical boundaries at GST as real exclusions. As mentioned in Chapter 5, some wanted to see the places where filming was currently going on: the studio building, outside locations other than the Street; they wanted to go themselves onto the Backstage Tour sets (which was forbidden). Many were disappointed they could not enter the buildings on the Street set (sixteen cases). The experience of being excluded from important spaces was repeated in interviewees' accounts of visits to other media sites (*Brookside*; *Emmerdale*; a *Star Trek* exhibition). In these ways, people experienced directly the spatial restrictions inherent in the media mechanism.

## Invisible boundaries

Invisible, implied boundaries between 'media' and 'ordinary' 'worlds' are as real at GST as visible, physical ones. For example, I observed on the Street set a cheque being presented by a cast member to a charity. Visitors held back from the presentation, silent as the formalities were completed. The 'actors' in the event then walked away, without acknowledging those watching; no onlookers called out to them. Even without any physical barrier, the visitors reproduced the segregation implicit in the event.

Both physical and social boundaries have symbolic significance and may be played with through 'symbolic reversal' (Babcock, 1978). Reversal of boundaries characterises a number of attractions at GST. The very idea of going 'behind the scenes' or 'behind the cameras' (as visitors put it) is a play with boundaries. Take, for example, the 'Newsdesk' room on the Backstage Tour. As visitors volunteered to read the news, there was an unmanned camera trained on the desk, linked to a monitor. The 'newsreader' read from a prepared 'bulletin'. The fun clearly depended on a shared sense of *transgression*: as one guide said, 'sometimes we do get a chance to go in front of the cameras'. Often, as the guide left the room, people would rush up behind the newsdesk to see themselves for a moment in the monitor. One man said to his girlfriend: 'I'd like to see you up there.' Others spoke of reading the news as being 'up there', *up there* where media production goes on. The newsdesk, in fact, is on the same level as the rest of the mock-up newsroom, so 'up there' could only be metaphorical! Such routine spatial metaphors condense the hierarchical relationship between the (higher) 'media world' and the (lower) 'ordinary world' (cf. generally Lakoff and Johnson, 1980: 17–19). To go 'up there' is to play out a 'symbolic reversal'. The terms being reversed were made clear by the script provided to 'newsreaders': 'Tonight we're asking the question: do members of the public make good newsreaders?' That is, can 'ordinary people' be 'media people'?

There were other symbolic reversals at GST. Elsewhere on the Backstage Tour you can 'appear' briefly in a *Coronation Street* scene through the Chromakey superimposition technique, used widely in television. The sense of reversal is vivid in this woman's description:

> I've enjoyed it all actually ( … ) being on stage [laughs] and it was, *actually they're filming me*, you know, they gave me a few lines to read, it was quite interesting actually, I enjoyed it, yeah. [added emphasis]

When another middle-aged woman, who had done this, got back to her family, she was beaming; they said to her, 'she's been on the real telly now … she's a star'. The humour registered both the symbolic reversal and the impossibility of such a reversal in 'real life'. Elsewhere, at the 'Telestars' booth, you can 'appear' in a videotaped 'episode' of *Coronation Street* with your name on the rolling credits. People outside the booth often watched an episode being put together, laughing when the 'actors' emerged: "'Excuse me, can I have your autograph, please?", roars of laughter' (Fieldnotes). The short, compulsory script had, as its theme, that the actors were hoping to move into the Street; as they bought a drink in the Rovers, they asked, 'do you think we'll fit in round here?' It was, as one woman described it to me, a 'video of us ['ordinary viewers', NC] moving into *Coronation Street*' (Fieldnotes). Two boundaries overlap here: not only the obvious boundary between reality and fiction (the impossibility of living in a purely fictional world), but also the social boundary around media production (the normal impossibility of being the 'type' of person who is 'in television').

Humorous play with media-related boundaries emerges everywhere at GST: in the graffiti on the backs of the old Street houses ('Nat and Lisa ON TOUR 1996'); in people's miniature performances on the Street (posing for photographs with deliberate artificiality: 'Is this my best side?'). The connection between humour and the transgression of boundaries has been developed in anthropological theory about 'symbolic reversals' (Babcock, 1978) and in Bakhtin's (1984) theory of the 'carnivalesque'. GST does not, however, involve the total symbolic reversal Bakhtin analysed in situations such as the mediaeval carnival.[88] Rather, it involves small-scale forms of play, less 'liminal' process than 'liminoid' activity in Turner's terminology (Turner, 1977; Deegan, 1989).

Even so, we should not underestimate the intensity which 'liminoid' activities at GST may carry. 'Sound World', for example, is ostensibly a show about television sound effects: the presenter gets various people from the audience to make sound effects manually, like 'foleys' in radio production, but of course without the right training or equipment (this is similar, but on a smaller scale, to the Monster Sound Show at Disney–MGM: Fjellman, 1992: 287). They try to make the soundtrack for a television crime drama. Then the soundtrack is played back ('Imagine you're at home watching the TV', says the presenter). The relation of the attempted sound track to the programme was so chaotic that it reduced most of the audience, myself included, to helpless laughter. Once again, the laughter registered play with a symbolic boundary – between 'our' (naturalised) incompetence in media production and the 'media world''s (naturalised) competence – a symbolic reversal, but with a touch of the 'grotesque' (Bakhtin).

In all these cases, the boundaries played with are invisible; no physical barrier is involved. Alternatively, a minimal physical boundary may be exaggerated, underlining its symbolic significance. In Chapter 4 we saw how, for some people, entering the Street set is almost a ritual moment. Between 1988 and 1992, however, this purely imaginary boundary between 'ordinary' and 'media' 'worlds' was formalised as a physical boundary. You were only able to get to the Street set by bus, via a spot called 'Checkpoint Charlie' (itself a set from a television drama). One woman who had visited then described it to me: 'there was like a German ... place, where they stopped you and they got a gun out at you and pretended you were on the line like.' The juxtaposition of 'border post' and Street set was hardly accidental: as the 1991–2 GST brochure put it, 'watch out for border guards ... keep those passports to Weatherfield [CS's region in the programme] handy, or you may not make it to the Rovers'. Now, even without a physical barrier, the boundary may still be marked in people's language, when they write of 'stepping *onto* the Street'.

Invisible boundaries around media production were also illustrated in Debbie's account of seeing the filming of a live weather broadcast for the popular *Richard and Judy* magazine programme (a weather broadcast well known for being delivered afloat in Liverpool's Albert Dock!):

> ... the weather was at twelve o'clock. And there was a great big crowd of people ( ... ) And out came the cameramen ... and he starts filming ... doing the weather ( ... ) it was ( ... ) a bit unbelievable really ( ... ) seeing him really like small, Yeah, he's on the telly, and then actually being there and like the camera crew are there and you're thinking, Oh, I wonder if I'll get on telly ( ... ) [one page earlier] I enjoyed seeing that, thinking, Oh Wow! That's on telly! And I'm standing there and ... Oh Mum, quick! Put on the weather! You know I was standing up there.

The excitement of that moment, Debbie said, was what started her interest in going to media locations such as GST. Exceptionally, Debbie found herself 'standing *up there*': the other side of the boundary between 'media' and 'ordinary' 'worlds'. Or at least so close to it that it felt almost as if she was on the other side: 'That's on telly! And I'm standing there.'

## Adjusting for limits

I have argued that at GST boundaries between 'media' and 'ordinary' 'worlds' are maintained. Indeed, by being played with, they are silently reproduced as legitimate. More speculatively, we can trace the social reproduction of those boundaries in the evidence interviews provide of visitors' wider dispositions. People adjust in advance to 'the way things are' at the level of dispositions, the 'habitus' (cf. Chapter 3). As Pierre Bourdieu put it:

> Because the dispositions durably inculcated by objective conditions ... engender aspirations and practices objectively compatible with those objective requirements, the most improbable practices are excluded, either totally without examination, as *unthinkable*, or at the cost of the *double negation* which inclines agents to make a virtue of necessity, that is, to refuse what is anyway refused and to love the inevitable.
>
> (1977: 77) [original emphasis]

People's talk about the media/ordinary boundary at GST provides interesting empirical support for this highly abstract formulation. For 'ordinary people' – that is, people who have never known any connection with the 'media world' – 'the most improbable practices' (crossing into the media world) are either excluded as 'unthinkable' or (through a 'double negation', as Bourdieu calls it) displaced by desire; necessary restrictions are converted into something 'loved'. Both forms of exclusion can be traced in the language of visitors. They denote, I suggest, a naturalised thought-pattern, something more than a simple recognition of practical constraints.

The 'unthinkability' of challenging the boundaries around media production may make actual access at GST a surprise ('I couldn't believe we were going to see all that': Debbie) or make its limitations readily explicable ('[Man:] I expected ( … ) when you looked through the curtains to be able to see ( … ) some of the sets, but I appreciate that that's not real'). More specifically, people discounted seeing filming:

Man        We wanted to see some action, some filming ( … ) not just to see the Street ( … ) Because you're not part of it ( … )

NC        Did you expect to see filming?

Man        No, you know deep down it would be too much trouble for them. It's not possible. But why couldn't they put on something?

(Fieldnotes)

There is tension here between a process of habitual discounting ('you know deep down that it would be too much trouble for them') and the desire for something more ('but why couldn't they put on something?'). This conflict was played out in many interviews. On the one hand, people gave various reasons why you can't see filming: 'you can't bring Joe Public in and do a job at the same time', 'difficult schedules they've got', and so on. Restrictions on entering sets were similarly explained: 'security', 'obviously, they didn't want people trampling ( … ) all the grass down'. Sometimes explanations were expressed as statements of principle: 'TV studios are hard to gain access to', 'it's not the way they do it'. At other points, the desire to go beyond the restrictions came through, for example: '[Woman:] You could put like barriers here at the end. Obviously, you wouldn't be able to get really close, but if you could actually see the type of actions that they get into like really in depth … ' Many people, then, are disposed to accept restrictions. These are often explained in technical or professional terms. Such talk (registering 'the way *they* do things') is a further way in which spatial and other restrictions around media production are naturalised. To clarify this, let us return to John's comments on preserving the 'mystique' of television (cf. Chapter 5). John talked of 'the mystique, the mystery, of the Street, the inaccessibility', as things which were connected. As a result, he did not want to enter the buildings on the Street:

I didn't think for one minute that I'd be able to get in ( … ) I actually felt
privileged just to turn the knob and try to get in [to the Rovers] ( … )
No, no, it was just brilliant to be photographed outside it.

For John it was a privilege just to be at the limit beyond which he knew he
could not go. To go there, and no further, was to acknowledge the set's
'magic': a clear case of what Bourdieu calls 'lov[ing] the inevitable'.

A further adjustment at the level of dispositions, which takes us beyond
Bourdieu's formulation, is constituted by people's attitudes towards *others*
who challenge the boundaries around the media sphere: the
pathologisation of those who come 'too close' to the media (cf. Chapter
3). Julie told me how people, including her family, thought her 'daft' to
want to go on game shows, or even to go to GST: 'a lot of people are not
like me ( … ) A lot of people seem to think you're silly just because you
want to go to these places, because ( … ) you want to do things ( … ) They
say, Oh, it's only a show.' Susan and Glenys mentioned that 'everybody
thinks we're mad' because of their intense involvement in *Coronation
Street*: they clearly had their own husbands partly in mind. But this
pathologisation cannot simply be accounted for by men's denigration of
women's pleasures. Michael, when he returned to GST for the second
and third times in a year, felt he had to pretend he was going somewhere
else: 'I cannot tell too many people that I have been to the Street three
times in '96 because they would say I am mad.' As he wrote defensively, 'I
am a fan and addict (not mad)'. John had people dismiss his account of the
moment when he crossed the media/ordinary boundary (see Chapter 5),
again because he was 'crazy'. Peter confronted me most directly with the
issue of pathologisation:

Peter      You think I'm crazy.
NC         No, no. Why should I think that?
Peter      Don't know, everybody else does.

Later in the interview he gave his response to that type of attitude:

Peter      It isn't only a show, it's a way of life. And then they just laugh at
           me. They think I'm crazy ( … ) Why *Coronation Street*? I said, why
           not? I've never been in trouble with the police or anything like
           that, never taken any drugs or anything. Why not *Coronation
           Street*?

Why not indeed? It is surely paradoxical to be addressed as 'mad' – a social
'outsider' – when your only fault is to get 'too close' to the principal shared
medium of our society, television. But it is through such pathologisation,
partly, that media power is naturalised. Peter had got 'too close' to the media

111

frame, as a viewer, by making his viewing a 'way of life'. As a result, he was 'out of place' (cf. Cresswell, 1996), trapped on the outside of a system of representation in which there was little role for him as an active producer.[89]

## THE MAGIC OF TELEVISION (REVERSED)

A connection needs to be made here with work on the media and desire. We have seen how access restrictions around the 'media world' are linked with the idea of that 'world''s 'mystique' and 'magic'. There is clearly, however, much more to the desires and fantasies mobilised by television than inadvertent reproductions of the media frame's symbolic hierarchy! Richard Dyer has written eloquently of the wider social functions of 'entertainment': 'entertainment offers the image of "something better" to escape into or something we want deeply but our day-to-day lives don't provide' (1992: 18). Drawing on Enzensberger's (1972: 114) notion of spectacular consumption as 'in parody form ... the anticipation of a utopian situation', Dyer analyses five separate dimensions of how entertainment works at a non-representational level: energy, abundance, intensity, transparency, community. These are related to five 'inadequacies' of actually existing society: exhaustion, scarcity, dreariness, manipulation, fragmentation (Dyer, 1992: 24). Dyer's powerful analysis helps explain the wider social resonances which entertainment has, regardless of whether it is produced through a highly concentrated form of symbolic power. We must not lose sight of the sheer pleasure in television which, for example, the full-length interviewees expressed, the sense of participation: as John put it of *Coronation Street*, 'I just feel part of it'. The 'magic' of television cannot be lightly dismissed as 'false consciousness'.

In considering, however, the 'magic' of television (its intensity) we must also keep in mind the inequality in symbolic power that lies just behind the magic. It was while reflecting on the inequality between media producers and audiences that Enzensberger wrote of entertainment's 'anticipation of a utopian situation'. This raises a further question: what happens when the symbolic hierarchy – on which the media's excess is constructed – is itself reversed, when we turn from the 'media world' to its obverse, the so-called 'ordinary world'?

The 'glamour' or 'magic' of television is part of what GST sells: 'the magical world of television' (GST Brochure, 1996), or, implicitly, 'TV's not *all* glamour' (guide's phrase on Backstage tour). While the terms 'glamour' and 'magic' were used by only a few visitors I spoke with (five cases), the *idea* of glamour – television as a separate, more intense 'world' – is readily traceable in what visitors said. Television is projected as a place of abundance, even excess. It is not only that television production is expensive (so are most forms of production, seen on a large scale). In television production, the *ratio* between the expenditure of scarce resources (money, time) and the resulting output seems different from that operating in the scarcity conditions of normal life. You are told on the Tour that Bet Lynch's wedding dress 'cost us £4,000 for one afternoon's filming' or that one character's make-up took three hours to apply, yet the character appeared on television for only four and a half minutes! People know that a high expenditure of labour-time may be required to produce a short period of 'media time': 'a split second', 'in a flash it was over … hardly anything there'. But this extravagant ratio between input costs and resulting 'media time' has wider resonances. It reflects the status of media time as ritual time, 'spectacular time' (Debord, 1983: para 153): time 'on the other side' of the media/ordinary hierarchy. The differential intensity of 'media time' itself registers the media's power.[90]

If 'media time' is extraordinary, so too is 'media space'. As the Tour guides tell you, 'you can go almost anywhere in TV': a marketing cliché which reflects television's imaginative power. More broadly, the distinctiveness of 'media space' was reflected in people's talk about the spaces where media production occurs, for example the size of sets: 'I know what TV's like, how small it can be.' The small size of television production sites is striking in relation to the intensity of their output:

> [Woman:] I mean seeing the actual length of this here [the Street set], it's hard to picture how much buzz there is, you know, with traffic ( … ) and ( … ) people crossing the streets, it's in such a confined space that there's so much action can go on.

The idea of spatial intensity was expressed also in a man's comment on the mock-up programme control desk:

> You're looking at the size of the rooms and it's surprising how much technology goes through out of a little room ( … ) obviously there's going to be so much going on out of that particular room, which I do find pretty impressive in itself.

Implicit here is a sense that the 'media world' (in all its dimensions: money, time, space) is somehow more 'intense' than the 'ordinary world'. GST, one woman said, 'was like another world' (Fieldnotes). Similarly, the media are associated with (symbolic) size: 'I've got photographs of Pat Phoenix at the time, *big* fur coat on ( … ), just there, like the *big* star, *big* fur coat and everything' (Peter, added emphasis). Or, as GST put it in their 1990/91 guide describing 'Telestars': 'your *big* chance to join the cast of *Coronation Street* on screen and take away a photo or video of your *big* television appearance' [added emphasis].

But what of the other side of the hierarchy? What of the 'ordinary world' that is the obverse of the 'media world' in the binary opposition? It was the Situationists (such as Raoul Vaneigem) who saw most clearly the impact of spectacular symbolic production on 'ordinary' life:[91]

> the mechanism of the alienating spectacle wields such force that private life reaches the point of being defined as that which is *deprived of spectacle*.
>
> (1989: 37, added emphasis)

Richard Schickel has argued similarly for the effects of media celebrity on our sense of identity: 'if we do not somehow insert ourselves into this [mediated] reality, we run the danger of being, in our own eyes, unpersons' (1985: 263, quoted in Priest, 1995: 167). Can we trace such a process in visitors' accounts of their own living conditions? Descriptions of meeting stars outside media locations are interesting here. Because they take place in 'ordinary places' without ritual framing ('just an ordinary newsagents', John; 'opening a freezer centre near us', Peter), the transition between 'ordinary' and 'extraordinary' world is abrupt. Here is Julie describing the former Street character Reg Holdsworth opening a supermarket:

> I must have been the only person in Leicester that didn't know that he was going to be at Tesco ( … ) I went up there to … well to get some shopping like you do. And I thought somebody was shoplifting like you do, because I could see this … security guard and somebody being ushered ( … ) So I said to my husband, Oh, somebody's been shoplifting. So I walked over and … *it was him*! … [Of] course, I just stood there, freezing, like watching … you know, just seeing what they were doing.

The star's presence transforms an 'ordinary' moment (going shopping 'like you do') into something extraordinary ('*it was him* … I just stood there').

A sense of the contrast between 'ordinary' and 'media' 'worlds' may easily shift into a sense that the 'ordinary' lacks something. A couple who had been to Disneyworld felt the Street set was too ordinary: 'when you're here it's just a street.' Debbie was disappointed by the *Emmerdale* site: the pub used for the fictional 'Woolpack' was 'just a normal pub'. Julie described the village location for *Heartbeat* in similar terms: 'It's only a very small place, it's unreal really when you see it ( … ) there's a shop that you see, well that's basically ordinary.' The theme of media 'excess' is here reversed ('it's only a very small place') and mapped onto an actual, living place. That place, by comparison to a media location, is 'basically ordinary'. Similarly with people. When a crowd waited for stars to appear at GST and saw someone who was *not* a star appear from the studio building, some commented: 'they're a nobody' (cf. for a similar phenomenon, Gamson, 1994: 136). Yet that person was of course, from another point of view, an 'ordinary person' like them.

114

GST and the Street set are places where, temporarily, 'ordinary' and 'media' 'worlds' meet. The 'geography' of the 'media world' encountered at GST is itself fascinating. The Street set itself is part of that geography, where 'they' film when you are not there. For John, this geography of where the stars move was like a world which he gradually explored:

> By the third tour I had got my bearings much more and ( ... ) I could actually see the door where the stars come into, I now know where the studio is, I know where they come into, I know where they park their cars, I know where the entrance is, I know where they go into the studios.

A similar fascination with media geography is found when people try to track down the locations where scenes of television programmes are filmed (such as for the 1960s BBC comedy show, *Steptoe and Son*), or when people search for the houses of rock stars, or tour the Hollywood streets where film stars live.[92]

In the 'media world' of GST, it is as if 'ordinary' things change their status. As people waited one evening for cast to emerge from the Granada Studios building, a Dyno-rod drains clearance van drew up in the parking area across the railings. 'It's a Dyno-rod' someone remarked to laughter; 'Yeah, but it's a *Coronation Street* Dyno-rod' was the reply. Alternatively, media things are noteworthy because they are 'ordinary after all' (cf. Chapter 5). I overheard two women talking as they looked into Fiona's Salon on the Street: 'They use the same shampoo as us then.' Anything touched by the 'world of television' may have special status: 'to see the clothes the stars wore at one time and another was thrilling' (Susan, letter). Yet, by a reversal that is fully consistent with the media frame's symbolic hierarchy, once you are in 'media space', even your 'ordinary' actions become significant. When Julie's tour party exceptionally was allowed onto the indoor sets, they acted out not scenes from the programme, but domestic life itself: 'pouring cups of tea ( ... ) pretending to iron'. The 'ordinary' then appears transformed in the 'media space' of GST. Looked at another way, *visitors* to GST – assumed not to be media professionals – are automatically defined as 'ordinary people'. When I asked one woman what type of person GST attracts, her answer was emphatic: 'ordinary people, ordinary people like what we are.' When, without introduction, I showed my mother a photo of the Street set from one of my visits, she asked: 'Is that the ordinary people going round?' Barbara projected the image of the 'ordinary person' onto the Street set itself:

> You have this sort of [short laugh] naive view that they're [the characters] going to be sat in watching the television but of course they're not because it's just like a set.

In fact, people rarely watch television on the programme, but between programmes Barbara imagined them doing just that:[93] she imagined them as 'ordinary people who watch television', the very thing that the cast are not.

GST is a place where people can participate imaginatively in the fiction of *Coronation Street* the programme, but it is also a place where a real social difference is negotiated in symbolic form: the difference between those 'in' and those 'outside' the media. Sometimes, if rarely, this difference emerges not as a symbolic boundary, but as a *material* boundary inviting actual negation. Debbie, who had enjoyed acting at school, felt this acutely. When she came home from GST, she felt depressed:

> I don't know, it sounds really silly, but once you've been there [to GST] or you're actually there, you feel as though, God, I really want to be on *Coronation Street*, I really want to be on the telly, I really want to act for a living. There's something there that draws you, all the excitement and you see what's going on. I think you really want to be a part of it.

When she got home, she put her name down at an extras' agency. Her long-term interest in acting perhaps makes her case particular, but her description of leaving GST has wider resonances:

> You don't want to come home and go back to your boring nine-to-five job or whatever. You know, I was really gutted that I had to come home and that was it, that was the end of it. Whereas up there you think, Oh God, I wonder if they need a cleaner or something, I'd go and work there so I can be there every day and see what happens, that sounds silly doesn't it.

The 'media world', in contrast to her everyday world of work, was a place of excitement. The difference was no doubt real, but it coincided with the symbolic difference inherent in the media frame. Even an 'ordinary' aspect of the media's 'extraordinary' world (being a cleaner) seemed better than remaining in the 'ordinary world'. Debbie imagined a fusion of 'ordinary' and 'media' 'worlds': she wanted to become an 'ordinary' part of the media world. Yet she also discounted this as impossible. I want finally to look at what happens when people attempt to act on such desires and appear on television.

## 'JUST ONCE TO BE ON TELEVISION'

Given the ritual intensity of 'media time', even the shortest appearance on television (for example, as an extra) can be significant: it crosses the boundary between 'ordinary' and 'media' 'worlds'. The desire to be an extra did not emerge in the short site interviews, but became significant in a number of off-site interviews. It is would-be extras who experience most forcibly the media's nature as a field of competition for symbolic power (cf. Chapter 3).

Peter had for some time applied unsuccessfully to be an extra on *Coronation Street*:

Peter      I approached Granada ( ... ) to be an extra. But they won't let me ( ... ) I wouldn't mind, just going into the Kabin and ordering ... a paper or something and then walking out, I don't want to speak or anything. Just ... once to be on television. On the show. I'd be happy then ... I think.

However small and 'ordinary' the action ('just ... ordering a paper'), it would be significant, if it meant having once entered the media frame. Debbie discussed her brother's appearance in an advertisement in similar terms:

Debbie      It was an advert that lasted, what, about a minute and a half if that, and all he did was ( ... ) come in, picked up the sofa and went away and he was up there all day. And he said it took all day to do it ... I can't believe that. [short laugh] ( ... )

NC      Did he think it was worth doing that?

Debbie      Yeah, he really enjoyed it ( ... ) he said it was a really good day out ( ... ) Ever since that he's sort of got pretty confident, he's really come out of his shell sort of thing. I don't know whether it's given him a bit of a boost, being on telly, that he's done that and whatever, maybe that's what it is.

Even doing something ordinary on television (lifting a sofa), however brief, is significant. When Peter did finally appear on television on a talk show, he felt (as Debbie's brother apparently did) that he had changed in some way:

Peter      Totally different now from the way I used to be ( ... ) I was so quiet, I never dreamed of working in the bar, I was ( ... ) always in the back scenes, come out on the bar now ( ... ) It did change me [appearing on TV] ( ... ) I'm in the open now, talk to anybody.

Patricia Priest's (1995, 1996) important study of US talk show participants points in the same direction. Her interviewees commented on the reactions of other people once they had appeared on television: even if they were identified with a group facing public hostility, they met positive responses, simply because they had appeared on television. Participants' feelings of empowerment derived not just from what they had said publicly, but from the transformative nature of television itself: 'I felt like I had contributed to society', 'when I think I'm useless ... , I think "But wait, I have touched these people"' (quoted, 1996: 74).[94] Of course there are differences between speaking on television in the first person and appearing as an extra in a fictional programme – thus, for most of Priest's interviewees, the importance of making a self-disclosure outweighed any specific desire to be on television (1995: 46) – but the structural pattern is similar. Both acts are ways of transforming one's relation to the 'media world'.

Other dedicated fans also wanted to be extras: Julie, Barbara, John, Debbie herself, Michael. Malcolm, who wrote to me, in fact succeeded in becoming an extra, after trying for many years. When I asked him to say what it was like, he wrote back: 'it's a job like anything else really. [I] am not nervous.' He had incorporated the 'extraordinary' into the 'ordinary' flow of life, it was 'ordinary after all'. Note that the desire to be on television is quite compatible with a cynical awareness of television's commercial basis (for example: Peter, Julie): another example of how cynicism at one level is compatible with belief at another. Being an extra – far from being an eccentric, vain pursuit – is simply one of many forms which the desire to participate in television production takes. You can be an active fan, collecting material about the show (as Peter does). Some programmes have allowed for people to travel to join their live audience: for example, in Britain, Channel Four's *The Big Breakfast* or the radio music programme *The Chris Evans Road Show*.[95] At least in imagination, you can write for your favourite programme, but in practice there are no outlets for *Coronation Street* fans' creativity here (unlike for example for the *Star Trek* fans studied by Henry Jenkins (1992)). Yet it is striking how a number wrote actively on other subjects (Peter, Chris) or imagined writing for the programme (Kim, John). Peter imagined a fictional substitute for being on television, acting out Elsie Tanner's 1989 departure from the Street:

> I'd love to do the Street on video. I'd have to have somebody with me though, so I can be walking down, that's the only way I can go down *Coronation Street*, if actually somebody videoed me walking down the Street ( ... ) I could do the Elsie Tanner, for one scene, couldn't I? Put my fur coat on, post my letters and jump in a taxi, and go.

It is, however, the normal impossibility of being 'on the other side of the cameras' to which people must adjust. It is this impossibility which is naturalised, so that imagining otherwise seems funny. Sometimes people joked when I interviewed them at GST, thinking the interview looked like a media event: 'I hope a crowd doesn't gather and think I'm famous at last.' While of course 'ordinary viewers' *do* appear on television – indeed daytime talk shows are an area now dominated by them – it is the normal impossibility of appearing that matters at the level of people's dispositions. As one US talk show participant said: 'I guess the average American doesn't think they could ever get on a talk show' (quoted, Priest, 1996: 71). Debbie's experience of being on a talk show is significant here. Watching a videotape of the programme back home shocked her:

> I thought, God, that's me, I'm on telly. God, that is so strange [short laugh] ( … ) I couldn't remember sort of like … being there, it just didn't seem the same watching it on telly, it was totally different [ … ] Or it's not like telly, it's like a sort of home video that someone's brought round that's done on a camcorder. You think, God, is that really on the telly? Is there millions of people watching it? Don't know, I honestly had to tape over it in the end, because it was making me cringe.

Debbie could not make a credible connection between the two states (being on television and being at home). She could not recall to mind what it felt like to be there. She started to doubt the status of the recording she saw: was it just a piece of 'home video' (made entirely outside the media frame)? Such was the dislocation caused by the absolute boundary between her 'world' (the world of 'home video') and the 'media world' (the world which 'millions' watch) that she destroyed her best evidence of ever crossing it. She destroyed her only durable context for retelling that event. Her 'tactical' act in relation to the media's 'strategic' storytelling frame therefore had to remain just that. As de Certeau wrote of the 'tactic' generally: '[w]hatever it wins, it does not keep' (1984: xix).

## CONCLUSION TO PART 2

Media production is both part of the social world and apart from it, separated by a naturalised, and therefore normally absolute, boundary. It is the absoluteness of that boundary that enables almost the whole social world (in all its complexity) to be taken for 'merely' an 'ordinary world', when compared with the 'media world'. That boundary is legitimated at GST, even as people play with it or participate imaginatively in the programme's fictional space. The material social processes that construct that boundary usually remain hidden. Media production remains protected by a 'territoriality' (Sack, 1986) that is both pervasive and effective. Visiting GST is, in Simmel's sense, an 'adventure':

> While it falls outside the context of life, it falls, with this same movement, as it were, back into that context again … it is a foreign body in our existence *which is yet somehow connected with the center*.
>     (Simmel, 1971: 188, quoted in Rojek, 1993: 103) [added emphasis]

119

The adventure of visiting GST is focused on the 'media world': the symbolic centre which the media project, the media's 'center out there' (Turner, 1973).

GST, it might be argued, is a privileged access-point for analysing the ritual aspects of the media frame, because of *Coronation Street*'s special status as a long-running popular programme, and perhaps also because of the programme's particular association with 'ordinariness' itself (cf. Jordan, 1981: 29). As the 1996 GST brochure put it, 'ordinary street, extraordinary story'. My argument, however, has been that what is registered at GST is a framework of meaning (a symbolic framework affecting both talk and action) whose importance extends beyond GST or *Coronation Street*: the symbolic hierarchy of the media frame itself. If so, visiting GST is an adventure which stands in for many others: an adventure around the contingent, but compulsory 'centre' of the media's symbolic production, a centre from which most people (as producers, at least) remain excluded.

# Part 3

# MEDIA WITNESSES: TWO DECADES OF PROTEST

# GENERAL INTRODUCTION

Part 3 investigates what we might call 'the politics of the media frame'. It analyses people's interactions with the media frame in contexts of 'political activism', including various forms of 'media activism'. Both terms are used in a broad sense: many of those studied would regard themselves as neither political nor media activists. Part 3 has two main themes: first, the complex ways in which the media frame may (at least, partially and temporarily) become de-naturalised in mediated social conflicts and, second, the practices of alternative mediation through which people may challenge, or disrupt, the naturalised assumptions associated with the media frame.

The first is examined through a detailed study of the protests against the export of live animals through the port of Brightlingsea in 1995. To develop the second theme, I analyse interview material from a number of protests from the past two decades of activism in Britain: the Greenham Common Women's Peace Camp (1981– ), 'awareness' actions that grew out of the Brightlingsea protests, the Pure Genius land occupation in 1996, and the work of two individual activists (referred to as Louise and The Umbrella Man). The general background to these events in terms of the growth of a protest culture in the 1980s and 1990s, fuelled by the deep unpopularity of the former Conservative government, has been given in Chapter 2. Detailed background on the events discussed is provided here and in later chapters. It is worth emphasising again the point made in Chapter 2 that my interests are different from those of political sociology. My concern is with political or social action solely as it relates to the 'phenomenology' of the media frame: what happens when people, who are normally outside both politics *and the media*, experience at close hand the media's operations and, perhaps, contest them.

Brightlingsea is Part 3's main case study, chosen because it illustrated clearly people experiencing the 'de-naturalisation' of the media frame. It was one of a number of protests during 1994 and 1995 at British ports and airports against live animal exports to continental Europe (especially veal calves and sheep). Groups such as Compassion In World Farming had campaigned against this trade for years. This campaign is one of many that have arisen in

Britain and other countries during the 1980s and 1990s around the environment, the treatment of animals, and methods of farming and food production (see Benton and Redfearn, 1996). The issue of live animal exports, however, attracted intense local hostility and national prominence only when major ferry companies – P&O and Sealink – boycotted the trade in October 1994, forcing its transfer to smaller ports. The little-known town of Brightlingsea on the English east coast suddenly received national and international media coverage, together with a number of other places, including the south coast ports of Shoreham and Dover and the small commercial airport at Coventry. This was mainly a British campaign, although there were some links between British protesters and activists in Belgium, France and elsewhere in continental Europe. The degree of media coverage for these local protests probably surprised those involved in the protests. It was fuelled partly by the context of the growing unpopularity of the government on many fronts, partly by the obviously 'non-political' nature of most of the participants, and partly by the widespread belief that the commercial interests behind the animal export trade had close links with members of the government and the Conservative party.

It might seem a large leap to move from reactions to a media leisure site, like Granada Studios Tour, to reflections on the media's presence in a protest situation such as Brightlingsea which, for many involved, was one of the most shocking events they had ever experienced. Each situation has, of course, its quite specific aspects, but the important larger point I want to make by such a juxtaposition is this: both contexts are evidence of a much wider process through which the symbolic power of media institutions in Britain has been reproduced. Paradoxical though it may seem, 1990s Britain is a place where there has been both (1) an expansion of more or less commercial sites for encountering the media process (as part of planned leisure activity) and (2) an increasing number of local conflicts where people have experienced the media process close up (and usually not voluntarily). That is not to say that we can read these processes together as belonging to any simple historical 'conjuncture', but at least the paradox needs to be grasped. I return to this broadly historical issue in the Conclusion.

The Brightlingsea study is based on twenty open-ended, semi-structured interviews conducted in people's homes between September 1996 and February 1997: twelve individual interviews, six double interviews (four with married couples, one with women friends, and one with a mother and son) and two group interviews (one with two married couples, and the other with a married couple and two women). The names of virtually all people interviewed from the Brightlingsea protests have been changed for reasons of confidentiality.[96] The exception was Maria Wilby, the leading spokesperson of BALE (Brightlingsea Against Live Exports) who received the highest public profile during the protests, and whom I interviewed in that context.

The Appendix gives further details of the sample, but precise ages and occupational details of individuals are not given, also to protect confidentiality (many of the sample being known to each other). This sample is older than the GST samples, but (as explained in the Appendix) this corresponds to the age profile of those protesting. Not all those people interviewed have been quoted in detail. Those who have been are as follows (with approximate age and class status):

| Angela | 50s | Lower middle-class |
| Clive | 50s | Lower middle-class |
| David | 50s | Lower middle-class |
| Ed | 20s | Middle-class |
| Edna | 50s | Lower middle-class |
| Eileen | 40s | Middle-class |
| Gill | 50s | Working-class |
| Harry | 70s | Working-class |
| Helen | 50s | Lower middle-class |
| Jane | 20s | Working-class |
| Jean | 40s | Working-class |
| Jennifer | 40s | Middle-class |
| Jenny | 60s | Lower middle-class |
| Jim | 60s | Lower middle-class |
| Martin | 40s | Lower middle-class |
| Margaret | 60s | Lower middle-class |
| Rachel | 40s | Middle-class |
| Sally | 40s | Lower middle-class |
| Samantha | 30s | Middle-class |
| Stephanie | 50s | Lower middle-class |
| Tony | 60s | Working-class |
| Vera | 70s | Working-class |

Details of interviewees discussed in relation to other protests will be given as they arise.

# 7

# BRIGHTLINGSEA: THE
# DE-NATURALISATION OF THE
# MEDIA FRAME

To hear or read the news is to live intermittently in a world one does not
touch in daily life.

(Edelman, 1988: 35)


You live your life, you're just an ordinary person just going along, and
then when something like this happens, it makes you realise, you know,
there are things going on in the world that you're just totally naïve to ( ... )
But we've touched it.

(Sally, interview with the author)


## INTRODUCTION

Of all the protest sites against live animal exports, Brightlingsea was the most
disrupted by the trade. A seaside town of 8,500 people on a little-known part
of the East Anglian coast, it is reached by one main road; where the road
approaches the small privatised port, it is no wider than a suburban street,
lined with houses and gardens on either side. The possibility that live animals
might be exported through Brightlingsea emerged on 10 January 1995. After
a packed public meeting where council opposition was declared, hundreds
blocked the road to the port and the first lorry was turned back on 16 January.
When two days later a lorry convoy arrived, escorted by riot police, a bitter
day-long confrontation ensued, a scene repeated in various forms until the
trade was withdrawn in October 1995. The protests received, at least in their
early stages, intense local, national and international media coverage. The
trade, and the protests, continue at other larger ports, but now receive only
sporadic media attention.

For Brightlingsea residents, the peacefulness of their town was important,
in addition to animal welfare. But the latter could hardly be ignored: the
sight, sound, and smell of animals crammed into lorries shocked those along
the route, often leaving them in tears. At Brightlingsea, unlike other ports,

protesters were close enough to touch the animals as they passed, certainly close enough to speak to the drivers. Events were played out on a small, almost personal scale: as Sally put it, 'the houses were close together, the people were close together, everybody could see everything'. Tension was greatly increased by insensitive policing: there were many allegations of violent assaults on young and old people, verbal abuse and general intimidation. Policing soon became, for many, a protest issue in its own right. For almost everyone – as the media emphasised – this was their first experience of protesting (true of all but three interviewees: Maria Wilby, Jennifer, Jane). People came in touch with a whole other world: of animal cruelty, police intimidation, morally questionable business practices, behind-the-scenes government influence. But at the same time – something the media did not highlight – it was generally also protesters' first direct encounter with *media reporting*. Within a few days of the original warning that the animal lorries would arrive, the first two stages of a 'social drama' (Turner, 1974: 38–44) had occurred: the initial breach of normal social relations and the escalation to a more general crisis. In 'major liminal situation[s]', Turner argued, society takes 'cognizance of itself' (ibid.: 239–40). My more limited claim is that protesters at Brightlingsea 'took cognizance' of a significant aspect of the social, namely the media. I focus not on how the media covered these events, but on how protesters – finding themselves suddenly 'subject[s] of media representations' as distinct from media consumers (cf. Benton and Redfearn, 1996: 58) – experienced, to varying degrees, the de-naturalisation of the media frame.

Even the act of participating in the protests disrupted an important assumption. For if, as William Gamson has argued for US media, UK 'media discourse systematically discourages the idea that ordinary citizens can alter the conditions and terms of their daily lives through their own actions' (1995: 97) – and this is fully consistent with my argument in Part 1 – then simply participating in a protest as an 'ordinary citizen' is potentially disruptive. It challenges the category of the 'ordinary person' so central to the construction of news events (cf. Edelman, 1988: 35–7). Many found themselves at odds with their own negative stereotypes of protesters, developed from the media and elsewhere. As Jim, a retired local authority worker, put it:

> It felt so foreign, didn't it? To be walking down the street with a placard. I mean, prior to all this, when we saw any protest on television, we always thought or assumed, Oh, protesters are wrong, the police are right.

Assumptions about the details of events previously seen on the media were challenged but, perhaps, something more fundamental also: the assumption that news events generally happen to *other* people. Protesters at Brightlingsea entered the media frame for the first time: 'the only time I've seen treatment [of people] like that ( … ) has been on television' (Clive).[97] It was as if people felt they were being socially recategorised.

The resulting de-naturalisation reveals the normal way that media power is naturalised, especially the routine trust on which the media's social authority is based. Similar disruptions of trust have been felt by those involved in other mediated protests. As one miner's wife involved in the 1984–5 Miners' Strike put it:

> When the strike began I felt at first that to some degree everyone up here had been cocooned against reality. The TV had always been accepted as *the thing that keeps you in touch with the world*: people would say, 'Let's have the news on to find out what's going on'. It was only as the strike went on that you discovered if you wanted to find out what was going on in your own world, among miners and strikers and in your own life, *what you saw on the news wasn't what was going on*. It was frightening gradually to realize the extent they selected what they were going to report.
> (quoted in Parker, 1986: 139, added emphasis)

She is speaking of a disruption of the whole interpretative structure through which she understands the media. As Angela, a Brightlingsea housewife in her fifties, put it:

> Initially why would you buy a newspaper, why would you put the news on? … You want to know what's going on in the world. But you know now that what you're being told [slight laugh] isn't necessarily right.

Previously, the media had put protesters 'in touch' with aspects of the world they would not otherwise experience directly. Now protesters were touching that world, and touching the mechanism of media representation as well.

## A SITE OF WITNESSING

By choosing this entry-point into the media's relation to politics, I am looking at the media process in a distinctive way: in terms of its geographical distribution and, above all, the significance of particular sites where non-media-people *witness* the actual process of making news coverage. Such sites are liminal: they involve a major change in people's relationship to the media frame, not least because the news in this case is about them. The spatial aspects of this are not incidental but central, provided we see them against the background (cf. Chapter 3) of the normal segregation of media audiences from media production. At Brightlingsea, there was a further shift in *imaginative* geography. Not all protesters were local residents, but for those who were it was their own town that was receiving national, even international, coverage. Applying Mackenzie Wark's distinction between 'map' and 'territory', the rather isolated 'territory' of Brightlingsea's daily life had joined the media-shaped 'map' of the nation (Wark, 1994: 62–3). Many told me how they were contacted by distant family or even strangers who had seen the town on television.

Highlighting the media aspects of the Brightlingsea protests involves some degree of abstraction from the ethical and political issues actually in dispute there, but this is justified by the fact that everyone I interviewed had some reaction to the protests' media dimension, and many seemed to have reflected upon it a great deal. Although other perspectives on the media dimension (for example, that of the police) might also have been interesting, I concentrated particularly on how it affected protesters, as it was they whose relationship to the media process was most likely to have been disrupted. I use 'the media' here, as elsewhere, in a broad sense to cover the principal mass media (television, radio and the press). Issues about each of these arise at various points, but it is above all 'the media' in a general, unspecific sense that was in question: the media as social frame (cf. Chapter 1). We must remember also the geographer Doreen Massey's insight about the complexity of what goes to make up any particular place (cf. Chapter 2): 'what has come together in this particular place is a conjunction of *many* histories and *many* spaces' (1995: 191, added emphasis). Before discussing the media aspects in more detail, I want first to sketch in some other important dimensions.

The Brightlingsea protests bear an interesting relation to literature on new social movements (cf. Chapter 2). While clearly 'political' in some broader sense, they fell outside standard notions of political action: they were a form of 'non-institutional politics' (Offe, 1985: 827). People's reasons for involvement varied greatly. For example, amongst my interviewees eight were already actively interested in issues of animal welfare, with two others having protested on other issues before; six became active on animal issues through the protests, while the remaining interviewees' involvement seemed mainly motivated by the impact on the town of the trade. Protesters came from a wide range of class positions: certainly the protests did not articulate the interests of a particular class (Offe, 1985: 833). In addition, the protests were planned by an organisation, BALE, without any formal representative structure (ibid.: 829–30). The protest actions involved both instrumental and expressive aspects (ibid.): blocking the roads, while initially purely instrumental, came increasingly (as people realised the lorries could not physically be stopped) to affirm collective action against the 'rationalised organisation' of economic life (Melucci, 1989: 12, 84). The protests acted as a 'symbolic multiplier' (Melucci, 1985: 813) which revealed, perhaps more effectively than formal political methods, the underlying principle at stake: civic ethics versus the purely economic 'rationality' of the food industry. Many protesters denied that what they were doing was 'political' (BALE's official position), yet a social challenge was mounted to economic forces most protesters regarded as having political (i.e. government) backing. There was also the wider 'politics' of discourse itself – issues about democracy and being heard – that were projected onto the apparently 'non-political' issue of animal rights. So, in various ways, the Brightlingsea protests fitted Ulrich Beck's broader thesis of how 'politics' have changed, when 'political modernisation disempowers and unbinds [official] politics and politicizes society' (1992: 194).

There were also parallels with older forms of popular action against economic processes. Just as Britain's eighteenth-century poor tried to prevent traders profiting from food shortages by road and canal blockades, travelling to traders' homes, and actions at markets (Thompson, 1971), so Brightlingsea protesters took action where their numbers seemed to count most: on the roads, whether along the route to the port, outside the homes of those profiting from the trade, or on nearby major roads. Intervening in events by 'get[ting] out on the street' (as one protester put it) to block them is hardly new, even if recently it has been relabelled as 'direct action'. 'Direct action' intervenes in the normal segregation of economic production from living spaces. It disrupts the economy's normal 'geography', our 'disembedding' (Giddens, 1990: 21) from the economic process, apart from that small aspect of it in which we may work ourselves. At Brightlingsea, people were brought face-to-face with the practices of the food industries (many, as mentioned, had no concern with animal issues before the protests).[98] And, by becoming involved in shared action, people temporarily realised common passions and beliefs. At the protests there was a 'liminal' sociality (Turner, 1974; Maffesoli, 1996) as people's isolation from each other was suspended: there was a sense for Brightlingsea residents of the whole town coming together, the 'camaraderie' of shared physical resistance.[99]

Brightlingsea is in some ways unrepresentative of contemporary Britain: it is almost entirely white, for instance (99.4 per cent, according to the 1991 UK Census, against a national average of 94.1 per cent: Essex County Council, 1993). Protest participation was weighted towards those without formal work, or with flexible work: housewives, the self-employed, the retired. However, 40 per cent of Brightlingsea's population participated in at least one daily protest (Benton and Redfearn, 1996: 54, quoting Tannenbaum, 1995): allowing for perhaps 25–30 per cent who could not attend (the 1991 census showed 17.8 per cent aged under 18 and 13.4 per cent with long-term illnesses), this is a strikingly high proportion of the population. The range of classes involved was noted by many: 'all walks of life', 'literally the whole range', both 'the roadsweeper and the schoolteacher'. The protests were seen locally as a struggle for 'the community' (Eileen), or 'the Battle for Brightlingsea' (as a locally-produced video was called). However, the protests included many from outside the town. Even on the protests' first day,

*Plate 5*  House window, Brightlingsea, June 1996

*Plate 6*  BALE members on hunger strike outside Essex farm, October 1996

there were non-residents attracted by advance television or radio coverage, including some interviewees (Jane, Martin, Samantha, and Stephanie). The proportion of 'outsiders' grew markedly in later weeks and months (estimated by various interviewees at between 20 per cent and 40 per cent), particularly from other parts of Essex or the adjacent county of Suffolk, but sometimes from other parts of Britain (especially other ports involved in the protests) and even abroad (Canada, Japan, Belgium). Some people felt that it was this national support that enabled the protests' eventual success.

People were shocked at Brightlingsea to encounter the force of the British state for the first time. Some referred to a loss of 'innocence'. Encountering police violence and intimidation bewildered people who had regarded the police as on their side: 'you couldn't believe it was your town' (Edna, Group 2), 'you felt as though you didn't belong to your country any more' (Clive). The experience was so dislocating that the best comparison might be wartime ('like living in a war zone': four similar examples), or even media fantasy (also four examples): *Close Encounters* or, more lightheartedly, *Starsky and Hutch*. The fact that the media provided ready metaphors for an experience so 'unreal' reinforces the point made earlier: that people were experiencing at first hand events that they had previously only seen in the media. The appearance of riot police on the first Friday night of protests had a particular impact. 'It was like a film set' (David, Group 1), vividly described by Sally, the owner of a small local business, in her forties:

> The police came round the corner in the dark with floodlights on, they were sitting on top of these big personnel carriers ... and they had binoculars and everything, and the big megaphones ( ... ) Oh, it was really really strange and it was huge great big beams, you know, spotlights ( ... ) going through picking out different people and giving descriptions ( ... ) And they were talking to the mike, There's so-and-so over there ... And so the police just went in in groups and picked out the people.

A more vivid description of the act of 'interpellation' in Althusser's sense (1969) could hardly be imagined. The protesters were interpellated as subjects of the modern surveillance-based state,[100] whose processes they had always before imagined applying to 'others'. Or, as a friend quoted by Rachel said: 'They're in riot gear and it's *us*!'

These disruptions had a symbolic dimension. As media coverage emphasised, Brightlingsea protesters were not those normally seen to be involved in 'actions', but 'ordinary people': 'ordinary people' left their homes and 'took to the streets' (Maria Wilby). Later this geographical disruption carried over to other public spaces, when people spoke publicly in market squares or demonstrated on motorways (see Chapter 8). For Jean, also a housewife in her forties, there was a vivid sense of the 'free space' that the protests involved:

> Every week, Wednesday when I go down there [to the Community Centre along the protest route], I always stand in the road and sort of look up and down and think, Oh yes, I've sat here [short laugh] ( … ) I never thought I'd do anything like that. But at the time I never thought about it, I just did it ( … ) Everybody did what they wanted.

The disruption was not only geographical: discursive hierarchies were challenged. Four protesters spoke to me of a new freedom to speak directly to people of higher status. This had implications for class and gender relations.[101] Here, Eileen (also a housewife in her forties) describes speaking at a televised public meeting against a (male) chief of police:

> It was … frightening because I'd never heard my own voice before ( … ) I was very shocked that I could be quite as eloquent as I was ( … ) Because I've been a Mum at home for 21 years ( … ) I think our menfolk found it a shock, he [her husband] found it a shock.

The protests, for Eileen, were a matter of 'being heard'. This was not only an issue of gender or class. Six of the interview sample across class and genders said they felt, following the protests, that Britain was not a democracy and that the protest was a response to that: 'deep down the protest is [about] being unable to protest' (Tony). The sense of being able to speak and act 'up' affected the town as a whole: Brightlingsea was transformed from a little-known seaside town to somewhere on the national, even the world, 'map' (ten cases). No one (including Maria Wilby, the only interviewee with prior knowledge of the media) expected the degree of coverage received. As Helen said, 'we had no idea it would cause such attention ( … ) we thought it was just a local thing': because it was local, *therefore* it would not receive media attention. But soon people were waking up to live coverage of their town on breakfast television. This affected many people's sense of the scale on which the Brightlingsea protests had an impact: '[it] brought the whole thing to worldwide attention' (Jenny, Group 1).

There were, then, many dimensions to protesters' 'collective action frame[s]' (Gamson, 1995: 89). Some, reflecting a year after the protests ended, even sensed that their whole lives had changed; others suspected that the impacts were not permanent, but this in any case is not my concern. It is the *immediate* sense of change that matters for my argument, in particular the sense of the de-naturalisation of the media frame. As in Part 2, we need to pay close attention to people's language to trace this process. How far people's different backgrounds (class, education, family) affected the degree to which they articulated the de-naturalisation explicitly is a complex issue, and I will come back to this.

## DIRECT CONFLICTS WITH MEDIA NARRATIVES

A good starting-point is people's experiences of contradictions with specific media narratives about the protests. This happened in four basic ways: (i) conflicts between what protesters saw happen and what was reported to have happened; (ii) conflicts between what protesters themselves said to media reporters and what they were reported as saying; (iii) questioning of the stereotypes employed in media narratives; and (iv) questioning of the general paradigms through which events such as protests are presented as news.[102] These types of conflict – which affected the sample as a whole – will be useful background to more profound forms of contradiction in individual interviews, analysed later.

Many were very active media consumers during the protests: videoing the news if they would otherwise miss it, reading more than one newspaper to get the best account, keeping press cuttings. Individual consumption was supplemented by exchanging video copies, or photocopies, of news items. Various media access-points (radio phone-ins, letters to the paper) were intensively used. There was also an explosion of unofficial media: newsletters, public meetings, information phone-lines, poems, songs, T-shirts, badges and placards. People were intensively engaged both with the official media and 'mediation' generally (Martin-Barbero, 1993). A common experience was frustration:

> One of the annoying things, talking about the media, is where we've been to an incident and actually seen things happen, and then you read a report in the paper, which is _totally_ wrong … You feel so frustrated, but there's nothing you can really do about it. They've got it in there ( … ) You feel, why should they [the media, NC] have that weapon in their favour and we can do nothing about it?
>
> (Jim)

A conflict is expressed here between what you 'actually' saw at the scene and how it was reported (on 'actually', see Chapter 6). The media's nature as a field of competition for symbolic power here becomes explicit: 'why should _they_ have that weapon in their favour?'

Differences with media coverage often related to violence alleged by protesters against the police. A number of people argued that such incidents were not reported, whereas violence by protesters was reported, creating a misleading impression (four cases). Some used the routine parallel of the football match: having a different view of a match you've seen from next day's press report. Others put it in less routine terms, as a clash between their sense of events, as eyewitnesses, and the edited media coverage watched at home:

> … it was ITV was the villain, have the news on, you'd get about ten seconds of what they were going to show about this. And smack! They cut the picture right out and go on to the next item of news. They used to quite often cut it right out. That's politics coming into it.
>
> (Harry, Group 1)

The materiality of the description (the sense of direct physical intervention in the media process: 'they cut it right out') is striking.[103] Later in the protests, as media coverage declined, some people outside Brightlingsea thought the protests there had finished: an even sharper conflict between protesters' and media versions of events. Protesters came to realise that you had to 'be there' at the protests to see things the way protesters saw them (six cases). This parallels how people talked at GST – the form of 'aura' associated with the site of mediation, the importance of 'actually' 'being there' at the site of mediation – but the effect here was not to confirm or enhance people's engagement with the media, but to disrupt it. We can put this also more generally. The media provide us with 'disembedded' access to distant events on the basis of 'trust', which can sometimes be 're-embedded' at access-points to the media mechanism (cf. Giddens, 1990). If going to see the Street set was, for most, a successful 're-embedding' of the media mechanism, 'being there' at the Brightlingsea protests was a failed 're-embedding'. Witnessing mediated events resulted in a more profound 'disembedding' of people's relations with the media.

Being interviewed by the media provoked this conflict in acute form. Virtually none of the protesters had been interviewed before, certainly not for a major news story; nor had many seen anyone else being interviewed and compared the original words with the mediated version. While some already knew that interviews are edited (three cases), others did not and were shocked (see below, Martin). Maria Wilby, as leader of BALE, was better placed than most to observe the impact of this on others. People often suggested points she should make in her interviews but, even if made, they might be edited out:

> A lot of people thought that what they saw on the news or read in the papers was the truth so when they didn't see everything put on there, they were absolutely gutted, a lot of them, because they really felt they were being misrepresented, mistreated and … were horrified really.

Editing seemed to disrupt a basic trust. For Harry (quoted above), the only explanation was 'politics', that is, an intervention beyond the normal media process. The wife of a miner involved in the 1971–2 UK Miners' Strike was equally puzzled by media editing and explained it equally generally:[104]

> Well I don't know, it's something I can't explain, but … when they're having interviews on the television with the miners they just seem to cut 'em off dead, you know, on to the next person, I don't know why, but … well I try to think but I just don't know, there seems no reason in it unless they think a miner's just nobody.
>
> (interview, 30 January 1974, quoted in Parker, 1974)

In both of these cases, editing was seen, not as a technical process, but as the sign of something more fundamental. The mere fact of editing in itself undermined a long-standing belief in the media's transparency. Not everyone, of course, experienced this shock in such extreme form, but none were insulated from it entirely.

A third type of conflict arose between the stereotypes of protesters in media coverage and protesters' own experience. In the interviews, the clichés so familiar from the past twenty or thirty years of British political discourse were frequently repeated: 'rentamob', 'loony lefties', 'youths with earrings', 'punks', and so on. Most people indicated that, before the protests, they would have been hostile to any protesters seen on television. Yet few protesters at Brightlingsea fitted the descriptions suggested by the conventional stereotype: they included pensioners, mothers with babies, doctors, a magistrate's wife, a senior policeman's wife! Existing self-knowledge clashed directly with the protester stereotypes: 'This is us! … This is no loony lefties or ( … ) Socialist Worker people, all the people that you've ever been led to believe are the only people who would "do that sort of thing"' (Rachel).[105] Some concluded that 'there isn't a typical protester' (two cases). Even if they did not, protesters came to grasp the *process* of stereotyping itself, and the media's role in it: 'we started to become mobs' (Jim), 'you'd think us loonies if you just watched it [television]' (Jean), 'you look at that [pointing to the television] and you're a mob' (Tony).[106] One woman questioned the implied stereotyping of the term 'activist': 'I don't consider myself to be an activist, because to me that conjures up somebody who does wrong things ( … ) I'm an active member of the public trying to make a protest' (Edna, Group 2). People also noticed an excessive (and, they felt, unfair) coverage of those younger protesters at Brightlingsea who fitted protester stereotypes more easily: 'we had lots of different people down there, but they're just the same as us ( … ) like scruffy clothes, long hair, black hair, pink hair ( … ) and that, everybody's there for a reason, they were all lovely' (Jean: three similar cases). Media stereotypes of protesters were further de-naturalised when Shoreham protesters (previously known only from the media) came to Brightlingsea:

> Everybody went Uhhhh! expecting these hooded, truncheon-bearing activists ( ... ) [laughs] What happened was a car of nice sweet old ladies from Shoreham came down to support us ... So that was a revelation because we realised that Shoreham was probably very very similar to Brightlingsea.
>
> (Maria)

An underlying similarity had been grasped, which seemed at odds with spurious similarities in the media coverage.

As a result, protesters' views of other mediated protests changed. A number spoke spontaneously, and positively, about protesters elsewhere, for example at the well-known Newbury anti-road protests (1995–6) (eight cases) or, historically, the 1984–5 Miners' Strike (three cases). Some concluded that the media continually obscure the fact that the typical protesters are 'ordinary people',[107] with the result that if you are 'ordinary' your political actions are not seen on the media. As Tony put it:

> They [the media] can't understand the likes of Gill and I getting into this. They want to see the bloke with the thing through his nose and the ears ( ... ) you know, they want to see them, we're nothing, we're, you know ( ... ) [an] old couple, who are harmless ( ... ) square pegs in round holes ( ... ) we're just ordinary, everyday, run-of-the-mill people.

Here, the process of stereotyping itself – the 'massification' it involves – is registered experientially. As Raymond Williams (1961: 289) famously wrote: 'to other people, we also are masses. Masses are other people.' The stereotyping of protesters, of course, occurs not only in the media, but the most direct way in which stereotypes were de-naturalised at Brightlingsea was through conflicts between media coverage and the experience of protesting. The result was to disrupt trust in the media generally.[108]

People, finally, began to question how news stories about protests are put together. Maria Wilby, as BALE media spokesperson, was keenly aware of how standard news items are constructed: for example, the way formulaic shots of police in riot gear were repeated, even though riot gear was only worn at Brightlingsea on two occasions, giving a misleading impression of continued high levels of violence. Others, without direct experience of the media process, commented on 'sensationalism' (three cases); excessive concentration on violence allegedly against the police (two cases); too much emphasis on trivial 'human interest' stories (three cases); the influence of news by entertainment values (three cases). Such questioning did not, however, all point in the same direction. One non-protester (husband of an interviewed protester) argued that the media exaggerated the conflict with the police and therefore worsened the situation. Others acknowledged that, whatever their opinions, the media needed to maintain a balance between different interests. When set against the media's generally naturalised authority, such comments signify an important shift, but not necessarily a full de-naturalisation. Ed (a health worker in his twenties), however, pushed the implications further:

> The news is giving people what people want to hear. People like to hear about demonstrators popping at [attacking] the police, but people don't like to hear about police popping at demonstrators ( ... ) *The news* ( ... ) *it's not actually what happens* ( ... ) and I don't think there's much you can do about it, they have control of what they put on at the end of the day, and they will put on the most newsworthy item, won't they? [added emphasis]

This is a powerful articulation of the media's reality as a mechanism of representation. Compare the comment of the miner's wife quoted earlier: 'what you saw on the news wasn't what was going on.' Such clear articulation was rare, but this was not because conflicts with the media's authority were not felt. We must keep separate two questions: whether such disruptions are registered at some level, and how they are articulated.

## BROADER CONFLICTS WITH THE MEDIA

Most people I interviewed said that, in some way, their consumption of news[109] had changed: the exception was Jennifer who, perhaps significantly, was the only interviewee to call herself 'political'. Some claimed the change was total: for example, 'I'm very suspicious of anything really now' (Angela), 'I question a lot more what they put on' (Jane), 'now I don't believe anything' (Christine). Others, while sceptical on detail, regarded media coverage of Brightlingsea positively overall (Vera, Tony) or at least neutrally (Jane). Vera and Tony, in particular, felt that, without the media coverage, the protests would have remained an obscure local conflict. Still others, while acknowledging how their media consumption had changed through protesting, said that, even before, they had been sceptical of the media (four cases): their disbelief had, however, become more active. This evidence from people's self-reporting is complex enough, but still leaves unanswered whether people's viewing practice had actually changed, a question I did not set out to answer. My main concern was different: revealing the more general assumptions about the media that were disrupted at Brightlingsea. I now turn to these in more detail.

Chapter 3's theoretical model suggests that involvement in mediated events would have broader implications than just questioning how specific events were covered. At stake was people's deep-seated, naturalised trust in the media, and beyond that, the symbolic hierarchy, and geographical segregation, between 'media' and 'ordinary' 'worlds'. If, as I have argued, the media's authority forms part of the 'habitus', then its disruption may be quite difficult for people to articulate as such: there is no ready language for it. My argument for the rest of the chapter will therefore proceed in two stages. In this section, I examine the overall range of interview material. In the following section, I look closely at the language of three particular interviews.

Hardly any protesters I interviewed had encountered the media process before. But they quickly became accustomed to speaking to camera crew and journalists. There was a 'camaraderie', partly because both protesters and media were shocked by the violence they saw. People became used to writing to local papers (especially the Essex *Evening Gazette* and the *East Anglian Daily Times*) and using local radio phone-ins (on BBC Essex and SGR, a commercial local station), whether to give their views or to pass on information about the protests: 'it [local radio] was our life line' (Clive), 'we all got into the habit of phoning as soon as we heard something that wasn't true' (Rachel). Protesters became 'closer' to the media in another way: they developed, rightly or wrongly, some sense of how the media work. In addition to the awareness of stereotyping already considered, many felt that the media were being censored, or at least distorted. The explanations varied from (1) the police's intentional inflation of incidents of alleged violence by protesters, to (2) the belief that reporters and photographers were intimidated by the police, to (3) an account that came close to the notion of 'primary definers' in *Policing the Crisis* (Hall *et al.*, 1978): that for legal and other reasons the media took police information on trust, while requiring protester information to be corroborated. People came to question, then, the naturalness of the news. Something similar happened with people's experience of participating in the media: many claimed they were barred from participating in local radio phone-ins or were shocked to find that television talk shows on which they appeared were not spontaneous conversations, but orchestrated by the presenter.

Almost all the sample spoke of a new mistrust in, or suspicion of, the media, and related this to their protesting experiences. This was true across all age groups. As Sally vividly put it: *'we've been behind the scenes* ( … ) *and we've seen how things that we did were reported and it's totally wrong to how it actually happened'* [added emphasis]. If, as Meyrowitz (1985) has argued, everyday television shows us aspects of public events that were previously 'backstage', so in this case witnessing the news events meant going 'backstage' behind the media process itself. People looked back on their previous media consumption as naïve: 'I used to believe everything that I read' (Margaret), 'I was an outsider just looking at it ( … ) I didn't really know what was going on' (Helen). Clive, Helen's husband and a retired local authority worker in his fifties, described the impact on his family. Previously he had been critical of his son for getting involved with 'troublemakers' at protests, and had in turn been criticised by his son:

> He used to say to me, 'Dad, you don't know what you're talking about.' He said, 'You've got to be in, to see what really goes on.' *And it wasn't until Brightlingsea started to happen ( … ) that I started to realise what he meant.* And now, since then, I've apologised to him and to several other youngsters ( … ) There is a lot more to it than meets the eye. It is not just a straightforward case of what the media try and make out sometimes. [added emphasis]

Some reflected on how the rest of the media audience, without the advantage of their experience as witnesses, must still be consuming media coverage in a superficial way. Others displaced their trust onto foreign media (sometimes assumed to have reported more of the protests than British media) or onto British media in the past. The implications of being 'behind the scenes' of the media process went deeper still. It was a disruption of the normal geography of the media frame; the separation between 'media' and 'ordinary' 'worlds' was broken. The normal situation was reflected when I asked Angela, a self-styled 'ordinary housewife', whether she had encountered the media before: 'I can't think where I might have [seen the media] … *there wouldn't have been any reason* for me to have been anywhere near a camera or … microphone' [added emphasis].

What was the impact, then, of being 'close' to the media? There was a range of responses. One possibility was to deny the media's presence had any impact on you: 'they were just there' (Margaret), 'I don't think I was too aware of the media that day' (Angela). But this apparent lack of response was itself, I suggest, influenced by a range of factors: perhaps a wish to avoid giving me the impression that they had 'acted up to the camera'; or, alternatively, a feeling that, because these were major events, the media *ought* to be there, their presence was natural. As Gill put it:

> Because everything down there was basically ( … ) alien to you ( … ) it just seemed a natural thing … The media, I suppose, if you ever thought about it, had to be there ( … ) and you thought it was the most natural thing to have your media there.

But articulating the impact of the media's presence is not necessarily straightforward, and this passage suggests one reason why. It was the whole situation that was disruptive: something 'alien', overwhelming in its strangeness. The media's presence in those strange circumstances was as natural as *your* presence there was unnatural, precisely the naturalised *segregation* between 'media' and viewer 'worlds' already analysed. That is why the impact of the media's presence could seem both obscure and profound, as in this passage where Eileen was corrected by her daughter:[110]

*Eileen*      … we were in such a state of shock that the media being there, you

just accepted, it didn't add to, it didn't detract, it was just somebody else you were talking to ( ... )

*Daughter*    No, you were excited that they came down because you didn't
think nobody would be interested ( ... )

*Eileen*    It was a very very strange feeling and it's one we've never ever
come to terms with.

The presence of the media – as a disruption of the 'habitus' – was disturbing
in a way that, because it was so difficult to articulate, could easily pass without
being articulated.

Others, however, registered the media's presence more straightforward
as exciting (six cases). These reactions are closer to what we might expect
from Part 2. There was the surprise of seeing the mass of satellite dishes
transmitting broadcasts, or seeing faces of reporters you knew from the
media. As Samantha described it:

> It was bizarre because the community centre was like there and we'd all
> meet there and you'd just be like milling around with them, like faces
> you'd see on television ( ... ) Obviously, if they wanted to know some-
> thing they'd talk to you, you know, you were under no false illusion that
> they don't really want to talk to you [short laugh].

The fact of the meeting was itself striking enough to be worth emphasising;
just as at GST people hoped to meet stars spontaneously, so here the (guaranteed) spontaneity of the encounter with media crews at Brightlingsea –
simply 'milling around with them' – was notable. But at the same time
Samantha was cynical: '[the media] don't really want to talk to you' as an
individual. In other words, as also at GST, the boundary between 'media' and
'ordinary' 'worlds' was maintained even as it was apparently breached.
Hence some, like Helen, were puzzled at the media's presence:

> I couldn't believe we were so important ( ... 2 pages) I mean every week
> or every month we had somebody down from some, either newspaper
> or television programme ( ... ) there was always somebody down here.
> And that really still did amaze me. Because I kept thinking, why is this
> all so important ... ?

The boundary between 'media' and 'ordinary' 'worlds' is not just physical; it
is a social and symbolic boundary between two orders of things, two orders
of people. If the media are 'there' with you, you must somehow be 'important'. And yet, Helen feels, she is not 'really' important: an unresolved paradox. At one level, she was sceptical about the accuracy of media coverage, but
at another level, the naturalisation of the media's symbolic hierarchy was
reproduced in her words.

We can trace that hierarchy in other things people said. Protesters realised that 'ordinary' events are not what the media usually cover, part of the media's 'sensationalism' (cf. Halloran *et al.*, 1970: 281). For anything to be on the media, it must be 'important', 'exciting'. As a result, actions during the protests would only be covered if they were 'out of the ordinary', 'mad'; more cynically, 'all you've got to do is pretend and you'll get media coverage' (Helen). This implied that successful actions from the point of view of media coverage would need to be *transformed* in some way – 'if it's big enough and loud enough, then it's news' (Rachel) – a problem if much of what you did seemed irretrievably 'ordinary'. People felt that 'ordinary' days at the protests could never be made newsworthy. But the risks of distorting events for the media were also recognised. As Gill put it, 'I didn't even agree … with all the protesters standing in one clump, because it's image ( … ) it turns it into something, you're not really serious, it turns it into something else'. These are exactly the type of pragmatic reinforcements of the media/ordinary distinction that I discussed in Chapter 3. Maria Wilby felt that seeing their lives reflected on the media was a fundamental and positive change for many people:

> It's amazing, instead of going home and watching *Coronation Street* and *Eastenders* and things, they'll go home and they'll watch *Panorama* and they'll watch *World in Action* and they'll watch *Newsnight* [the last three all popular news programmes] *because they've seen their own things on there*. It gives you this ability to relate to it … I think a lot of people think that programmes like that 'are all above me' but once you've seen things that you know about on there, you realise that you've just got to listen and it'll go in. [added emphasis]

Again, although it is not certain whether this alteration in viewing actually happened,[111] Maria's comment registers precisely the categorical distinction in question. Seeing your 'own things on there' marks a significant shift in how you and your 'world' are categorised.

This shift was, I suggest, linked to the wider recognition (already noted) that those involved at Brightlingsea did not confirm the media stereotype of protesters; they were 'ordinary people'. Protesters often described themselves as 'ordinary' (ten cases), even 'normal, boring, ordinary' (Rachel). The fact they were involved in public events was itself a shift in categories. Nevertheless, the normal hierarchy of the media frame went on being reproduced, or (adapting Zizek) 'people were still doing it' (cf. Chapter 3, 'Ordering'). So people drew on the capital of 'media people' (including television and sports 'personalities') to help their cause. Helen told me: 'we thought it would help bring more importance to it, if we could get *people that the media knew* ( … ) [if they] were supportive of us, then that would help people realise that we weren't stupid idiots, we were people that really cared' [added emphasis].

Those who were positively stereotyped because they were 'people that the media knew' could rescue 'ordinary people' from being negatively stereotyped, transforming them from 'stupid idiots' into 'people that really cared': a subtle, but hardly trivial, legitimation of media power.

Implicit here is an argument about language. On the one hand, I am arguing that the symbolic hierarchy of the media frame affects everyone and its disruption at Brightlingsea was registered by everyone at some level. We can look for this in the 'small words' people used. As noted in Chapter 6, 'actual' and its cognate expressions can mark something the significance of which is taken for granted, for instance because a naturalised boundary is challenged or approached. Thus when Clive heard his wife interviewed live on radio from the protests, he '*actually* heard her voice ( … ) she *actually* said ( … )'; similarly, Eileen had phone calls from friends abroad who had '*actually* seen it [the protest]'; Jean described how, while protesting, she saw the protests '*actually live*' on the television of a house along the protest route. More generally, people marked the significance of their experience at the protests through the word 'actually': 'we've actually seen things happen', things that 'I actually experienced', 'all the things we'd actually seen'. Here is Sally describing the taking of an unpublished press photograph:

> A photographer was actually there and ( … ) one of the policeman had hold of her hair ( … ) and he actually took a photograph of this girl, and we never saw it in the press anywhere.

To be at the site of the mediated events was 'actually being there' (five cases). Similarly, the fact that things breach or approach the media/ordinary boundary makes them notable in themselves, 'just' as they are ( Chapter 6). This may apply to actions ('just going down there', 'just standing there', 'just how we felt', 'just an ordinary protest', 'we were just there'). Or it may apply to people: 'just Mrs Ordinary Public', 'just ordinary people' (seven cases). As Jane (a factory worker in her twenties) put it, when describing her shock on arriving at Brightlingsea and seeing those involved: 'I thought, God, yeah, it's like real, this is just people, you know, just come out of their houses ( … ) this is just people come out onto the streets.' Or, as banners at Shoreham and other protest ports put it, 'NO JUSTICE JUST US'.

The 'banality' of people's descriptions of their actions was often insistent, as in Angela's words:

> *I haven't done anything other than be there* and voice an opinion and hold up a placard and go out and create awareness ( … ) And I don't think that's anything more than the normal person who is trying to … bring attention to something would do. [added emphasis]

Such banality is, however, deceptive. Not only is there a degree of self-discounting, but, in projecting the banality of being 'just us', for example, the protesters challenged the mass of social categorisations which coincide in the 'ordinary' or the banal. It is no paradox that the actions involved were themselves 'ordinary'. For what was at stake was the categorisation of social action itself, precisely a changed relation between what was 'ordinary' and what was not.

So much for the traces of the symbolic hierarchy of the media frame in the language of the whole interview sample. More difficult to analyse is how the de-naturalisation of the media frame at Brightlingsea was articulated differently by individuals of different genders and classes, educational and family circumstances. The interview sample is too small for definitive conclusions, but we need to explore at least what are the relevant factors.

Maria Wilby, BALE's principal spokesperson, was one of the interviewees most articulate about the media generally. She was 30, middle-class, a former therapist whose education had continued with college work training after school. She had already had a sense of the media's workings before the protests from her and her mother's activities in the campaigning charity Compassion in World Farming. This did not mean that the media presence had no impact on her, especially as the person doing the bulk of the interviews: indeed at the outset the pressure was 'overwhelming'. However, events moved so fast that she did not feel the nervousness she would ordinarily have expected before 'the BBC'. Others assumed she already had media training, but gradually realised she was 'just an ordinary mum' (as Maria put it). Maria was the main force behind BALE's successful media strategy and developed a clear understanding of how news stories were constructed. She alone of all the interviewees questioned the media frame's key term, the 'ordinary person': 'I think Brightlingsea was enormously successful in the fact that so-called ordinary people got up and took to the streets.'

Jean was a working-class housewife in her forties with no experience of the media before the protests. She finished education at secondary school. During the protests she held back from appearing on the media in an individual capacity, even on radio phone-ins. While certainly aware of specific media distortions, she did not express any general view about media coverage of the protests or the operation of the media in general: in fact, she consistently discounted the value of her opinions on the media and the value of what she did at the protests. However, a clear sense emerged that the experience of protesting had changed something in her:

> It's quite funny talking about this ( … ) it seems strange [short laugh] …
> You can see how it's affected me [short laugh]. Well I think it has. For the good, I think really, as I say. I feel honoured to have been down there ( … ) I'm glad, I wanted to be there. I'm glad I was there, because ( … ) it's going to be history, isn't it? ( … ) so I can say to my grandchildren I was there. [short laugh]

144

There is a powerful tension in this passage. On the one hand, Jean clearly felt she had something important to express ('You can see how it's affected me ... I feel honoured ... I'm glad'). This is connected to her sense that the protests will be 'history'. The connection between historicality and major media coverage emerged elsewhere in Jean's interview: 'I used to see my Mum on [television] a lot ... And I used to think, Ooh, that'll go down in histor.'[112] On the other hand, this sense of importance is countered by an impulse to discount what she says. Given this and her lack of any explicit critical position in relation to the media, the significance of her experience became condensed into one phrase: '*I was there.*'And yet, in that phrase, she indicated what mattered most: she *was* 'there', temporarily the other side of the boundary between 'media' and 'ordinary' 'worlds'. She was, in that sense, briefly part of the space where 'history' – or at least 'actuality' – is made.

Gill and Tony, a working-class couple in their fifties, provide another, but contrasting case of where the articulation of disruptions to the media's authority was cut across by other factors. In their interview there was a tension between a general disillusionment with the media, and a sense that they must hold on to their trust in the media. Mistrust of the media showed up in many instances (I quoted Tony's comments on stereotyping above), but they said they found it difficult to 'pinpoint' particular cases of distortion. Tony at one point discounted his criticisms of the media as caused by the exhaustion felt on returning from the protests each day. He was more critical of viewers themselves: 'how stupid we are, because ( ... ) we don't pay no attention to anything that goes on around us.' Perhaps this reluctance to be fully critical of the media reflected their sense of how dependent they were on the media:

> You must have the media, because otherwise with a little sleepy town like Brightlingsea, you wouldn't know ( ... ) Let's face it, *that's how the ordinary people gets to know things.*
>
> (Gill) [added emphasis]

Whether or not Tony and Gill could articulate their criticisms of the media clearly, perhaps they did not want to.

What people are able to articulate, what they are willing to articulate, and what – at some, not fully articulated, level – they feel, are three different things. The individual factors underlying these variations across the interview sample cannot be fully mapped here. However that may be, such differences in articulation may amount to a further dimension of the naturalisation of media power. As with any form of power, its impact depends on how far people can articulate their relation to it.

## DE-NATURALISATION: SPECIFIC CASES

### 'I honestly question virtually everything now'

Martin was lower middle-class, in his forties, living in a medium-sized town outside Brightlingsea. He described himself as 'a product of Thatcher', having done well out of his small business. He finished education at technical training college. Both his lifelong attitudes to the police and his attitudes to the media were transformed by the protests. An avid news consumer for many years, he had considerable media exposure during the protests, being interviewed on radio, press, and television. He had become mistrustful of 'media people': '[they] are like politicians ( ... ) they never answer a question and when they ask a question, that's not the question they're asking.'

He expanded on his changed attitudes to the media:

> I'm sorry, the media saw what happened at Brightlingsea and they haven't reported it correctly. They knew what was going on, they witnessed what was going on, and they shied away from it, that's wrong, that's not what they're there to do ( ... ) It's sanitised ... we're being told what we need to know ( ... ) They've got to be honest with me. And they've got to report things as they happen, not their impression of how it's happening ( ... ) We need to know. And if we can't get it from the TV or the press, there's nowhere else we can get it from ( ... ) If I hadn't have gone there [Brightlingsea], I would still be sitting here, thinking, they got what they deserved.

Here there is a clear sense of loss of trust. Why? Because the media saw what happened and they didn't report it: they were *false witnesses*. While Martin accepted that it was his particular experiences at Brightlingsea (of police harassment, and so on) that led to this change of view, his mistrust had become quite general. Note his ironic view of his past viewing self: 'I would still be sitting here ... .' Like Gill and Tony, he knew that he remained generally dependent on the media for his information: 'there's nowhere else I can get it from'. The only way out was to be present at the scene being reported, to be a witness himself. But that implied that his current, better understanding of the world, which he valued, had been achieved not through media reports, but in conflict with them. After revising his view of how police–protester incidents were covered in the media, Martin went back to review media coverage of the 1984–5 Miners' Strike, identifying 'the way things were stage-managed', that is, by the police for the media. He drew the same conclusion about the anti-Poll Tax 'riots' in the early 1990s. As to his media consumption, while he remained 'a news junkie', he no longer watched documentaries, since he felt that 'you're getting the presenter's view of it':

| | |
|---|---|
| *Martin* | I honestly question virtually everything now ( ... ) We don't use [television] so much. But we talk a lot more, sometimes my wife and I, you know, we're going into the small hours. You start off with an article and that, sometimes silly articles and that, and the more you talk about it, you then start pulling up the alternatives, and what ifs ( ... ) |
| *NC* | And you didn't do that before basically? |
| *Martin* | No, I read the paper. I didn't believe half of what I read, but I didn't really need to question it ... and you know I was a fully paid-up member of the hang 'em, shoot 'em ( ... ) community ( ... ) No, actually the whole thing down there, it's not changed my life, but it's changed my attitude towards things. |

Notwithstanding Martin's qualification ('it's not changed my life'), his loss of trust was substantial and sustained by active media consumption and discussion. He had changed the type of media consumer he was, a striking shift given his long-held attitudes on specific issues and his long-term engagement with media news. Before, his scepticism was proverbial ('I didn't believe half of what I read') and inert ('I didn't need to question it'); now it was active.

Martin's critical attitude to the media did not, however, involve a wider disillusionment. One reason, perhaps, was that he could talk actively about his mistrust with his wife. In any case, his pleasure in information enabled him to enjoy his new, critical position.

### 'It's almost futile watching it'

Samantha was a middle-class former care-worker, married with children. Like Martin, she lived outside Brightlingsea. Her first contact with the protests was through a television image: the image of a Shoreham protester smashing a lorry windscreen that was later – controversially – used in a report of events at Brightlingsea (see Rachel, below). Her interview revealed a shift in attitude as striking as Martin's, but achieved at the cost of much greater tension. For Samantha, the shock of the police action she saw was great, but her attitude to the media was also disrupted. Like Martin, she looked back ironically on her previous position as a naïve viewer with 'opinions', but no real understanding:

> It's all been such a mega learning process, it really has. Because I'd never encountered any of it before. You know ( ... ) you sit in your little armchair and watch the telly and have strong opinions and all of a sudden it's like smacking you in the face, you know, and this is like reality.

The physicality of the language is striking. She was quite explicit about how her views on the media had changed generally:

| | |
|---|---|
| *Samantha* | I just look at it on the telly and I don't believe what I see now. I always think there's something else behind it ( … ) |
| *NC* | Generally, you mean? |
| *Samantha* | Generally. |
| *NC* | Not just about animal rights? |
| *Samantha* | Oh no, no. Anything. Yeah, anything at all. Because ( … ) you know how it's all been manipulated and used and changed ( … ) So really in a way it's almost futile watching it, because, yeah, is it the truth? |

However, unlike Martin, Samantha had no context in which to place her scepticism. She lived outside Brightlingsea amid apathy from family and friends; nor had she previously been an avid news consumer, for whom active criticism might be a pleasure. She was left with her doubts and a sense of the futility of watching. Her sense of normal reality was undermined: for many reasons, perhaps, of which mistrust of the media was only one. This is how she described returning home from the protests:

> But then you come away from it ( … ) and it's like ( … ) you've had reality all the time ( … ) and you come back, but this has always been my reality [short laugh]. You know, the village, home, and everything ( … ) [later in the interview] Yeah, it's changed me so much. In some ways, I wish I'd never gone. Because *unless you then join the rest of society* ( … ) *and deny what you've seen*, and go into that blinkered life like this … you can't help but be affected ( … ) You know, I can't even sit and watch things like … the adverts. It's like they annoy me ( … ) and it's like, God! I want to be a bit more superficial but I can't be like that any more ( … ) I can't really get back into what I'd call normal life, I can't fit in ( … ) I seem to be seeing everything from a different tangent … like real [short laugh]. [added emphasis]

It is as if the axis on which she viewed the world had tilted, and become permanently out of line. There was no way back 'to the rest of society'. Her old 'reality' was not, in fact, reality. With this realisation had come a general sense of the media's power: 'The media have so much power and if they like have sort of a political persuasion, it's like mega power, you know, isn't it? [short laugh] Mega, mega power.' Samantha was not the only interviewee to talk about the power of the media in a general way, but her stark language goes beyond the proverbial. This starkness was matched only by Rachel's comments, to which I now turn.

148

## 'You're not saying it right'

Rachel was a social services worker in her forties (cf. also, Couldry, forth-coming). She was middle-class, living with her husband and children in Brightlingsea. She wanted to be involved in the protests from the outset, but was ill. However, since she lived near the route where protesters, lorries, and police passed, she was still able to question media reports:

> It was a morning ( … ) and police vehicles started to come really thick and fast ( … ) because I stood at the window and watched them ( … ) And I put the news on [the radio] and I'd seen over the previous hour lots of people walking up, so I figured [they were going] to meet the lorries out of Brightlingsea ( … ) But the SGR [local commercial radio] said that there was a large gathering in Brightlingsea … it was after the riot police ( … ) and it was being policed by twenty-six police officers in normal uniform … So I phoned the news desk and I said, 'I'm just en-quiring how you know that there's twenty-six police officers in normal uniform?' And they said, 'From the police press officer'. And I said, 'Well, I think perhaps the information you're getting is drastically wrong, because I've just counted twenty-three full VG vans go past my bedroom window and the lorries haven't even come' ( … ) And also by the time I got through to the newsroom there were officers walking ( … ) they certainly weren't in normal uniform ( … ) And they looked so sinister. And I was so incensed, because SGR was putting out 'twenty-six police officers are policing this huge crowd in _normal uni-form_', it's like they were stressing it. And I wanted them to put me on the radio to say, 'This is just not true'.

This was one of many conflicts between her or her friends' accounts of the protests, and media reports (in both national and local media). It was the most acute, because it revealed explicitly how the media report had been constructed: from a _police_ press briefing. Worse, her perception that events before her eyes were abnormal (and therefore of media significance) was contradicted by the apparently objective radio statement suggesting policing was normal (an important point after the furore which the introduction of riot gear had caused a few days before). She realised that she could not alter the report.

When around the same time Rachel saw pictures of people she knew in the national press, surrounded by police, apparently involved in conflict, she was concerned that people who didn't know them would misunderstand the photos:

> I was privileged because I knew who they were. But nobody else would … they [the media] could have put any sort of headline on those

pictures and told a completely different story ( ... 1 page) I wanted to be able to have a voice to say, 'you're wrong! You're wrong, you're saying it wrong, you're presenting it wrong ... From the information I'm getting from the people I know and love ... you're not saying it right'.

Like many others, Rachel knew the impact of media stereotyping, but she expressed its consequences in a particularly intense way, with a sense of paradox: *this* is reality, yet *this* (something different) is (mediated) 'reality'.

She lost her trust in the media, and expressed this in terms, which clearly register the symbolic disruption involved:

| | |
|---|---|
| *NC* | What effect do you think it had on you, being so close to the media? ( ... ) |
| *Rachel* | I think it completely took away ... any awe that I may have had ... respect isn't the right word. |
| *NC* | Awe rather than respect? [ ... ] |
| *Rachel* | Yeah, I suppose yeah, because things on the telly aren't always real, are they? It's all exciting, and it happens to other people, so the opportunity to be right in the midst of it ... didn't have an effect that if you'd asked me two or three years ago, it might have done. I'd have said, 'Ooh, I'd have pushed myself, or I'd hide so that nobody could see me' ( ... ) I don't think my reaction could have been predicted at all ( ... ) You know, [I would have said] 'I'd have hidden and not had anything to do with it, out of coyness' or 'I'd have been really brave and I'd have said something, I'd have told them what I really thought'. But it was still with that sort of feeling, [a click sound, indicating surprise] 'Ooh! these big people have come from the television!' you know. |
| *NC* | So what had changed? Why didn't you feel that this time, do you think? |
| *Rachel* | Because they let me down, I think. Because I had enough short-term experience of what they were doing ... to feel that ... they weren't getting it right. It still needed me to tell my friends what was going on ( ... ) I think, resentment, that we were totally at their mercy, as to whether anything was said at all. |

Her loss of trust is presented by her as part of a complex shift in attitudes. She felt the media were 'not getting it right': it is down to her (with her special knowledge) to tell the true story, revealing the lack of control which she normally had over what the media do. Her old attitudes to the media had changed. Previously she had felt more than respect for the media: she had felt 'awe', expressed in her sense of the symbolic size of 'media people' (cf. Chapter 6). She articulated her old attitude through two alternative effects the media would previously have had on her: either she would have avoided the media through nervousness; or she would have overcome that hesitation, 'pushing herself' and 'telling them what [she] really thought'. Either way, she would have acknowledged the boundary which media participation represents: 'it was still with that sort of feeling, "Ooh, these big people have come from the television!".' Now she had lost that awe and, she implied, respect as well.

Perhaps the complexity of her present attitude can be expressed as a conflict between different aspects of her trust in the media (cf. Chapter 3). She still confirmed the 'ontological' aspects of that trust (the sense that media are in touch 'with reality'), yet its 'ethical' dimension had crumbled. One phrase expressed the tension well: 'things on the telly *aren't always* real', yet (she implies) they should be and she once would have thought they were. On the one hand, the media world is 'all exciting and happens to other people', a separate and 'higher' world. On the other, the media can no longer be relied upon: 'it still needed me to tell my friends what was [really] going on.' Rachel's account of 'reality' had to be maintained in competition with the media in whose naturalised status she still partly believed, but which she no longer trusted. As a result, she said, 'I doubt everything … that I hear'. Like Martin, she had reinterpreted the events of the 1984–5 Miners' Strike:

> I doubt totally now what was said then, and the way things were policed. And I understand that when somebody says, 'You presented that wrong, that isn't the right time sequence', then I know that's probably likely that they changed it. Because I've seen it here, seen them use one lot of film, inferring that what they're showing happened at Brightlingsea when that happened at Shoreham, where they've completely juxtaposed picture and sound.

Rachel is referring here to the belief, which others shared, that in some television coverage of Brightlingsea, an old picture of a Shoreham protester smashing a lorry window was shown as if it had happened that day in Brightlingsea. Her realisation of the false editing process broke for Rachel the symmetry between media coverage and 'reality' that she relied upon: quite simply, 'they *changed* it'. She returned to this later in the interview:

> … the choice is still theirs [the media's], they control totally, right down to the simple things and how high their ladder is or whatever, to whether they even bother to show it or whether they repeat a film of three weeks ago, but put today's commentary on it.

From being a naturalised window on the world, the media had become a series of 'things' people do, a process: 'they control totally, right down to the simple things'. This process had a geography – the camera was placed here, and not there – a geography that Rachel wanted to contest. The 'black box' (cf. Callon and Latour, 1981: 285) of the media process – previously masked behind a structure of trust – had been opened, revealing it as a mechanism of *re*presentation.

## 'Her picture in the paper, but her on the corner'

Rachel registered, more explicitly than anyone else, the symbolic disruption which her experiences as a protester involved: it is worth exploring this further. She described how she saw outside her bedroom window the local 'lollipop lady'[113] surrounded by police for no apparent reason, and then saw a similar photo of her in *The Independent*:

> And Sandra the lollipop lady who speaks to us every day and remembers my kids' names and everything, is totally surrounded by uniformed po-lice officers, and she'd done *nothing*, she was standing on the kerb, and it was just so bizarre that Sandra was *in the paper* ( ... ) I can't even describe how utterly inappropriate it was. Because Sandra stands down there, Sandra Jones with her lollipop.

There was of course genuine anxiety at Sandra's situation, yet something else breaks through: the sense of shock that the 'ordinary' world Rachel inhabited was temporarily part of the 'media world', which everyone in the country could see. Compare Rachel's description of seeing her friend's husband in the paper:

> And the other picture was again so very very poignant and ... it just said it all, is Geoffrey, who is ... is just Geoffrey, he's got two little boys and he's just normal and he works ever so hard and he's in a sea of police of-ficers and he's pointing ... shouting at them ... and the futility of it ( ... ) But he was so recognisable, you just opened *The Independent* and there's Geoffrey in *The Independent* [laughs] ( ... ) It was just so ... I can't de-scribe it, but just two ... very very very very normal boring ordinary people ( ... ) And that for me epitomised it all. Her [Sandra's] picture in the paper, but her on the corner.

What Rachel 'can't describe' is what necessarily can't ordinarily be described: a temporary fusion of 'ordinary' and 'media' worlds that over-rides the naturalised boundary of the media frame. As noted in other cases, the shock of this – its 'impossibility' – is expressed precisely in the insistent banality of the language: it was 'just Geoffrey', 'just normal', 'just two', 'very very very very normal'. Yet paradoxically this 'ordinary world' had become mediated, creating a gap which was strange: 'her picture in the paper, *but* her on the corner.'

For Rachel, the symbolic disruption was also articulated more directly. I asked what it was like watching television coverage of the protests in the evening, having taken part in them during the day. This was her reply:

> It's a bit like a child. I can remember Andrew when he was a baby ... [longish pause] We've got a big mirror in my bedroom, a big Cheval mirror, and he would look at himself in it, and he would have a little mirror [Rachel acts it out] ... and it's a bit like that, his puzzlement, total puzzlement really, incomprehension, that you can go from one image where you're totally surrounded, you see that was what was missing on the news, when you watch it on the news ( ... ) I wasn't surrounded, physically surrounded by it, whereas half an hour or three hours ago, whatever it was, or yesterday, you were totally surrounded, you were bombarded, you were squashed, you couldn't breathe, you were frightened, the noise was incredible. And none of that is on that flat picture on the screen ( ... ) I suppose that is the closest I can come to it ... Andrew as a little one sitting with these mirrors ... and just checking whether it's him in that one and him in that one and how can he be? You know it's just that sort of puzzlement really.

In this extraordinary description, a great deal is condensed. There is, first, what we might call a paradox of representation: *this* is reality (being 'totally surrounded' by the protests' physical reality) and yet *this*, something different, is mediated 'reality'. The paradox is so great that Rachel explains it through another paradox (of identification), imagined through the mind of her infant child. Rachel's direct concern is not her identification with a media person, but the disruption of her trust in the media world as a whole. Perhaps, however, only a paradox of identification (her child's confusion of identity before the mirror) could express the 'depth' of the disruption Rachel felt.[114]

Why did Rachel find the conflict between her experience at the protests and her experience as a viewer so disturbing? Because, I suggest, it breached the naturalised assumption that her experience of watching (watching the demonstration on the screen) and what happened to her earlier (standing on the road, in front of the lorries, surrounded by the police) were experiences *of the same thing*. But they were not. What you watch is only – can only ever be – a mediated version of what you have experienced. The naturalised assumption which underlies the media's social authority – that it presents 'the real' – is false.[115] This fundamental disruption of the media's representational authority (with its ethical, ontological and symbolic dimensions) is still, however, some way from the issues of identity suggested by the image of the child in front of the mirror. Yet Rachel's language certainly recalls Lacan's (1977) analysis of the 'mirror phase' to a startling degree. Rather than pursue issues of individual psychology (not my purpose: see Chapter 3) I simply want to point out that the connection between the media frame's symbolic hierarchy and paradoxes of identity is a direct, even a banal one. That hierarchy divides up people into two categories of different value: 'ordinary' people and 'media' people. There is no significant difference between them, except the structure of differences legitimated through the operation of the media frame. The media frame is like a distorting mirror in this sense, reflecting the viewer back, distorted, to her- or himself, as *'merely* ordinary'. To question the trust on which the media frame's social authority is based (as Rachel did) is, therefore, implicitly to question the assignment of 'merely ordinary' identities which it involves.

And yet, when I asked Rachel for her overall reaction to her experience at the protests, what she expressed was pride:

> I feel so much more confident in myself because of that real experience. And I'm not ashamed of what I did at all ( … ) I'm really really proud of it ( … ) Because I was successful as a person, I was successful as part of a group, and I made, we made such a difference, I don't think what we did was totally unimportant at all.

Her pride drew, in part perhaps, on a 'reality' *outside* the 'media world'. Unlike Samantha, she could place her sense of disruption – her anger at what she felt was the media's betrayal – in a wider context. Her family was reasonably sympathetic. She could, as she put it, 'tell my friends what was going on'. As a result, perhaps, she could live with the disruption of her relations to the media, in spite of expressing them more vividly than anyone else.


CONCLUDING COMMENT

In this chapter I have analysed how, for Brightlingsea protesters, the media frame was, in various ways, de-naturalised.

Although the argument has been at times abstract and complex, it relies (like Part 2) on a double test. It uses both the spread of language in the general interview sample and close analysis of particular interviews where thought-patterns are stretched rhetorically under the pressure of emotion (confusion, anger) and of reflection. It has, I hope, provided insights into an 'object' which it is perhaps impossible to describe explicitly without some distortion: the process whereby, at a particular time and place, the habitus (the media's naturalised authority) is disrupted.

# 8

# ACTING WITHIN THE
# MEDIA FRAME

It's all changed because we're just like complete ordinary people with no experience of the media or protest or anything .

(Louise, interview with the author)

Looking back I had always believed that the news cameras were somehow magic and appeared when something important happened ... Our local farm and football field were important to everyone I knew ... but the news people never mentioned [our protest] ... The moral of the story is, don't wait for TV news people to come to you. Take what is important to them ... Direct Action on the airwaves is what it's about. Join us. Just do it.

(O'Connor, 1995)

## INTRODUCTION

In this chapter I want to explore more fully than I have so far a principle underlying my theoretical model: the idea that, although the symbolic hierarchy of the media frame is a naturalised pattern which structures talk, belief and action on a large scale (it is part of the 'habitus'), it is always through local practices that it is reproduced. As a result, there is always the possibility that people, by acting and thinking differently, can challenge or disrupt it. The legitimacy of media power is not monolithic, although it is certainly pervasive.

This theme began to emerge empirically in Chapters 5 and 6, for example, when we looked at non-media people who want to change their 'position' in the media process, to become active producers in some way. We saw, however, that the desire to become an 'extra' remained quite ambiguous in its consequences. The very terms in which the desire was formulated often reproduced aspects of the underlying symbolic hierarchy, not surprisingly since the possibility of individuals effectively challenging the power of entertainment institutions remains difficult even to imagine. In the area of political communications, however, the possibilities of conflict and opposition are more clearly delineated. You can certainly imagine putting out an alternative representation of a political event on a small scale, and even developing an alternative source of news: this desire has motivated many oppositional groups. But, if I am right about the *naturalised* status of media power, even these challenges will be marked by the symbolic hierarchy which they contest. This is an important, but neglected, cultural dimension of oppositional action in contemporary mediated societies. I want to explore it through various examples of recent activism, drawing on interviews I conducted around the time of my Brightlingsea study. It is impossible here to do more than indicate possible avenues of research in what is largely unexplored territory within media sociology. As Tony Dowmunt has pointed out (1993: 14–15), the study of mainstream media outputs has for too long been artificially separated from the study of alternative media practices.

Two themes will run through the details of this chapter. First, the disruptive significance of place. Particular locations, and particular uses of location, may have significance because they disrupt the normal 'geography' of the media frame. This can be seen, for example, at Greenham Common and Pure Genius, where places not usually open to media coverage were used. It emerges also in tactics of media activists: 'the Umbrella Man' who goes to sites in the media eye (Parliament, for instance) in order to insert his message into media coverage; or in the attempts of Brightlingsea protesters to develop alternative forms of mediation, through messages on roadsides. In these cases, the normal spatial configuration of the media frame (producers/consumers/texts) gets distorted, or at least negotiated. Recalling the typology of Chapter 2 (pilgrimage, witnessing), we can call these forms of 'active witnessing' or 'tracking'. Another theme, implicit at various points, will be the contestation of the symbolic category of the 'ordinary person'. Greenham Common women fitted the category in one sense (as non-media people), but were excluded by media discourse from it in another sense (since they were rejected as socially, even sexually, abnormal). Brightlingsea protesters fitted willingly into the social category of 'ordinariness' – the media cliché of 'ordinary people on the streets' – but gradually began to reject the position of ordinary (non-media) person. Pure Genius residents accepted neither of these aspects of 'ordinariness'. This questioning of the category of the 'ordinary person' is just one example of Alberto Melucci's argument that symbolic action may begin to 'alter how people's experiences are perceived and named' (1996: 185).

Contesting the media's 'magic' (to return to the second quote at the head of the chapter), like any disruption of the habitus, is both simple *and* profound. The ironic banality of video activist Paul O'Connor's adaptation of the Nike slogan ('Just Do It') captures this well.[116] As before, I will explore these processes by looking at people's language and actions, the background expectations and categorisations which shape them. Actions which disrupt the symbolic hierarchy of the media frame may emerge without being articulated as such. This is what we would expect if the media's concentration of symbolic power is naturalised.

## GREENHAM COMMON

From summer 1981, hundreds of women went to live at Greenham Common Women's Peace Camp around the perimeter of the Greenham USAF/RAF base, protesting against the Cruise missiles to be held there and the nuclear arms race in general. Although the base was closed in 1994 and most women had left by then, some still live at Yellow Gate camp outside what was once the base's main gate, continuing their protest against militarism and the nearby nuclear weapons establishment at Aldermaston. The Camp received major national and international media coverage.

The example of Greenham Common is important because it represents in extreme form the processes studied in Part 3: first, in the early years, the de-naturalisation of the position of 'ordinary person/woman' in relation to the 'media world'; and second, in the later years, the attempt to develop alternative forms of mediation, even in the face of media silence. My account will necessarily be brief: for more details, see Couldry (1999b). I rely, for the early years, on testimony in already published accounts (Harford and Hopkins, 1984; Liddington, 1989; Roseneil, 1995; Alison Young, 1990). My comments on the later years relate exclusively to Yellow Gate. I draw on a recent history of that camp (Junor, 1995) and my own interviews with its members in September, 1996: I interviewed Rosy Bremer, Sarah Hipperson, Katrina Howse, Jean Hutchinson, Aniko Jones and Peggy Walford (actual names).

The Greenham Common encampment was a site of 'discursive dissonance' (Roseneil, 1995: 143) along many dimensions – social, spatial and symbolic – a liminal, almost utopian site (Hetherington, 1998: 129–30). Greenham women disrupted a familiar, gendered geography of public and private spheres: both as women displaced from the private space of the home and as women (and private persons) living beside the 'masculine', public, emphatically non-domestic space of a nuclear weapons base (Cresswell, 1996: 97–100). The effect was amplified by intense media coverage, which was extreme in its pathologisation of the protesters (Alison Young, 1990). But Greenham was disruptive also at another level. It was cut off from the normal domestic setting with its taken-for-granted media inputs: without electricity, there was no television, although some no doubt had newspapers or radio. Some women made this point humorously with a mock 'television made out of a cardboard box, with a piece of wire for the aerial' (Jinny List, quoted in Roseneil, 1995: 79). Yet the Camp lived under intense media coverage in the early years. As Sasha Roseneil put it (summing up the whole range of disruptions at Greenham): 'she [Greenham Woman] was a woman who transgressed boundaries between the public and private spheres; she made her home in public, in the full glare of the world's media, under the surveillance of the state' (1995: 155–6). These two facts – the lack of normal media consumption and the abnormal media coverage – differed markedly from the regular pattern by which domestic, private, non-mediated space (where you normally watch from) and non-domestic, public, mediated space (places you normally watch) are constituted as separate sites of discourse. This 'geography of normality' (Cresswell, 1996: 95; cf. Chapter 3), which helps sustain the symbolic hierarchy of the media frame, was itself turned inside out at Greenham Common. By insisting on speaking and acting from where the nuclear weapons were (their 'actuality'), rather than where they are normally debated (Westminster, television studios), Greenham women challenged the assumption that effective national debate was possible without experiencing the weapons' physical presence (cf. Roseneil, 1995: 115). In effect, they challenged the assumption of all media debates: that audiences can adequately participate by watching at home. In so doing, Greenham women made concrete the implicit geography of the media frame.

In addition, Greenham (like Brightlingsea, but even more dramatically) disrupted the 'common-sense' understanding which the media help reproduce (cf. Brunsdon and Morley, 1978): that most people act within a sphere (the 'local', the 'private', the 'ordinary') separate from 'national' matters. Greenham introduced 'ordinary women' into an extraordinary place: the place of 'public affairs'. To 'be there' within the mediated space of Greenham was to cross over into the space (indeed the storytelling frame) of national events. Not that this disruption was explicitly planned as such, but it was reflected in what Greenham women said and did. Language in leaflets mobilising women to Greenham frequently addressed 'ordinary people', 'ordinary women', as did publicity. The press release for the 1981 March to Greenham, from which the encampment developed, summoned 'ordinary women' and continued: 'some of [the women on the march] are already known to the media, most [are] just the unknown women who will be coming on the march to tell the world what they think of our society's priorities' (quoted, Roseneil, 1995: 35). Note the suggestion that 'ordinary women' are not yet 'known *to the media*'. This reflected how the march's organiser, Ann Pettit, regarded herself:

> Everybody had gone there [the starting-point] feeling sure that what they would find would be female experts of some variety or other … And it was such a revelation. We were such a revelation to each other. Because I looked around and my first thought was, 'Oh, my God, they really do all look so ordinary'.
>
> (quoted, Liddington, 1989: 228)

The revelation, paradoxically, was that the marchers were 'ordinary women' doing something extraordinary *for them*: taking public, potentially mediated, action (the initial marchers were disappointed by the lack of media coverage: ibid.: 230). They were not the people 'normally' involved in politics, but 'a ragged, motley, little ( ... ) band of women, dressed in all sorts of odd garments' (ibid.: 229). A visual stereotype is being contradicted: in part, a media stereotype of people in 'public life'.

The accounts of women who hesitated before going to Greenham confirm what Chapter 3 suggested: that 'common-sense' notions of what 'ordinary people' do are not simply reflected in, but themselves partly *reproduced by*, media coverage. One woman said she had heard of Greenham women through the media but was daunted from going: 'I couldn't fit myself into that [picture] because I was so normal' (quoted, Roseneil, 1995: 52). Another said: 'I had all these images of all these women. Yes ... I was in awe of these women ... And what could I do? What was my measly contribution to all this wonderful work that was going on?' (quoted, Liddington, 1989: 269). 'Awe' was the word Rachel used in relation to the 'media world' (Chapter 7). The obverse of 'awe' is feeling you are 'too ordinary' to take part. As Sarah Hopkins put it, 'most of us felt torn ... We were attracted but at the same time scared of something that seemed so spectacular' (Harford and Hopkins, 1984: 21).

One reason therefore (of course, only one among many) why the symbolic actions at Greenham had such an intense impact on those involved was a sense of being involved within the media-sustained 'action frame'[117] of national, even world, events. Guy Brett, discussing artworks at Greenham – such as the personal objects women attached to the perimeter fence – described them as 'signs capable of acting directly on events' (1986: 133). 'Acting directly on events' is what public figures do: 'ordinary people', usually, watch news events or are 'affected' by them. This assumed sense of difference is part of the taken-for-granted background assumptions associated with the media frame: political and discursive hierarchies are mutually reinforcing. Acting in the 'arena' of Greenham (Roseneil, 1995: 155) mattered, at least in part, because it breached the implied boundary between 'media world' and 'ordinary people' (in particular, 'ordinary *women*'). Breaching that boundary was an act of representative significance. This, I suggest, is part (again, I stress, only part!) of the context for Mary Brewer's moving description of attaching a pincushion made by her grandchild to the Greenham fence:

> I'll never forget that feeling ... the lovely feeling of pinning things on ... It was even better than holding your baby for the first time, after giving birth ... [holding your baby] is a self-thing – a selfish thing between you and your husband, isn't it? The baby. Whereas Greenham – it was for

women; it was for peace; it was for the world; it was for Britain; it was for us; it was for more.

(quoted, Liddington, 1989: 244)

In that moment of action, there was the chance of doing something, for once, that signified 'directly on events', a moment of ritual action whose 'frame' coincided with the boundaries of the media frame itself.

Since 1984, however, the Camp at Greenham Common has received virtually no media attention. In 1994, when Blue Gate – the last remaining gate apart from Yellow Gate – closed, it was announced as the end of the camp (cf. Junor, 1995: 268). And yet resistance to militarism at Yellow Gate has undeniably continued on a small scale, with illegal entries to Aldermaston and RAF Burghfield, court and other actions, all without significant media coverage. This resistance has been effectively 'deleted' (Law, 1994: 111) from the media's 'mode of ordering', performed within what Noelle-Neumann (1974) earlier called a 'spiral of silence'. What is it like to continue with public action knowing that you are at the centre of a 'spiral of silence', when in effect you are told 'whatever you do, we will not take notice ( ... ) you have been silenced out and nobody's going to know that you're going through this' (Katrina Howse, interview with the author)?

Yellow Gate women regard the media silence as a 'censorship' or 'state erasure' of the camp (Junor, 1995: 81, 107, 154), provoked both by their own resistance to the state and the fact that they are women. At times they have sought to resist this silence directly, for example, by complaints against misreporting by the BBC and the tabloid *Sun* (ibid.: 192, 225). But they know that media silence's social impact runs deep: for most people, they have ceased to exist. They still, of course, want what they do to be known, even though the actual audience for their actions (including those just discussed) is extremely limited. How then do they conceive of their communicative practice, their way of 'putting information out' (Rosy Bremer)? It makes most sense, I suggest, as *symbolic resistance* to the media silence. While not motivated directly by a desire to enter the media process, such actions can only be fully understood against its background, rejecting as they do the principle of conventional media. As Aniko Jones put it, 'we have to get to people on our own terms and we have to give out information and we have to be the source of that information, not the media'.

This strategy of *alternative mediation* can be traced for example in a series of writing actions inside the base and elsewhere:

On May 26–27 1989 six women from Yellow Gate went into the USAF/RAF base at Greenham Common, to expose the INF Treaty as a betrayal of people worldwide ... We painted the exterior of three hangars which house the cruise missile convoy, and the runway ... We wrote 'The Treaty is a con – stop your killing' and finished up writing other messages which we felt needed to be written.

(the late Helen Thomas, in Junor, 1995: 153–4)

Such acts of writing seem paradoxical at first. They are acts of communication, yet, since they occur in media silence, very few receive them. They seem to leave the media silence unchallenged. Helen Thomas's words, however, suggest an alternative perspective: 'this action was done in an atmosphere of continued censorship by the peace movement *and the media in general*, which makes us vulnerable to the police, military and other threats to our safety' (ibid., added emphasis). The media silence was, then, a significant part of the context for the writing actions. At one level, they work as a direct act of communication to agents of the British state. At another level, they work because the very act of writing (purely symbolic though it is) breaches the closure of communication channels about its nuclear weapons that the state seeks to maintain. Yellow Gate assert that channels of communication *are* open, a claim of representative importance.

Yellow Gate's actions show one form which alternative mediation may take in extreme circumstances. More broadly, Greenham women's actions throughout its history can be understood, in part, as 'tactics' of resistance within the 'strategic' context of the British media frame (de Certeau, 1984), actions from the 'edges' of society, where society's symbolic geography is vulnerable to challenge (Stallybrass and White, 1986; Sibley, 1995; Cresswell, 1996). The concept of 'tactics', as has often been pointed out, does not imply an actual destabilisation of power, but a way of living or dealing with it. I return to this idea later in the chapter in relation to other attempts to deal with exclusion from the media process.

## BRIGHTLINGSEA: THE AWARENESS ACTIONS

At Brightlingsea too, media silence played an increasing role in influencing protesters' actions and pushing them into forms of 'alternative mediation'. In the protests' early weeks, media coverage came automatically. As Maria Wilby put it: 'when they're coming to you, you just have to be there and ( … ) be prepared to speak.' What happened when this media interest waned? I am concerned here less with BALE's formal strategies to maintain coverage (effective though these often were) than with more informal strategies, particularly those aimed to generate 'awareness' outside Brightlingsea.

As media coverage declined, and most people outside Brightlingsea believed the protests had ended, a sense developed among protesters that their actions had to extend beyond Brightlingsea itself. Since there was no end to the exports in sight, they needed to spread 'awareness' of the protests to people whom media coverage was not informing. These 'awareness' actions took various forms. First, protests along major roads outside Brightlingsea, either along the route which the animal lorries took or along other major roads (the A120, the A12). Protesters stood with banners on bridges or along the hard shoulder. Second, protesters walked to Dover (another major port for live animal exports) which linked up with Shoreham protesters and obtained local media coverage. As they walked along major roads and through the town centres along the way, they canvassed members of the public. Third, there were protests outside the houses of those benefiting financially from the live export trade: the wharf-owner and the leading exporter. Once again, these protests took place on the roadside in front of the houses' grounds.

One interest of these actions is the challenge they mounted to the status of major roads as '*non*-places', the anthropologist Marc Auge's (1995) term for contemporary spaces such as roads and airports, where your passage is controlled by abstract instructions rather than by any embodied sense of place. The roadside protests outside Brightlingsea converted non-places into sites of discourse. There are parallels here with the road actions of Greenham women: the following of weapons convoys across Britain to draw attention to their passage (Roseneil, 1995: 111–12; Junor, 1995: 44, 243, 287).

The actions outside Brightlingsea were attempts to mediate the protests through spreading 'awareness'. They were precisely alternative forms of 'mediation' or 'broadcasting':

> But we had no coverage for all that [in Brightlingsea], so what we were doing was taking it out of Brightlingsea and saying to people that this was going on ( … ) It's just an extension of the media really. If you think the media fails you ( … ) you've just got to do your own thing ( … )
>
> (Samantha)

> You had to do this, to get it through to the public, because though [the protests] had been going on in the other places, it wasn't got through to us. We didn't know about it. And if we didn't take it farther out, those people wouldn't know about it.
>
> (Vera)

Even if there was media coverage (as Vera implies), it could not be relied upon to have any impact: the protesters themselves needed to 'take it further out'. As Tony put it: 'even though it comes on television, everybody doesn't watch the news at night ( … ) If it comes on television, it's on for ten seconds ( … ) unless somebody gets killed or something like that.' For many interviewees, creating 'awareness' became a basic principle of action: 'I would go on anything if it brings awareness' (Christine). It had its clearest form in the 'awareness stall' taken by Sheila and Mike Gerard (actual names) to various towns in Essex and Suffolk: 'always out of Brightlingsea' was Sheila Gerard's phrase. But such 'awareness' work faces great difficulties, since it attempts to work in parallel to the electronic media. Lacking media coverage itself, it cannot gain from the automatic morale-boosting effect which media coverage gives (Gamson, 1995: 94). 'Awareness' work can be justified only by its actual, not its assumed, impact, something always difficult to gauge; it suffers from the geographical limits of scale which, to a large degree, broadcasting transcends.

And yet such alternative mediations matter symbolically because they cut across the media-ordinary hierarchy: 'just getting through to people' (Clive), 'just spreading the word' (Helen), 'just talking to people' (Jane). They are actions which assert, quite simply, that individuals, not only the media, are essential 'points of translation' (Callon and Latour, 1981) in the spread of information. However localised, they represent a shift beyond the position of 'ordinary viewer' de-naturalised at Brightlingsea.

## INDIVIDUAL TACTICS

I want now to explore some further shifts away from the position of 'ordinary person/viewer' in the practice of two activists. While of course we cannot draw any definitive conclusions from individual cases, they suggest something important about the symbolic context within which 'alternative mediation' is possible.

The chapter's opening quote comes from Louise, a self-employed university graduate in her twenties, whom I interviewed in November 1996 (for further discussion, see Couldry, forthcoming). She had gone with a friend in 1995 to a protest against live animal exports at one of the ports:

> ... we'd never protested or anything before. We just saw the TV coverage of [the port] ( ... ) and watched the coverage, just saw just so so many normal ordinary people, you know, we'd always thought of protesters as being not like us [short laugh] and we just saw ( ... ) ordinary people ( ... ) It was just like seeing the ordinary people and just thinking, we can do that.

'Just', as noted in Chapter 6, marks the boundary between the 'ordinary' and what lies beyond: 'just saw just so so many normal ordinary people.' Clearly a number of senses of the term overlap here (cf. Chapter 3, 'Ordering'). Before, Louise had thought of protesters as 'weird', 'like the edge of society'. Seeing images of 'ordinary people' protesting flatly contradicted this.

She avoided the cameras at the port through shyness and to avoid bad publicity for her business. But what she saw (including police behaviour) was so shocking that she decided to buy a camcorder 'to capture it all on camera'.

From talking to others, she got the idea that she could take her camcorder to her local livestock market and film the conditions there:

> I used to avoid it [the local market] ( ... ) but all of a sudden, through having seen everything at [the port], through having a camera and through having spoken to someone else about markets who was going there, we thought, Yeah, we can do that, you know, *we're ordinary people, but we can go and make a difference*. [added emphasis]

Note the turn of phrase: she is 'ordinary' *but* she 'can go and make a difference'. Gradually she became more active, until she was deliberately using her camcorder to generate local news. Her interview was striking for showing how her media practice emerged against the grain of long-term assumptions about her relationship (or lack of it) to the media process. As she put it: 'we had no idea we were *even worthy* of coverage.' She was also afraid: 'the whole idea of going to the media ( ... ) I wouldn't dare, because that's going to be printed, what I say is going to be printed, what if I say something wrong? It sounds very naïve now.' Before, she had operated in a different 'discursive domain' (Stallybrass and White, 1986: 80) outside the media process, the other side of a boundary policed by restrictions and fears (once again, implicitly, the theme of pathologisation). Now, however, she felt able to act.

As her confidence grew, she not only generated media stories but informed other activists about her work. Her relation to the media frame changed. Reversing her earlier fear of saying the wrong thing, she found herself thinking: 'if I say the right thing here ( ... ) I'm going to inspire these people.' A position of silence – of 'deletion' (Law) – was transformed into one of action.

While Louise's practice depended on the use of media technology (and in that sense is not a form of alternative mediation), a very different type of activism uses the already established story-frame of media events. 'The Umbrella Man' (pseudonym used at his request) has been campaigning and protesting in Britain for more than five years. I met him first in summer 1996 at a meeting about Pure Genius and subsequently at other events (including actions connected with Brightlingsea). He was 61, living in an Essex town just north of London. He took early retirement from his job as a local authority carpenter. The name, 'The Umbrella Man', comes from the 'umbrella hats' he wears to protests. The idea originated from a joke hat bought at the seaside: a base supporting a sunshade, shaped like a small umbrella in the colours of the Union Jack. Each hat, indeed most of his clothing worn at public events, is covered in campaign stickers or messages. All the campaign material he wears relates to campaigns in which he has himself actively participated.

His practice operates outside conventional definitions of politics. His importance for my argument, however, depends not on making claims for his political effectiveness, but on his intervention in what we might call the 'politics of speech'. His clothes are part of that, using conventional signs of loyalty ('red, white and blue') and visual humour as the backcloth for a message that otherwise would not be heard. He has an acute sense of the social differentials which determine who is normally seen and heard:

> It's sad to say you don't always see the truth. Because ... *the camera always moves into a different direction* and they're looking for a bit of news ( ... ) they always talk nice about the Queen and Royal Family and everything else ( ... ) they always show the goody-goodies, the upper crust, but *the ordinary people* ( ... ) the only time you can gather is to wave your flag to the Queen and the King or whoever. [added emphasis]

He understands therefore the way those who act 'out of place' are pathologised (cf. Chapter 3), and knows also the power of media stereotyping and resists it: 'they can't call me a thug or a bully or out of work ( ... ) because they tend to paint people with a brush and then they push them aside. Well they can't do that to me.' The Umbrella Man is unusual for the range of his involvement in contemporary protest campaigns: these include purely local campaigns (on practical measures for the elderly and the disabled); national campaigns on social issues (hospital closures, pensioner rights – he is a committed trade unionist); and those 'direct action' campaigns connected with the environment and animal rights that have attracted national media coverage in 1990s Britain – not only Brightlingsea, but the anti-road protests at Newbury in 1995–6, the Pure Genius land occupation in 1996, and the campaign against the second runway at Manchester Airport in 1997. His work spans the full range of contemporary 'political' activism in Britain, outside, that is, the official political process.

The Umbrella Man's main media tactic is to make himself readable by the media within the context of some larger story whose prominence is already guaranteed. In that context, he performs actions, and projects an image, that he wants to get noticed. The idea that only things 'out of the ordinary' attract media interest emerged at Brightlingsea (see Chapter 7). The Umbrella Man faces a greater difficulty, in that he is often trying to publicise campaigns which are not the subject of major current coverage at all; he needs, therefore, to use the context of other events which are. That is why many of his actions take place near Parliament on major media days such as Budget Day. These provide a story-frame within which his actions may get 'picked up'. That means working closely with the spatiality of media production. Here he describes an action on Budget Day 1996, performed in Father Christmas uniform (adapted by covering it with campaign stickers, flashing Christmas tree lights and placards highlighting the plight of pensioners):

*Plate 7*  The Umbrella Man interviewed by Japanese TV outside Houses of
Parliament, Budget Day, November 1997

*Plate 8*  Banner at entrance to Pure Genius site, London, June 1996

I decided to do something different so on my own, all the cameras came out, they all went on to [College Green where MPs are normally interviewed for television] and I thought right, let's go for it. And I've got this little push trolley, you know, that the old people carry and I've got all my balloons [with the Unison union logo] and boards ( … ) so I crept across and *all these cameras shot up* as soon as they saw this Father Christmas coming along the footpath, right? And the trouble was they were *picking me up* and forgetting [the MPs] who were *in front of their camera*, so the MPs didn't like it … the camera *going onto me and not them*, that's what it's all about ( … ) And at least again a few pictures were taken and they were used *elsewhere* [outside the UK]. [added emphasis]

Media space, for him, has become a space of action. He contests the spatial segregation on which the media's social authority is based: 'the camera going onto me, not them, that's what it's all about.' His actions – in the very places where the media mechanism is concentrated – arise, perhaps, from something like necessity; they are a response to the 'ordinary person''s normal lack of resources for entering the 'media world'.

What he does, then, is 'tactical' in de Certeau's sense:

The place of a tactic belongs to the other. A tactic insinuates itself into the other's place, fragmentarily, without taking it over in its entirety, without being able to keep it at a distance. It has at its disposal no base where it can capitalize on its advantages, prepare its expansions, and secure independence with respect to circumstances … it is always on the watch for opportunities that must be seized 'on the wing'.

(1984: xix, note omitted)

'Tactics' are spatial – they intervene in the empty spaces left in wider strategies – and so too is The Umbrella Man's practice: 'it's very important to know who's going where and where you're going to be to make it worthwhile.' But crucially, he intervenes, not in media texts, but directly in 'media space', the quite specific physical spaces where media attention is concentrated. The way he describes his actions fits well with de Certeau's spatial metaphor:

While I'm playing the field, I play it for everybody. I always say to pensioners, I don't just belong to pensioners, I belong to everybody who needs support and at the moment that's what I'm doing, I'm playing the field ( … ) I'm making the most of what I can do.

He uses the media as a 'strategic' space, within which 'tactical' play is possible.

In this way he tries to send a signal which can be picked up by at least some of the audience: 'I think [my appearing on TV] actually gets home, they say, "Oh, saw you on the telly" ( ... ) it gives them hope.' Other interviewees mentioned the impact of his appearances, registering his status as a sort of alternative celebrity. For example, Jenny from Brightlingsea (Group 1) who knew him personally:

> ... it said [on TV news] something about Hillingdon railway station, protests get wheelchair activists, I said where is he? There he is, lying on the railway platform padlocked to the train. The very next day 10,000 people in Trafalgar Square protesting for pensioners' rights and money. I said to [husband], where is he? He said, you won't see him among ten thousand people but there's the umbrella ( ... ) And that really has made us ... sort of look at different things, you know. I say, what's all that about? ( ... ) I think it's sharpened our awareness about all sorts of other issues because you wonder ( ... ) what really is going on there?

Recall Maria Wilby's comments quoted in Chapter 7: 'once you've seen things that you know about on there, you realise that you've just got to listen and it'll go in.' Jenny's language registers with surprise and pleasure the fact that someone she knows is 'on there'.

## PURE GENIUS

From May to October 1996, a few hundred people occupied a derelict London site on the Thames by Wandsworth Bridge. Those who stayed after the occupation's first two weeks named the site 'Pure Genius' after the famous marketing slogan for Guinness beer. The Guinness conglomerate was the owner of the site.[118] I interviewed twelve residents over the summer of 1996.

The occupation's specific aim was both to protest against Guinness's plans to develop the land as a supermarket (which neither local residents nor the local council wanted) and to draw attention to ecologically sounder ways of living (often labelled 'permaculture') and the undemocratic nature of the official planning process. There is an important difference between Pure Genius and the other collective protest actions I have analysed. Unlike Greenham (the first mass action of its kind) and unlike Brightlingsea (conducted by people largely isolated from other direct action), Pure Genius took place in the context of a sustained protest 'culture' during the final years of Britain's long Conservative regime (see Chapter 2). Some of Pure Genius' residents had been involved in, for example, the anti-road protests at Newbury. That recent history of activism provided a context for the occupation in a number of ways: first, a developing philosophy of 'direct action' as political practice and way of living; second, the connection of direct action with the tactical use of the mainstream media; third, the contestation of conventional notions of 'ordinary life' through symbolic action (a process started at Greenham, but continued at the anti-M11 roads protests and elsewhere).[119]

Being at Pure Genius, like being at Greenham, meant leaving behind the normal world of domestic media consumption ('holed up in a flat with your telly': Stephanie, a resident, interview with the author). George MacKay, discussing recent British 'cultures of resistance', quotes Iain Donald of the Dongas Tribe making a similar point in broader terms:

> We considered the resumption of ... traditional gatherings as important for re-energizing ... sacred sites, for getting people back on the old trackways to celebrate the land ( ... ) *to get people away from their TVs* and out of their houses and cars and into contact with the land ...
>
> (quoted Mackay, 1996: 147) [added emphasis]

Living 'in contact with the land', whether nomadically as the Dongas Tribe do or in one place as at Pure Genius, of course has wide implications, but it is significant that the land is a marginal space in part because it involves rejecting domestic media consumption, it is a space (apparently) beyond media culture.

As elsewhere, my concern is not with the occupation's media coverage (substantial and generally sympathetic), but rather with how actions at Pure Genius were orientated to the media frame. The occupation followed substantial planning by the national campaigning group, The Land Is Ours ('TLIO'). Many of this group, including its leader George Monbiot, had media experience. Monbiot in particular is a *Guardian* columnist and ex-television producer. After a successful temporary occupation of land near St George's Hill, Weybridge in 1995 in homage to The Diggers' occupation there during the English Civil War (Hill, 1975: 110), TLIO decided to attempt a less temporary occupation. There was a clear media strategy, explained by another leading TLIO member, Tony Gosling (actual name), when I interviewed him during the occupation:

> ... a lot of us in the organisation have experienced working in the media and so we ( ... ) prepared a group of people who would be media spokespeople who we would feed the various media to, because it was a real frenzy in the first few days ( ... ) We prepared all the arguments beforehand ( ... ) This was a bit of a history lesson for them [the media] as well, because what we were doing essentially is ( ... ) an important piece of civil disobedience ( ... ) It's not just a piece of vandalism ( ... ) So we made sure we acquainted a sizeable group of people with good background as to why we were doing that action, why we were doing it there, why were doing it now.

The message for the media – 'this is not just a piece of [stereotypical] vandalism' – was expressed in press releases explaining that the occupation began on the anniversary of land occupations in London soon after the Second World War as part of a campaign for better housing for returning troops and their families.

TLIO gave media training to Pure Genius residents because they were aware of the discursive inequalities associated with the media. As Gosling put it:

> A lot of ordinary people find that cameras pointing at them, microphones ( ... ) very intimidating. And what we did is we made sure that we had a good core group that would be prepared to meet the media and meet their questions and armed with the facts.

In addition, the Wandsworth site was chosen as 'a very high profile site': on the Thames, along a busy connecting road, and close to central media operations. The strategy was reflected in the words of Simon on site:

> Well it's a very *media site*, isn't it? ( ... ) I think they're doing it in the city to be a media sort of site [ ... ] I mean it's in the middle of London isn't it? And it's ... easy for people to get to and we've decided that if you want support it's best to go to the media. [added emphasis]

By 'easy to get to', he means easy for the media to get to, close to the nodes of media production and distribution (cf. Brunn and Leinbach, 1991: xvii–xviii). This was central to the occupation's role as an act of 'showing'. Gosling again:

> One thing you can do with the land is ( ... ) to show alternative visions, alternative lifestyles ( ... ) And I think this is a crucial point, that we're really throwing the spotlight on one particular situation which is ... mirrored in situations in many other parts of the country, but this is a particularly bad one. I mean essentially, I think, the occupation is largely symbolic.

Unlike the actions at Greenham Common and Brightlingsea, therefore, we cannot understand the Pure Genius occupation at all without reference to the media context within which it was conceived.

This media-based strategy involved a large group living on an open-air site near the centre of London. For those who chose to stay after the first two weeks and the initial media attention, a sense of greater permanence was important. The derelict site was planted, installed with toilets, public areas, and so on. This suggested a permanency which conflicted with the likelihood that Guinness would eventually expel the occupiers. It also conflicted with the fact that, for purely media purposes, the occupation only needed to be temporary. The media strategy's short time-frame (tied to the media's 'attention span') conflicted with the much longer time-frame of what was being 'shown', a way of living (cf. Featherstone, 1997: 55–60). Yet this tension emerged as the long-term social consequences of opening a site in the centre of London (its attraction to homeless and other displaced people) proved beyond Pure Genius' resources to handle. This tension between temporariness and permanency was already inherent in TLIO's original strategy; it is a condition of much 'mediated' campaigning, reflecting their two-sided nature as 'both immediate and media-ted' (Routledge, 1997: 362).

Two interviews with Pure Genius residents, in particular, are interesting here for the distinctive way of interacting with the media frame that they suggest. This combines explicit distance (a recognition of the media as a mechanism) with a tactical closeness (a willingness to integrate the media's possibilities of projection into one's daily actions): a self-reflexive media tactic.

Andrew was 48. He had travelled for many years, but had also lived in more conventional domestic settings. He had protested at Newbury, Solsbury Hill and elsewhere. Far from being uninterested in the media, he once ran an alternative magazine himself. In recent years he has done media interviews (for Channel Four, CNN): 'I can't go anywhere without being in a video or on TV', he told me. Like The Umbrella Man, he had become, in a sense, an 'alternative celebrity'. While he regarded media news as ridiculously limited in its coverage ('a media circus'), he had no difficulty in imagining using it. He saw the media as a very important, and global, 'story tool'. His willingness to use the media was implicit in how he understood his daily practice at Pure Genius:

> I see the need to protest ( … ) in a way that … notice is taken of it ( … )
> We try to reflect [our position] in the strength of the day or in the strength of the week, but we try and make sure that it's remembered ( … ) but without being violent.

'Remembered' here clearly includes media coverage. Andrew was well aware of possible misrepresentation but, even if the verbal coverage was negative, the *image* presented to the media audience might be positive. Like Tony Gosling, he understood the Pure Genius action as a form of 'showing', expressed in a metaphor where the power of the media (and the mirror-image it implies: cf. Chapter 7) is given a positive sense:

> … when it boils down to it, it doesn't matter what people look like or what they dress like ( … ) there's so many like-minded people but they need something to spur them on, they need something *to give them the mirror image* ( … ) to give them an example of the power ( … ) It's so that they can see that they can be empowered ( … ) it does create the focus

> ( … ) We've got to *show* it's like this, to me that's why the mirror is so important. [added emphasis]

Stephanie was 34 and after university worked in publishing and charity work. She rarely consumed the media: 'you're involved, you're informed already.' Her orientation to the media frame, however, combined a confidence in projecting to a wider mediated audience with a sense of the media's responsibility to reflect that message back:

> … we must use them [the media] ( … ) to point out that these things are only being done because they have to be done. There is a need … for direct action to be opening up the sort of democracy that has long been missing ( … ) So the media has a responsibility to tell people that things can be done and that there are groups of people … who … will accept anybody if they have got the same vision and are working towards the same ends ( … ) It will happen if the media help to show people how it will be achievable. And the fact that we sit here in Wandsworth *now* saying … we've got to banish the car from inner cities ( … ) It's getting to the situation now where people just simply have to do it and … there are st too jumany people for the media to taint with the same brush … they can't just write us all off.

Once again, although well aware of the risks of media stereotyping, she had integrated those risks into a self-reflexive practice on site. What matters, she implies, is not so much access to the media, as the projection of actions through them:

> We're very open here. You know, there was a slogan around at the beginning, when there was so ( … ) much media, it was, *If you're not proud of it, don't do it* ( … ) Be aware that everything is very public … and that's been the basis of this site. [added emphasis]

She imagines a wider sense of connection across the media audience:

> People come in, they might be a bit wary, they might think people look a bit strange, but by the time they go out they're just amazed that people are friendly, we're not threatening … and those people won't look at Newbury ( … ) and things on the telly in the same light … and they might even recognise some people and they'll feel part of it, they'll feel strangely attached.

This is precisely the attachment that Jenny felt when seeing The Umbrella Man on television: an attachment in spite of stereotypes and dominant media narratives, a 'strange' attachment.

172

Stephanie and Andrew have developed a practice which seeks to use the media's potential for projection, while at the same time (at least to some degree) de-naturalising the media's authority: a politics of everyday life, which is also, implicitly, a media politics.


## CONCLUSION TO PART 3

The Pure Genius occupation is just one example of a wider shift towards media sophistication in recent UK protest actions. Events are staged – such as the early days of Pure Genius, or protesters emerging from the underground tunnels of the Fairmile anti-roads protest in early 1997 (the event that made its main protagonist, 'Swampy', famous) – with a clear awareness of their media impact, their status as image. They are actions which are both 'immediate and media-ted' (Routledge), both embedded in a locality and readable – on a different scale – as media stories.

The wider social impact of such actions is difficult to gauge. Whatever their disruptive potential, they have been adopted by parts of the media as a new form of 'actuality',[120] with their protagonists (such as Swampy) co-opted, and subsequently vilified, as temporary 'celebrities' (Vidal, 1998). There are dangers in exaggerating such protests' long-term political impact. We can interpret them in cultural terms as resulting from growing media awareness and sophistication, which Abercrombie and Longhurst (1998) have argued translates into a readiness to perform in a real or imagined media context, a media-related 'narcissism'. The last point is, however, quite speculative, and needs more empirical research. Less speculatively, the actions discussed in this chapter must be put in the context of the alternative media that have developed around British protest culture in the 1990s. New print journalism outlets (for example *Squall* and *SchNews*) have explicitly criticised and ironised mainstream media outputs. *SchNews* at various times has staged live readings of its editions, parodying the rituals of television news. Distribution networks for activist camcorder footage have also developed, both through public showings (Exploding Cinema in London, Conscious Cinema in Brighton) and through the video magazine *Undercurrents*, based in Oxford (which unfortunately ceased publishing in spring 1999). The development of a tradition of non-mainstream video news parallels earlier developments in the US (Caldwell, 1996; Engelman, 1996: 239–44; Kellner, 1990). There is clear evidence of growing media sophistication among activist groups on how to obtain coverage, how to deal with journalists, and so on (Harding, 1997; Road Alert!, 1997). What is striking about such media activists is their apparent lack of respect for the 'objectivity' of mainstream media, or its symbolic authority. As Harding (who was the founding editor of *Undercurrents*) puts it, 'once you've accepted that the production of video stories is subjective, then you can really get started in the exciting world of manipulating the media' (1997: 22–3). At one level, this is pure instrumentalism. But it also suggests a rejection of centralised media's authority to speak for all. Of course, the media's differential symbolic power cannot be conjured away so simply: when elsewhere Harding says that getting your footage on television is 'one of the most exciting kicks for a video activist' (ibid.: 89), he unwittingly reconfirms that power. At the level of practice, then, the long-term impacts of this new media activism are uncertain. Elsewhere, for example in 1970s France,[121] brief traditions of alternative mediation have left little permanent impact on media power. It is clear, however, that the language and actions of media and social activists are a fertile area for detailed empirical work.

I want to end Part 2 by focusing on a tension implicit throughout. On the one hand, there has emerged at various points a sense of discovery when 'ordinary people' seem to have broken through to a greater engagement with the mediated public sphere: Jean's sense of pride in 'being there' at Brightlingsea where her action counted, Samantha's traumatic but compelling sense that at Brightlingsea she saw 'reality' for the first time. Worth remembering here are a Greenham protester's words as she reflected on how she laid stones at Newbury War Memorial to protest against the forgetting of militarism's horrors: 'yes this is real. I did know why I was here. I think we all did. It was so damned real, it turned my guts upside down' (quoted in Harford and Hopkins, 1984: 58–9). But there have also been moments when the media sphere's exclusions have emerged with special starkness: Rachel's sense of the media's power ('they control everything'), Tony's feeling that as an 'ordinary person' his protests are largely invisible, Katrina Howse's knowledge that Yellow Gate has been largely 'silenced out'. It is with this unresolved contradiction – between the rush of 'reality' available at media sites, and the silence of the 'ordinary world' which the media cast into shadow – that contemporary 'struggles for visibility'[122] are engaged.

Part 4

# THE FUTURE OF THE
# MEDIA FRAME?

# 9

# CONCLUSION AND
# PERSPECTIVES BEYOND

This book has looked at how the media's particular symbolic power is legitimated, and it has done so by analysing talk and action orientated to the media in a general sense. This has involved focusing on an object of study which is untypical for media sociology, neither consumption nor production, neither 'text' nor 'audience'. I have focused on an intermediate region that I called in Chapter 1, for convenience, 'interactions with the media frame', or rather on a particular type of interaction in which the naturalisation of the media process is suspended or disrupted in some way. The aim has been to find a way into studying the workings of media power that takes account of how deeply the media are embedded in social life.

There have been two sides to my argument: first, the development of a theoretical model of how media power – that is, the differential symbolic power of the media as an institutional sphere – gets reproduced as legitimate, and naturalised; second, detailed empirical work on people's talk and action, and the background assumptions that are reproduced in them. Unusually, this empirical work has crossed the divides between studying fictional media and factual media, mainstream media consumption and alternative forms of mediation. Although rarely studied together, each is part of the vast, uneven pattern of social interaction across space which we simply call 'the media'. In this chapter, I want to summarise my main argument, bringing out connections between its theoretical and empirical aspects, before suggesting some possibilities for further research and considering this project's implications for the future of media theory.

## REVIEW OF THE ARGUMENT

### Theoretical model

In Chapter 3, after introducing my project in the first two chapters, I analysed the naturalisation of the media's differential symbolic power in terms of five 'dimensions'. These are 'ideal types' isolated for the purposes of clarifying their interrelations, and in any particular context they will be traceable in various combinations. They are features not only of media discourse but our interactions with the media process in the widest sense. By the 'media', as explained in Chapter 1, I mean the 'common-sense' definition of the principal mass media – television, radio, and the press – although aspects of my argument may be applicable to other popular media such as film and music. (It has not, however, been part of my argument to make that wider claim.)

The first dimension I discussed was *framing*. 'Framing' refers to the media's role in sustaining the frame in which our experiences of the social occur. The media are a defining frame through which what is shared by everyone is marked off from what is private and particular (cf. Silverstone, 1981). This function underlies a number of other concepts, 'liveness' and 'prime time' for instance. *Ordering* refers to the hierarchical implications of that framing function. There is a hierarchy between two constructed terms – 'media world' and 'ordinary world' – which is continually reproduced both symbolically and through the practical details of how information is made and circulated. This hierarchy is registered in many practices. Some (such as the language patterns analysed in Chapters 6 and 7) are so banal as to be barely noticeable: the way we talk about media people or places in the media, for instance. *Naming* refers to the media's authority as the principal source of social facts ('facts' here is understood in a broad sense to include the sense of 'actuality', which can cover both strictly factual information and central social fictions). It is here that the media's differential symbolic power seems to be most open to argument, since specific conflicts between media and other information sources may arise. However, our general trust in the media is deep-seated: it is a particularly important form of functional dependency in a 'disembedded' society (Giddens, 1990). Specific conflicts with media 'facts' are rarely sufficient in themselves to disturb that generalised trust.

The 'framing', 'ordering' and 'naming' dimensions reinforce each other, constituting together what I have called 'the symbolic hierarchy of the media frame'. This hierarchy is reinforced further by a dimension that is usually hidden: *spacing*. The media's institutional sphere is normally segregated from the rest of social practice (unless you happen to be one of the media's major sources, such as a senior politician); contacts between the two 'worlds' are ritually managed. All contemporary societies involve a complex grid of spatial segregations, but what distinguishes those separating the media sphere is their symbolic significance. The boundaries around the media sphere reduce the chances of the media's authority being ever de-naturalised: actual separation, in other words, reinforces the notion that there is such a thing as the 'media world'. The fifth dimension, *imagining*, refers to our imaginative and emotional investments in the symbolic hierarchy of the media frame. The media/ordinary boundary may be implicated in our sense of identity as 'ordinary people', and in our sense of media people or the media world as somehow special, so that contact with them seems compelling and desirable.

These five dimensions, however, do not represent the only ways in which media power is naturalised. We all contribute to that naturalisation in our competition for, or play with, the symbolic power focused within the media sphere; such competition is generally masked, rather than seen directly for what it is. Those who get too close to challenging their assigned position as 'ordinary people' may be pathologised, labelled as 'mad', 'freaks', and so on. There are also other dimensions which I have not had space to consider – for example, the complex relations between the media sphere and other institutional spheres (the state, corporate economic power, the family) – but which others have analysed extensively.

My model, in other words, remains precisely a *model*, an abstract way of bringing out the complexities in a process of naturalisation which would otherwise be an undifferentiated object: 'media power'. The value of the model depends on how well it helps us articulate what people actually do, think, and say in their dealings with the media process, the question addressed in Parts 2 and 3.

## Granada Studios Tour: the meaning of mediated place

Part 2 analysed what it means to visit Granada Studios Tour, Manchester (GST), the site of *Coronation Street*'s external set. This is Britain's most important and commercially developed media tourist site.

In Chapter 4, I argued that visiting GST should be interpreted not only in terms of the affirmation of broad social identities (Northern, working-class, or soap fan), but also in terms of its status in the symbolic hierarchy between 'media' and 'ordinary' 'worlds'. Walking down the Street set and identifying its features both commemorates people's practice as viewers and allows a negotiation of that hierarchy. The set of *Coronation Street* is an automatically significant place to visit – it has 'aura', it is a 'ritual place' – because visiting it involves, first, crossing the usual separation between media sphere and the rest of social life (back to the 'spacing' dimension) and, second, a ritually managed crossing of the symbolic boundary between 'media' and 'ordinary' 'worlds' ('ordering'). Hence, it is credible to speak of such journeys to GST as secular 'pilgrimages' in a particular sense. In addition, to confirm that the Street is 'there', as fact, is a 'reembedding' (Giddens, 1990) of our trust in the media mechanism itself (the dimension of 'naming'), even if it takes place in relation to a media fiction. The imaginative pleasures of GST are grounded in the real power differentials negotiated there.

Chapter 5 explored further the interrelations between 'fiction' and 'reality' at GST. Visitors are well aware of the fictive status of *Coronation Street* and its set. But the place where that fiction is *produced* remains compelling: it is the 'actual' site where filming happens (fact!). Meetings with cast members at GST are also much more than 'para-social' identification: they help to stage the Street set's authenticity as a real place of filming (MacCannell, 1976), and they are also contact-points with the 'media world'. The complex negotiation of media power in these meetings is paralleled by Billig's (1992) analysis of 'ordinary people's' talk of meeting royalty. However, the negotiation may not always be smooth. I discussed its potential disruptiveness in relation to three interviews. John and Debbie wanted to maintain the normal separation between themselves and the actual processes of media production, while for Sarah visiting GST had disrupted her belief in television, highlighting its 'falseness' and its power. These are exactly the tensions inherent in the media's symbolic hierarchy itself: tensions which may become explicit if the media frame's normal spacing is collapsed.

In Chapter 6, I analysed how the boundaries (spatial and symbolic) between 'media' and 'ordinary' 'worlds' are reproduced at GST. One (easily neglected) form is routine language patterns which mark that boundary. Another is play with that boundary through symbolic reversals, which effectively legitimate it. I also examined how the physical exclusions around media production enforced at GST are reinforced, first, by visitors' discounting the possibility of crossing them in advance and, second, by the pathologising of those who seek to get 'too close': an interesting empirical parallel emerged with the workings of Bourdieu's concept of 'habitus'. Returning to the dimension of 'imagining', I also discussed people's sense of the 'magic' of the 'media world', and its obverse: the feeling that the everyday world of social life is somehow 'lacking', 'merely ordinary'. GST is a point, primarily, of ritual contact, which helps legitimate the actual boundaries surrounding media production. Those exclusions become explicit, however, in GST visitors' talk of becoming television 'extras', and the disappointments that result. Even there, however, their language often serves only to reproduce the media/ordinary boundary.

## Exploring the politics of the media frame

Part 3 analysed a number of political sites where people came close to the media process in some way: principally, the protests against live animal exports at the English port of Brightlingsea in 1995, but also the Women's Peace Camp at Greenham Common (1981– ), the Pure Genius land occupation in London (1996) and the work of various individual activists.

Chapter 7 developed a broad picture of the processes through which, for protesters at Brightlingsea, the media frame was de-naturalised, along with many other aspects of social life. Almost everyone I interviewed had their trust in the media disrupted. As media narratives clashed with people's 'direct' experience, there was an intensified 'disembedding' (in Giddens' sense) from the media process. Being close to the media, and having one's trust in them shaken, had implications also at a symbolic level, revealed most precisely in the interview with Rachel. The extent to which the de-naturalisation of the media frame was articulated (rather than merely registered) by interviewees varied, however, for a number of reasons (including family context, education and class). The disruption of media power, like any disruption of the 'habitus', inevitably leaves uneven traces. Perhaps those with least connection to the media sphere may also be those least able to articulate a challenge to that exclusion.

Chapter 8 analysed people's moves to challenge media power, whether implicitly or explicitly, through becoming active themselves within the media frame: in other words, processes of alternative 'mediation' (cf. Martin-Barbero, 1993). A range of examples were discussed. First, Greenham Common Women's Peace Camp, which implicitly challenged the geography of media debates about nuclear weapons, normally conducted in studios or Parliament, by forcing debate to focus on the site of the weapons themselves. Second, the actions by Brightlingsea protesters to produce 'awareness' outside Brightlingsea; these tried to challenge declining media coverage in the later stages of the protests, for example through demonstrations along major roads. I also discussed two individual activists: Louise, a camcorder activist tracking a livestock market, who turned from being a silent protester to using tools of media production herself, and a campaigner for pensions and disability rights, called The Umbrella Man, who inserts himself into media coverage of large events in order to get his own message across. Finally, I analysed the Pure Genius occupation in London (1996), which continued Greenham's challenge to media geography through an action explicitly planned as a media event. Interviews with Pure Genius residents suggested the emergence of a new attitude towards the media frame (what I called 'self-reflexive tactics') that combined a willingness to use the media to project messages and a deep cynicism about the media's social authority. As I made clear in Chapter 8, these are only some of the avenues for research into alternative forms of mediation and media activism that could be pursued, but they are sufficient to illustrate how media power leaves important traces in activists' practice.

## The mediated landscape of 1990s Britain

In the 1990s, Britain has seen two apparently very different processes. On the one hand, there is the growth of leisure visits to media locations (large enough in some regions, such as Yorkshire, to affect significantly how they are marketed for tourism); GST, on the other side of the Pennines in Manchester, is simply a well-established example of a wider trend. On the other hand, there has been a long series of local conflicts over political, social and environmental matters which have not only received media coverage, but have provided opportunities for people to see the workings of media production at close quarters.

As I remarked earlier (Part 3, Introduction), the juxtaposition is on the face of it paradoxical. A number of heterogeneous processes are involved. First, the realisation by media organisations and the tourism industry of the economic value (both in terms of direct income and wider marketing) of exploiting the connections between media production and place. The strategic fit between the interests of, for example, Yorkshire Television and the Yorkshire Tourist Board is significant, and has to be placed in the context of the wider diversification of tourism since the early 1980s (Urry, 1990). Second, and quite independently, there has been the eruption of numerous small-scale local conflicts (often claiming to be 'non-political', but political in their implications). This occurred under a highly unpopular Conservative regime that even many of its supporters admitted had been too long in government, but similar actions have continued since the election of a Labour Government in May 1997. Third, and connecting the first and second points, such protests have increasingly been interpreted by the media as the actions of 'ordinary people'. In this sense, there is a connection with other representations of the 'ordinary person' in media discourse in 1990s Britain: the growth of so-called 'reality television' in many forms, from surveillance footage to jokey compilations of home camcorder material to the sudden explosion of serialised 'docusoaps' that aim to show the 'reality' behind the scenes of 'ordinary people''s working lives (cf. Kilborn, 1994). This links in turn to economic factors – since those programmes are cheap to produce, and they sell well – and technological factors (such as the development of light, affordable hand-held cameras of professional quality): see further below.

Resulting from all these various factors, then, is, on the one hand, the increasing thematisation, and public awareness of, the media production process and, on the other hand, the mediatisation, perhaps even spectacularisation, of certain aspects of 'everyday life'. In spatial terms, the result is to complicate the separation of the media process from the rest of social life. We should, however, be cautious about reading into these changes any broader political or cultural implications (it is, I would argue, much too early to be clear about these). Nor should we interpret them as a dismantling of the overall 'division' (Baudrillard) within social life which the media process involves; as the details of Parts 2 and 3 show, this is far from the case.

Two things in this complex and changing landscape, however, remain fundamental: first, that in these various situations it is the differential symbolic power of media institutions that, overall, continues to be reproduced; and, second, that it is only by studying the media as a vast, dispersed process of social interaction (rather than simply as an abstracted collection of 'texts'), that we can grasp the range of ways in which this reproduction occurs.

## Extensions of the argument

Every empirical study implies many others which would correct for its own particularities. GST is, arguably, quite a privileged entry-point for analysing the symbolic dimension of the media frame, because of *Coronation Street*'s special status as Britain's longest-running television soap. Would other media tourist sites be different in this respect? That is an important question, although different from the main question I was addressing: this was to establish how, by studying patterns of language and action across a whole range of interviewees, we could get some purchase on the slippery notion of media power and its naturalisation. Similarly with Brightlingsea, Part Three's main site, I am not necessarily claiming that it is a typical protest site (although Brightlingsea protesters' experiences had parallels with those of Shoreham protesters: see Stephens and Shehata, 1995). But it is an example of how my theoretical framework can be applied with interesting results.

This book will, I hope, encourage empirical work that explores its implications further. One area to explore is how far my analysis would be corroborated with different ranges of interviewees. For example, for reasons deriving from the particularities of the case studies chosen, a majority of my samples were women, very few were non-white, and at Brightlingsea a majority were aged 40 or above. More broadly, as I mentioned at the beginning of the book, there is enormous scope for developing *transnational* comparisons between the ways in which media power is socially embedded in different 'media cultures'. My focus has been British, but the potential of this type of analysis is much broader than that. When applied internationally, the varying relationships between media, state and corporate power, for example, would become crucial, as well as questions of cultural and ethnic identity.[123]

I have also abstracted to some degree from processes of family and peer-group interaction, and it would be interesting to see how this might affect the ways in which media power is reproduced. However, as I remark in the Appendix, we must get away from the idea that group talk or ethnographic fieldwork offers a key to unlock such processes which other forms of qualitative analysis lack. My arguments could also be developed in terms of psychoanalytic and other psychological perspectives. If I am right about the pervasive and intricate ways in which media power gets reproduced, then these must have some relevance to individual psychology. Although I have touched on this at various points, I have decided not to pursue this interesting question, if only because it raises a far larger question about how psychoanalytic theory, on the one hand, and sociological and anthropological theory, on the other, can be successfully integrated. That would need more space to resolve than I have here.

Talk and action, space and power, symbolic hierarchy and material exclusion: these are the overarching concepts which have shaped my approach to the media in this book. In this, I have strayed a long way from the usual paths of media sociology or media studies: the 'text', the 'audience' and the 'political economy' of media production. The links have been mainly with theoretical frameworks *outside* recent media studies – sociology, geography, anthropology – although, as explained in Part 1, there are also important continuities between my argument and, for example, work on fans.

I am not suggesting, of course, that studies of the text and audience, or political economy analysis, are unimportant. All are necessary in thinking about the media field as a whole; it would be interesting, for example, to study in more detail how within media texts various processes related to the naturalisation of media power, and even challenges to it, are played out. The book started with one such example from *Wayne's World.* My aim, however, has been broader: to set out an approach to media power which can provide a more satisfactory context for specific media analysis than has been available before. In the rest of this chapter, I want, first, to make some further connections between my approach and likely developments in media provision, and then finally to review where all this leaves us in relation to, perhaps, the central ethical question facing media sociology: debates about the public sphere.


## THE FUTURE OF THE MEDIA FRAME

> Modes of viewing are not simply things that technology does to us ...
> Nor does television change when new alternatives are available. Rather,
> television seems to change, but only on its own terms ... television now
> creates and sanctions specific rituals, ones inextricably tied to new video
> production and home entertainment technologies.
>
> (Caldwell, 1996: 283)

We are in the early stages of a long-term, radical change in media provision, comprising first a multiplication of contents – a shift from scarcity to plenty (cf. Thompson, 1990: 212) – and, alongside that, a multiplication of the ways in which media consumers can access media materials ('interactivity'). What impact will this have on the central issue of this book, the media's concentration of symbolic power? Will it lead to its dissolution or its reinforcement?

It is, of course, too early to know and, if I am right about how deeply embedded media power is in social life, resolving this will require a great deal of empirical work. It is not something that we can know 'in advance' from theoretical pronouncements or futuristic blueprints. It is worth, however, setting out here some relevant issues, in order to show the complexity of these questions. As always, we cannot assume that technological changes have automatic cultural impacts: what matters is 'technology-in-use' (Neuman, 1991: 18).[124] My discussion will concentrate on the medium which may change most fundamentally: television.

## Video, satellite and cable

Let's start with the changes in media technology and media provision, which have been familiar for some time: video, satellite and cable. Many have argued that video – first, the introduction of videotape for production purposes in the 1960s and its subsequent general use inside and outside television institutions and, second, the widespread domestic use of video recorders and players (VCRs) from the 1980s – has irrevocably changed television, and perhaps the media frame as a whole. This argument is especially important in the UK where VCR ownership is higher than in the USA or the rest of Europe (Curran and Seaton, 1997: 202). (It is interesting that both my GST and Brightlingsea samples showed higher VCR ownership than the UK average: see Appendix.)

VCRs have enabled the 'timeshifting' of media consumption. We can watch 'prime time' broadcast television without necessarily assuming that large numbers of people are simultaneously watching what we are watching. Sean Cubitt has developed this point, arguing that 'because [timeshifting] takes issue with the presence of television, it alters the possibilities of identification with the screen, the implied unity of the audience, and even with ourselves' (1991: 37). This is an important argument, because it engages precisely with television's framing dimension. In fact, however, I want to argue that the implications of 'timeshifting' are more complex. First, the possibility of ritual simultaneous viewing remains (for example, Princess Diana's funeral in September 1997, watched reputedly by two billion people worldwide). Second, 'simultaneity' in a broader sense is still important, even if it does not always involve exact simultaneity or continuous 'liveness'. To take the example of popular British soaps, *Coronation Street* and *Eastenders* have a place in the social 'frame' which is sustained by many institutions beyond broadcasting: speculation and comment in the press and magazines, for example. Having a VCR, in any case, surely *increases* your chances of participating in the ritual of (broadly) simultaneous viewing: when you discuss last night's episode at work, does it matter whether you watched it live or a few hours later, when you got home from work? 'Timeshifting' in a broader sense is certainly a significant phenomenon – causing, for example, the gradual undermining of the social ritual of broadcast news bulletins – but its impact derives not from VCRs[125] but from the likely long-term impacts of continuous news information services (teletext and the Internet).

Video has had other impacts which perhaps are more fundamental. Videotape has enabled a new flexibility of inputs to mainstream television production; and VCRs have made possible using your television to watch material not sourced from broadcasting. Potentially, these are radical changes, and this was precisely how video activists from the 1960s onwards (for example in the USA) saw them: see Caldwell (1996). Video changes the flow of what we see on television into a process in which non-media people can, in principle, intervene (Cubitt, 1991: 137). However, the wider cultural impact is much less clear. As Caldwell demonstrates for the USA, the technical possibility of extensive external video inputs to broadcast US television long predated their reality (1996: 264–83), partly because further technological changes (portable camcorders, digital editing techniques) were necessary, and partly because the culture of US network television had to change first. Once inputs from outside broadcasting institutions were accepted, this was a significant shift, just as the recent acceptance of video inputs from non-media professionals into UK news bulletins has created opportunities for social activists (Dovey, 1996: 129–30). The footage of the non-media person at the scene has a status in broadcasting which was simply not possible before video (ibid.: 130): what Dovey calls 'the inscription of presence' or, using my term, a 'witnessing' which is incorporated into the media text. Even so, the long-term implications are uncertain. In the shorter term, I suggest, the impact of video has not been to undermine the media's framing function. As Caldwell argues (see quotation at the beginning of this section), video technologies have been absorbed relatively easily within mainstream television's rituals. It is true that since the 1980s portable camcorders have made possible a decisive breakthrough in the history of access television, allowing non-media subjects to be responsible for filming themselves. In the UK, the BBC2 series *Video Diaries* and *Video Nation* have begun to involve the subjects in editorial decisions: these programmes involve personal statements by non-media people direct to camera. But we should not exaggerate their impact; they occupy only a very small percentage of overall media output. As Dovey remarks (1996: 117–18, 125), a much more prevalent use of 'external' video material on television has been the growth of so called 'reality TV'. In the UK, this ranges from programmes involving surveillance footage (some serious – *Crimewatch*; others entertainment – *Police Camera Action*) to light entertainment based on private camcorder footage (*You Have Been Framed*) to 'soapumentaries' (serialised documentaries based on real-life situations) to 'soap operas' that present 'real life' (such as BBC2's *The Living Soap* and MTV's *The Real World*).[126] 'Reality TV' in the UK and other parts of Europe followed developments in US network television (on which see Caldwell, 1996; Nichols, 1994) and has a clear economic rationale: low costs, high popularity.

The broader impacts of 'reality TV' on the media/ordinary hierarchy are fascinating but, I think, quite ambiguous. On the one hand, such programmes are a significant shift in the nature of media outputs, reducing the amount which is actually 'produced' by media institutions. The fact that these programmes are often popular may suggest that some sort of negotiation of media power is involved. In addition, the status of 'witness footage' complicates the media/ordinary hierarchy to some degree. Yet the result may still be to reinforce that hierarchy. All the above programmes remain editorially controlled by media institutions. The 'reality' they present is precisely non-media ('ordinary') reality: significantly, as one commentator has remarked, we have yet to see unfettered behind-the-scenes coverage of the *media production* process (Christy, 1998). In fact, it could be argued that such programmes, by affirming television as the site for watching such 'reality' footage (for example, surveillance film), simply extend the ambit of the media's 'naming' authority; they legitimate television as a ritual form of public surveillance.

The position is also quite uncertain when we turn to satellite and cable television. These have grown more slowly in the UK than elsewhere, but by 1997 around 27 per cent of UK homes had satellite or cable reception (Office for National Statistics, 1997: 150). As yet, satellite and cable competition has not reduced the broadcasting channels' viewing share comparably to the 1980s fall in US network TV's audience share from 90 per cent to 64 per cent (Caldwell, 1996: 11). This may change, of course, when satellite and cable material becomes more widely available through digital television packages, but meanwhile it seems that the impacts of channel multiplication on the nature of the television audience have been exaggerated. In 1996, 90 per cent of total UK viewing was still of broadcast channels, in spite of many other channels being available (Curran, 1998: 176: cf. for other European countries, ibid.: 177–9, and for the US, Winston, 1998: 315–20).

We need to look ahead, however, to a time when a choice of hundreds of channels becomes the norm in Britain and in all other richer countries. Will this lead to the 'death of homogeneous Britain', condemning each of us to a 'sad little viewing community' (Jeffries, 1997) or, less dramatically, to the audience being primarily a mass of market segments ('narrowcasting')? Some things will certainly change. Viewing patterns will become detached to some degree from channel loyalties, especially as all programmes are repackaged in new digital television 'multiplexes'. Will this mean that viewing preferences become detached from national media provision? This will vary geographically, depending on many factors such as language, ethnic and cultural differences and the historic strength of local media industries. Even as audiences are split, however, between more channels, the framing function of certain programme streams is likely to continue, even if its distribution becomes more complex. Age-targeted channels such as MTV, far from suggesting that television's framing function is dead, involves perhaps focusing it more precisely for a particular age group. A factor often forgotten is actual audiences' *resistance* to fragmentation. William Neuman, drawing on the long US experience of multiple channels, argued that the evidence for real audience fragmentation was inconclusive (1991: 127–8), partly because of the overlap of contents between channels, but more importantly because, as channels multiply, the more viewers need their choices to be simplified. As Neuman put it:

Packaging, formatting, filtering and interpreting complex flows of information represent value-added components of public communications. In a more competitive, complex and intense communications environment, that value-added component will be equally important to the individual citizen, *if not more so*.

(1991: 163, added emphasis)

We cannot assume, just because an almost infinite range of variant viewing practices becomes possible, that it will become actual.

## Digital media

Some of the same points apply to more recent, and anticipated, expansions of media provision: the development of multimedia and the onset of digital television. These, however, constitute a much more fundamental change in the nature of television and other media. Digitalisation of communications enables new, fully-integrated services (combining television with many other information and entertainment flows). The ultimate convergence of all communication forms within one broadband service accessed through one medium (whether television or, perhaps, the computer) will clearly have major implications for 'the media' (as I have defined them), and indeed all cultural consumption, although its full realisation is some time in the future. Television, radio and the press would no longer be distinct media. More importantly, digital media are likely to involve much higher degrees of viewer *interactivity* than earlier forms of television, radio and the press (certainly, this is central to the recent marketing of digital television in Britain).[127] The vision of media interactivity is an important one, which Neuman expresses well: 'today the issue of shared, non-interfering, two-way communications again arises as a practical possibility' (1991: 68; cf. Negroponte, 1995; Toffler, 1980: 169–76; Pool, 1983). It has deep roots, not least in a reaction to the concentration of symbolic power in media institutions: a similar issue, perhaps, to that arising in relation to 'reality TV'. 'Interactivity' is likely to remain central to media debates for a long time.

But leaving aside the uncertainties about how quickly interactive digital media/multimedia will spread (cf. Thompson, 1990: 214), what exactly is the 'interactivity' on offer? Does it mean a move towards genuine two-way communication (viewers able to *input* visual and aural material through the set)? If so, this would be a very major shift in the apparently irreversible trend within modernity towards a 'non-dialogical' mode of publicness (Thompson, 1993: 187). This of course would involve redistributing resources of media *production* (fictional, factual), something which is definitely not yet on offer from the media industries. Or does 'interactivity' simply mean an increased ability to make viewing choices, or access information, within option frameworks that are already fixed (Drew, 1995: 75), a much less radical change?

It is undeniable that, as media shift to being a broader stream of information and leisure flows accessible at the consumer's option, the consequences for the media's authority and attitudes to the media process will need to be explored through further empirical work. But we should not assume that the result will inevitably be to undermine that authority. One possibility, as Castells has argued (1996: 372–5), is that the concentration of so many communications streams in one 'super-medium' may only *enhance* that supermedium's framing potential, even if within a media field whose complex landscape we have yet to map.

## The Internet

The concept of 'interactivity' leads directly into consideration of the Internet, where it has found its natural expression in many writers' claims that computer-mediated communication constitutes a radical new alternative to, perhaps even a replacement of, the public sphere as constituted by existing mainstream media, particularly television. Mark Poster, for example, has claimed that the Internet represents a 'second media age' when '"reality" becomes multiple' (1995: 85); Howard Rheingold, a little more cautiously, has written of a reinvigorated virtual public sphere with a new sense of community (1994: 14). My remarks will necessarily be brief and will focus on the Internet's role in public rather than personal communication.

The importance of the Internet to my overall argument derives from two fundamental features. First, the degree of interactivity it involves: not only will particular software allow individuals an interactive, personalised information and entertainment service, either through their own individual selections or through 'personalised' browsers, and so on, but the decentred nature of Internet communication means that it has the potential to be genuinely interactive. As Howard Rheingold put it, 'every citizen can broadcast to every other citizen' (1994: 14), or at least in principle they can. The Internet's structure determines that a sender can send information to the whole network at once and any receiver can do the same, including by communicating back to the original sender (ibid.: 118–19). Second, the Internet enables new large-scale information transmissions beyond national or geographical borders and outside the broadcast media: think, for example, of political and campaigning groups' uses of the Internet through Web sites and alternative news information services such as PeaceNet (Frederick, 1994; Rheingold, 1994: 261–8). Of the activists considered in Chapter 8, both Pure Genius and Greenham Common Women's Peace Camp (since 1998) have had Web sites. The speed and ease of most connections on the Internet enables something like the 'broadcasting' of information by those outside the media sphere: as transmission speeds increase, this may involve broadcasting live visual and aural material on a regular basis (footage of a protest action, for example). This will bypass the media frame, but with a sense of immediacy and directness that may rival it. Such Web 'broadcasting', if it became widespread, would make the Internet into an alternative public sphere of considerable importance.

There are, however, reasons for caution, and not only the familiar, but still crucial, question of access: the skewing of access (even as it grows) towards those of higher social class and/or income,[128] and towards men rather than women.[129] Access, we should also remember, does not necessarily mean active use. It is reasonable to predict that regular Internet use, even in the richer countries, will remain concentrated in a minority of the population for a long time (Castells, 1996: 358–64), but this remains to be seen. A more fundamental point, however, is that, given the vastness of the Internet already (and it will go on growing exponentially), people's ability to access *particular sites* (for example, sites not wholly geared to commercial interests or routine information provision) will depend on many factors: their computer literacy, the effort they make to find them, or the way their search tools are structured. Strikingly, the Microsoft-produced Web site, Microsoft Network ('MSN'), assumes that most users will *not* be able to find what they want on the Net without help, hence its coordination into 'shows' arranged into 'channels'. Laura Jennings, vice-president of *The Microsoft Network*, summarised the logic:

> If you don't know what you want here's a metaphor *that feels like radio or television* ... There are so many choices that a small number of portal sites – gateways, sites like [Microsoft Network] that have a spread of information – are a great starting point ... *There are these critical entry points and if you're not* [on] *one of those then the average user is not going to find your site*.
>
> (*Guardian*, 6 February 1997, Online Section, added emphasis)

The irony is unmistakable. For many users, the Internet will already have been configured along the lines of older broadcast media, with commercial decisions pre-structuring the choices. This is not to minimise the positive potential of aspects of the Internet – for example, the space it allows for non-commercial, non-centralised political networking on a global scale – but it is to suggest that its reality as a fully interactive public sphere may be much more limited than cyber-visionaries proclaim.

Clearly the Internet's increasing growth will affect our common-sense definitions of what constitute 'the media' – the question I addressed in Chapter 1 – and further research will be necessary into the Internet's impacts on media power. Clearly also, just as the introduction of broadcasting changed the previous configuration of 'the social' in complex ways, so too will the new combination of electronic and digital media that, in the next century, becomes the norm, at least in richer countries and for their better-resourced members. Individuals' ability to access information and entertainment (at least, in purely quantitative terms) will become massively greater and more flexible. The new digital 'supermedium' may become the single medium not only for public, but also for a large number of private, communications, a fundamental shift. Paradigms and background assumptions about what 'the media' *are* will surely change in the long run. But the fundamental question in all this, which I must simply pose here rather than answer, is: how will these changes affect the distribution of symbolic power? Even if the contours of the 'media world' and the 'ordinary world' become reconfigured in various ways, will the boundary between them disappear? Will fragmentation and atomisation lead to an undermining of media power and social power generally? Only if we assume a model of social integration based on shared 'values' (a sort of dominant ideology thesis: cf. Chapter 3, Conclusion), but that has not been my assumption at all. Technological hype apart, can we not argue that the massive multiplication of media sources will lead to the entrenchment of a new concentration of symbolic power in the media sphere (and its naturalisation)? Current rhetoric about the virtual age, perhaps, only paves the way for this transition.

In thinking about the future of the media frame in terms of developments of media technology, there is always of course the danger of mediacentrism. To analyse more fully the future status of media institutions, we would need to return to the point suggested in Chapter 1: the study of 'the media' as part of a wider history of social mediations (Martin-Barbero, 1993). This, in turn, would take us into other territory: changes in the authority of, and the trust vested in, all social institutions (Fukuyama, 1995; Giddens, 1990), changing forms of 'reflexivity' (Lash and Urry, 1994), and so on. As I argued at the end of Chapter 2, media sociology can make a complex contribution to these debates, and this book, I hope, has gone some way towards making that connection. More research is clearly needed.

## THE FUTURE OF MEDIA THEORY

A newspaper represents an association; it may be said to address each of its readers in the name of all the others and to exert its influence over them in proportion to their individual weakness. The power of the newspaper press must therefore increase as the social conditions of men become more equal.

(Tocqueville, 1994 : vol. II, 115)

I have argued for a sociology of the media as a vast, historically continuous process of 'mediations' (in Jesus Martin-Barbero's useful term). This approach brackets the analysis of specific media texts and how they are culturally absorbed (if they are), and insists that such analysis needs a much wider context, that owes more to history, sociology, anthropology and geography than it does to literary models. The idea of textual analysis as an *exclusive* paradigm for what media analysis should be is as outdated as the idea that social and cultural life can be studied simply in terms of bounded, autonomous 'communities' (the village, the town, the nation). There is no autonomous media text, and so there is no media 'text' in any conventional sense, except as projected by the textual scholar's imagination.[130]

Experiences of media tex*tuality* occur locally and as part of a much wider process; the boundaries around any particular textual site are always liable to be exploded. Only in this highly qualified sense can we speak of the media text. The anthropologists Arjun Appadurai (1990) and James Clifford (1990) have each captured different aspects of this with their concepts of 'mediascapes' and 'travelling cultures'. We travel across the surfaces of media cultures, but at the same time we continually rework them for ourselves in talk, actions and imaginings. Changing the scale of media analysis in this way is necessary, and has been under way for some time (see Chapter 1 and cf. Abercrombie and Longhurst, 1998). The danger, however, is that we lose a sense of the power which particular media images, particular narratives or textual fragments may have: what Barthes (1977) called the 'rhetoric of the image'. It is Barthes (1973: 129), in fact, who is the alternative source to Bourdieu for the concept of naturalisation (history turned into nature, the level of 'myth') that I have drawn upon. I do not want to lose sight of that textual dimension. That is why, although specific media 'texts' (in the above, qualified sense) have not been analysed in this book, I do not wish to displace textual analysis so much as to provide a different context in which it can take place.[131] That different context is, quite simply, to study the 'mythical' status of media institutions themselves, the way their complex history has been turned into nature.

The historical balance-sheet of the mass media is of course hardly simple: as John Corner (1995) and Paddy Scannell (1989, 1996) have rightly emphasised, mass media have changed social territories and made possible new forms of 'communicative entitlement' (Scannell). But, at the same time, media history is, at its root, a history of the continued, even intensified, naturalisation of *inequality*: inequality in who can effectively speak, and be listened to. This inequality is focused on the concentrated symbolic power of media institutions themselves: media power. What is the place of media power in a wider account of social life? How is it legitimated, how is it lived with? These are the questions which I have tried to answer.

To emphasise media power in this way is to continue the themes of early media sociology, but to draw out its account of media power more broadly (those broader aspects were of course always there: see for example Hall, 1973, 1977). I make no apologies for that continuity. Foregrounding media power means foregrounding issues of *participation* which have often been neglected in media analysis before and since Hall's intervention (cf. Barbrook, 1995: 4). The reasons for this continued emphasis on the power of media institutions are worth restating in a more general way than I have done so far. Historically, we need only recall the liberal historian Alexis de Tocqueville's paradox in his study of nineteenth-century America: that as 'the social conditions of men' become more equal in other respects, the differential power of the media that 'represent' them increases. This automatically raises issues about participation in the media, or rather the lack of it. Philosophically, the central reference-point remains the questions raised by Jürgen Habermas (1989) [1962] in formulating his concept of the 'public sphere'. Whatever his account's limitations, and there are many (see Calhoun, 1992), it still, in some form, provides the starting-point from which the analysis of media power begins. As fears for the collapse of public television, for instance, grow in America, Britain and elsewhere (see, for example, Blumler and Gurevitch, 1995; Engelman, 1996), it is all the more important to keep the public sphere debate alive. In fact, it is at the general level of media power (in the sense I have used the term) that it is most persuasive.

It matters for the quality of public life that its central institutions – the media – involve an asymmetry between a relatively small group of producers and participants, and a vast mass of non-producers (cf. Garnham, 1992: 361). It matters, similarly, that this asymmetry is naturalised and challenges to it de-legitimated. We cannot adequately analyse the media's impact on public life without considering the social processes through which the media's own differential power is reproduced. Talk is not in itself democratising if it circulates within an effective hierarchy of speaking positions (cf. Nancy Fraser's (1992) critique of Habermas' original historical model of the public sphere). It has recently been argued that this hierarchy may be shifting, for example in new types of talk show (see Livingstone and Lunt, 1994), but the debate remains complex and unresolved. We must therefore keep hold of the ethical issues implicit in Habermas's original arguments: his notion of a democratic public sphere as a discursive space with 'procedures whereby those affected by general social norms and collective political decisions can have a say in their formulation, stipulation, and adoption' (Benhabib, 1992: 87). This principle remains of fundamental importance as a regulative ideal, even if (see Thompson, 1993: 186–7) it can no longer be formulated by reference to an ideal of unmediated face-to-face communications. As Nicholas Garnham has argued, *some* notion of 'the reciprocal duties inherent in a communicative space that is physically shared' is necessary even for contemporary societies that are massively dispersed and media-saturated (1992: 367). On the contrary, that structural shift makes those questions all the more urgent. As Garnham (ibid.: 373) asks: 'how much room for manoeuver [do] agents actually have in a symbolic system within which both the power to create symbols and access to the channels of their circulation is hierarchically structured?' These issues affect not just mediated politics (where most discussions of Habermas have concentrated) but the whole media field, including 'entertainment' (Dahlgren, 1995, ch. 5; cf. McGuigan (1996) on the 'cultural public sphere'). The ability to participate in the production of shared fictions remains fundamental to any sense of belonging, and therefore to 'citizenship' and 'identity' themselves.

General issues of participation in, and exclusion from, the media are as important here as specific issues of representation in particular texts or types of text. It is important to remember the connections with the broader radical tradition of media analysis: for example, Situationism's theory of the 'spectacle' which attacked the concentration of symbolic power in a separate, exclusive sector of society (cf. Chapter 2); and Brecht's call for the conversion of radio 'from a distribution system' to 'a gigantic system of channels ... capable not only of transmitting but of receiving, of making the listener not only hear but also speak' (1979–80 [1932]: 25, cf. Enzensberger, 1972).

These are the philosophical and political issues which underlie my interest in the reproduction of media power. They are issues which, at least explicitly, have been associated more often with 'political economy', than with 'cultural' approaches to studying the media, and yet my own analysis (since it includes nothing about the economics of the media industries) would no doubt be called 'cultural'. There is a problem, however, with this artificial way of demarcating the tasks of media theory. The apparently unbridgeable divide between 'political economy' and 'cultural' approaches to the media must be consigned to the past, even as it is being entrenched still further.[132] I have argued throughout that media power is constituted *both* through institutional structures, and the unequal distribution of access to the means of media production which they entail, *and* the broadly 'cultural' processes which help reproduce the media's legitimacy. There is no contradiction, therefore, between 'political economy' approaches which concentrate on the first and 'cultural' approaches which concentrate on the second.[133] On the contrary, they require each other. The power of media institutions is both a cultural and an economic phenomenon. To claim that either has analytic priority is as absurd as a sociologist of religion arguing that studying the economics and organisational aspects of religious institutions is somehow 'prior' to studying the cultures of belief which help sustain them. The media have their own 'culture of belief', and we need to study it.

Doing so means thinking seriously about space and the media's impacts on the territories which they play a central role in mapping. I have begun to explore in this book a number of spatial themes: journeys to media locations and their significance, being present at sites of media production, the ways in which memory (whether of television fiction or political events) is preserved, and (implicit throughout) the question of what and where counts as 'real'. Many forms of media analysis could help develop this analysis of 'media territory' further, but I have emphasised the directly spatial since it has been the most neglected.

However we approach media power – whether from institutional or cultural perspectives, or from both – making this our focus involves a choice, ultimately a political choice. It might be argued that such a choice rests on an outdated reference-point, what John Corner in his important recent discussion of public sphere debates has called an 'abolitionist fantasy' (1995: 43). But that would be to misunderstand the type of argument I have developed here. Far from looking back wistfully to a pre-media age, the point is that we need to grasp more clearly than ever before the implications of the fact that contemporary societies have, as their universal starting-point, the concentration of symbolic power in media institutions. To analyse the social impacts of this power is simply to address directly a dimension of our present, which helps shape us all. To question media power is, indeed, to question who 'we' are.

# APPENDIX:
# METHODOLOGICAL ISSUES

## RESEARCH METHOD

### Theoretical outlook

Every piece of research involves choices, and there is no point pretending they are objective. A value-free standard for choosing research topics in sociology does not exist (Gouldner, 1962). My research has been orientated explicitly towards the identification of power inequalities and their social consequences (cf. Callon, Law and Rip, 1986; Fairclough and Wodak, 1997; van Dijk, 1996). That does not, of course, exempt me from considering the power inequalities implicit in my own position as social analyst. I return to this below.

Before that, I want to explain the methodological stance I have taken in this work. It has been deliberately eclectic. This is, I believe, the most sensible strategy when so many issues in media sociology, and in particular those regarding questions of media power, remain outstanding (cf. Chapter 1). Glaser and Strauss' well-known (1967) model of 'grounded theory', which draws on multiple theoretical perspectives, and therefore multiple methods, remains as good a starting-point as any.

There is, however, one underlying principle in my research which needs to be made explicit: the idea that we can develop a large-scale theory about the media's general social impacts and the reproduction of media power through analysing media-related talk and action in specific contexts. In other words, I assume that 'macro' issues can be illuminated through the study of 'micro' contexts (cf. Billig, 1997; Giddens, 1984; Knorr-Cetina, 1981). There is nothing paradoxical about this, since as Knorr-Cetina has argued we should regard the 'macro' 'no longer as a *particular layer* of social reality *on top* of micro-episodes ... rather, it is seen to reside *within* these micro-episodes where it results from the *structuring practices* of agents' (1981: 34, original emphasis). It follows that studying 'ideology, power and politics' necessarily involves understanding 'the articulation of micro and macro issues and processes' (Morley, 1997: 127–8).

That still leaves unanswered the controversial question of what sort of connections there are between interviewees' talk or action and wider social regularities. In the absence of any consensus, I have drawn on a number of different traditions within social theory without claiming to be following strictly in the footsteps of any of them. *Symbolic interactionism* provides a useful starting-point, because of its basic principle that culture is not an abstract entity, but 'is derived from what people do' (Blumer, 1969: 6). Understanding cultural processes accordingly involves studying the 'formation' of action, that is:

> [observing] the situation as it is seen by the actor, observing what the actor takes into account, observing how he [sic] interprets what is taken into account, noting the alternative kinds of acts that are mapped out in advance, and seeking to follow the interpretation that led to the selection and execution of one of those prefigured acts.
>
> (ibid.: 56)

This makes clear the importance of looking closely at the accounts interviewees give of their actions. *Ethnomethodological* approaches to talk (Garfinkel, 1967; Heritage, 1984), by contrast, have prioritised not so much agents' explicit meanings and explanations as their shared 'background expectancies' (Garfinkel, 1967: 50): the shared, taken-for-granted rules which lie, as it were, 'behind' any specific actions or interpretations. These expectancies have both a normative status (defining how agents are expected to behave and think) and a cognitive status, since they constitute what is understood to be going on between people (Heritage, 1984: 83). This almost 'ontological' dimension to everyday talk is a useful principle to keep in mind in analysing what happens when people's background assumptions about the media are disrupted. I draw on aspects of both approaches in my own analyses of people's talk and actions. I have also drawn on insights from the large field of *discourse analysis*, particularly Michael Billig's work. Billig has emphasised studying people's 'rhetorical' practices as a way into power and ideology (1997: 222). Ideology, he argues, is embedded in particular processes of arguing and thinking, rather than in stable 'attitudes' that are necessarily fixed beyond particular interview contexts (cf. Potter and Wetherall, 1987). Particularly important for my research is Billig's recent argument that ideology and power are reproduced in language that passes without argument: 'in the unnoticed, small words which seem beyond rhetorical challenge and which are routinely and widely repeated' (1997: 225), such as apparently 'dead' metaphors (cf. Lakoff and Johnson (1980) on the largely unnoticed patterning of metaphorical language). Similarly, I analyse media-related talk for evidence of forms of thought manifested across whole interview samples, rather than (necessarily) for evidence of fixed attitudes attributable to individuals. It is through these forms of thought that the symbolic hierarchy of the media frame is reproduced. The same point applies to actions. What Billig calls 'banal practices' (1995: 95) may be very revealing of patterns of thinking; in fact, they comprise one of the ways in which patterns of thinking, categorisation and so on, are reproduced. An example is the practice of phoning home from the *Coronation Street* set (see Chapter 4 for discussion).

This description of my approach might seem rather abstract, but my underlying aim is purely pragmatic. How else are we to trace how the legitimacy of media power is reproduced except by looking very closely for patterns in what people say and do? At the same time it is important to avoid the naturalistic assumption that studying 'naturally occurring talk' reveals what people 'really' think or that the social can be 'directly' accessed at certain points (see Willis (1980), Hammersley (1989) for critiques). Such assumptions seem to lie behind recent, rather dogmatic claims in media sociology that, for example, only ethnographic research or group talk can give us access to the workings of media cultures (Drotner, 1993: 35; Gillespie, 1995: 54–5; and cf. Abercrombie, 1996: 178). Privileging ethnography as a method is particularly unhelpful, not least because the conditions for true ethnographic fieldwork are so rarely met; misleading claims of 'ethnographic' status in media and cultural studies have rightly been criticised (Gillespie, 1995: 23; Nightingale, 1996: 110–12). If we take the case of Granada Studios Tour (GST) (see Part Two), hundreds of thousands of people from all over Britain visit it each year. There is no serious possibility of doing 'ethnography' at such a site: you could hardly follow a sample of visitors home to analyse the full context of their visit, nor would many people have agreed to my following them around the site on what was their day out! GST, like many leisure sites and like the political sites analysed in Part 3, is a *hybrid* site where people from many backgrounds and lifeworlds *intersect*. 'Ethnography' is not a helpful model for studying such sites (note also Lofland and Lofland's (1984: 17) comments on the difficulties of 'participant observation' at protest sites). Detailed, theoretically informed analysis of people's talk about the site – 'triangulating' where possible between different forms and situations of talk – is a more useful and practicable model.

### Interview format

My principal data were open-ended, unstructured interviews, supplemented by some fixed questioning on background material. These interviews were generally with individuals, but included some group discussions.

In the GST case study, people were interviewed on site in groups, couples or individually (there was no reason to exclude group talk, of course). The longer off-site interviews were all individual, except for two friends who had visited GST together and a husband and wife couple. Logistical difficulties prevented my forming a group from the other, geographically scattered off-site interviewees. At Brightlingsea (the main site in Part 3), group interviews on a larger scale would have been possible. But in any case my preference at both sites was for individual interviews. While group interviews can reveal how people make collective sense of media material (Buckingham, 1987; Liebes and Katz, 1990), there are circumstances where individual interviews may be a better source: for example, where it is more private forms of sense-making that are being studied or where there is some moral or social difficulty in talking about one's consumption practice (Lindlof and Grodin, 1990: 13; cf. Lofland and Lofland, 1984: 14). I suspected that, for many visitors to GST, the personal meaning of their visit was *not* something they normally talked about socially: if so, group interviews might be just as artificial as individual interviews. A number of interviewees' comments bore this out. At Brightlingsea, I was seeking people's detailed reflections on events that were often painful and difficult, reflections that I suspected they might not wish to share in group situations (some group interviews were, however, held at Brightlingsea as a 'control' device). All interviews, whether group or individual, are, of course, to a degree artificial situations.

## Sampling strategy

The case studies are based on the analysis of almost 900 single-spaced pages of interview and letter material. How was this obtained?

In the case of GST, most off-site interviews were obtained through responses to advertisements placed by me in the letters page of two soap magazines: *Inside Soap* and *Coronation Street* (issues 58 and 33 respectively). (*Inside Soap* is a fortnightly magazine with major national circulation (approximately 200,000). *Coronation Street* is a monthly magazine with more limited circulation.) The notice read:

> Have you been on the Granada Studios Tour? If so, researcher Nick Couldry from Goldsmiths College, University of London would like to hear from you. Nick is collecting people's accounts of what the Tour meant to them for his research on trips of different kinds. Please write (no limit on length) to: [PO box address].

Twenty-one people replied with accounts ranging from one paragraph to four pages. Clearly this method ensured that *off-site* interviewees, at least, were not a random sample: first, they were likely to be keen soap fans (readers of soap magazines) and, second, they were those who had the time and inclination to write to a stranger, and then meet with him.[134] Accordingly I do not claim that the off-site interviews are necessarily typical of GST visitors as a whole.

On site at GST, the flow of visitors was so great and so variable that statistically significant random sampling was impossible (cf. Lang and Lang, 1991:

197). Instead, I aimed to sample within the overall range of visitors across the relevant factors of 'time, people and context' (Hammersley and Atkinson, 1995: 46). Interviewing was spread over three weeks (two during the school summer holidays – peak visit times – and one in later September). I aimed to match my interview sample to my own observations of the age, gender and group composition of visitors overall. I also aimed to represent ethnic minorities and overseas visitors in my sample, although from my observation they were a small minority (less than five per cent). Large visiting groups (including groups of schoolchildren) are underrepresented in my sample, simply because their visits were more difficult for me to interrupt than those of others. In addition, the majority of site interviews (seventy-four out of eighty-four) were conducted on or near the *Coronation Street* set, thus deliberately biasing them against GST visitors who ignored it or left quickly. This followed from my aim of analysing the talk of those interested in the *Coronation Street* aspects of GST, rather than the overall visitor population.

At the political sites, the 'snowballing' method of sampling was adopted (Denzin, 1978: 80–81). Initial visits to Brightlingsea established that people would probably be interested in talking about the protests, and advertisements to obtain interviewees were therefore unnecessary. I developed two initial contacts (one active in the protesters' group – Brightlingsea against Live Exports, 'BALE' – one not) and at a BALE meeting I asked people to let me know if they were interested in being interviewed. In order to avoid my sample being weighted too heavily towards those (predominantly female and/or retired) present at BALE meetings held on weekday mornings, I contacted some protesters from categories underrepresented in the initial sample: men, people under twenty, people living outside Brightlingsea, and protesters who were less close to BALE. The adjusted sample reflected these groups.

GST site interviewees were approached without any preparation. People probably therefore framed the interview initially as 'market research' or perhaps, because I had a microphone, some form of 'media interview' (although of course I denied this). I aimed in conducting these interviews to allow for the relaxed, free flow of talk. Other interviews were almost always preceded by a letter indicating the areas the interview would cover. Interviewees in one case study were not told about the existence of the other, nor were they told that my overall research project was concerned with issues of media power; this disclosure might have misled interviewees and at worst distorted responses (Hammersley and Atkinson, 1995: 72–3, 265).

Longer interviews were open-ended and unstructured, although I did not hide the fact that I had a general protocol of areas I hoped to cover. My interview protocols aimed to cover a wide range of topics that might have a bearing on the central subject. Brightlingsea protesters, for instance, were asked, not only about their reactions to media coverage of the protests, but about how they came to be involved, their interpretation of events, their involvement in other protests, and so on. The GST on-site interviews inevitably operated under rather different constraints: most people felt time pressure to continue with their visit (visits are expensive and time is limited). In the first week a formal list of questions was visibly relied upon, but in later weeks I followed my protocol from memory, so as to encourage more open-ended answers.

## Power relations

All the interviews inevitably involved power relations between me and the interviewee(s). Any interviewee will to some degree monitor the impression (s)he is giving to the interviewer (Denzin, 1978: 127) and this will be affected by power differentials, or other perceived differences. One important dimension of difference in the GST interviews was that of *class* and *region*: as a middle-class Southerner, I differed from a majority of my interviewees. *Gender* was a differentiating factor in both case studies, since the majority of interviewees were women. It is impossible in any case to remove all power differentials. Some are inherent to the interview situation, viz. the additional discursive resources available to the analyst (Fairclough, 1989: 167). In this research, some interviewees (in spite of my denials) probably perceived me as 'part of the media', the very power nexus whose reproduction I aimed to analyse. Where this seemed a particularly significant factor in the interview, it is noted. I had, however, anticipated from the beginning that the power relations I was studying might themselves be reproduced through the interview situation. This is only a particularly clear example of the issues arising in all interview situations.

## Generalisability

Part 1 develops a theory of the naturalisation of the media's symbolic power which is highly general, although it emerged from my empirical research. My specific case studies, by contrast, relate to specific vantage-points on the social terrain rather than a statistically significant sample of the whole population, and so cannot prove the general validity of my theory. This is not a problem, however, but a condition of all 'grounded theory' (for an interesting discussion of the tensions between interpretive field work and the generation of theory, see Sperber, 1985: ch. 1). Such theory inevitably aims for a generality wider than the contexts in which it was formulated. The issue, in any case, is not whether the case studies are statistically generalisable, but whether they make the theory more persuasive (cf. Bryman, 1988: 90; Alasuutari, 1995: 155–7).

As mentioned earlier, I do not claim that everyone interviewed is typical: some quite obviously are exceptional, for example some GST visitors interviewed off-site. But again that is not a problem. There is a necessary dialectic between mapping overall patterns of talk and thought on the one hand, and making detailed sense of more exceptional material on the other. It is the latter that enables us to articulate discursive structures that underpin the wider patterns, precisely because it is in the exceptional cases that more argumentative weight is placed on those structures, in a way that highlights both their consistencies and their contradictions.

Ultimately of course there is an unavoidable risk in every interpretation. As always in constructing a theory, 'we are building a world and then attempting to convert that world into a reality by enrolling others in it' (Callon, Law and Rip, 1986: 228). This case is no different.

## INTERVIEW SAMPLES

### Granada Studios Tour

Of the eleven people interviewed in nine off-site interviews, eight were female and three male: this gender imbalance reflected the prevalence of women visitors to GST. None was aged over 60 but, subject to that, they represented a spread of ages (two were at school, four aged between 20 and 40, and five between 40 and 60). They also represented a range of class positions: four working-class (working in catering, printing, or (Julie) married to a carpenter), four lower middle-class (nurse, clerical worker, two teaching assistants) and three middle-class (a health professional, the daughter of an electrical engineer and the daughter of a care-home proprietor). Four came from the North of England (including one man now living in the South, who regarded himself as 'Northern'), four from the Midlands and three from the South. They represented, therefore, a range of ages, classes and regions. As regards education, two were still at school, five had finished their education at school, three (Beth, Peter and John) had work qualifications from training colleges, and Sarah alone had a university degree.

Of the eighty-four site interviews, twenty-four were effectively individual interviews (generally because the rest of the interviewee's party was elsewhere or (s)he was accompanied by a young child: solo visitors were rare). The remaining sixty-three were mainly conducted with pairs of interviewees (forty mixed couples, seventeen female pairs and two male pairs) apart from four larger mixed groups. Since some men took to answering for themselves and their female partners, male talk is to some degree overrepresented. However, this should not be exaggerated, since, in most interviews with male-female couples, both spoke. There were only two cases where a couple explicitly disagreed over the significance of their visit.

The total site interview sample (those who spoke) was 143: 65 per cent women and 35 per cent men (this gender spread broadly matched my own observations of visitors). Sixty-two per cent had travelled from the North of

England, 13 per cent from the Midlands, 12 per cent from the South, 9 per cent from elsewhere in the UK, and 4 per cent from overseas. The age and class range of the sample can only be estimated on the basis of my observations and internal interview evidence, since I kept personal questions to a minimum. On that (limited) basis, I would estimate that those under 20 and those over 60 were in the minority (15 per cent and 18 per cent respectively) and the majority were between 20 and 40 (31 per cent) or between 40 and 60 (35 per cent); as to class, approximately 50 per cent were working-class, 30 per cent lower middle-class and 20 per cent middle-class. These estimates are not relied upon in my detailed argument.

The letter-writers overlapped partly with the full-length sample. Sixteen were female and five male: seven wrote from the North of England, four from the Midlands, five from the South, two from the rest of the UK and three from overseas (two from Eire, one from Canada).

A striking feature of both on- and off-site samples was that ownership of domestic media technology was above the national average. For example, all the off-site sample and 93 per cent (N=69, calculated by household) of the on-site sample owned VCRs, approximately 40 per cent of both samples had a computer (N=69), and the same percentage had access to cable or satellite television (N=75). The 1997 UK national averages, by comparison, were 82 per cent (for VCRs), 27 per cent (for computers), and 27 per cent (for cable/satellite access) (Office for National Statistics, 1997: 141, 150).

## Brightlingsea

I interviewed thirty-two people in twenty interviews (twenty women, twelve men). The Brightlingsea sample was older than the GST samples: twenty-one were aged over 50 (sixteen under 65 and five over 65) and eleven were aged under 50 (six in their forties, two each in their twenties and thirties, and one teenager); of those under 65, five had already retired. In terms of both gender and age, the sample broadly reflected the composition of the protesters themselves. Because most animal shipments occurred during weekdays, participants (after the first two weeks of protests, when many took holidays) were disproportionately those without formal employment or with flexible employment hours (including retired people, housewives and self-employed small businesspeople). In terms of class (judged by occupation), eight were working-class, fifteen lower middle-class, and nine middle-class (professional or managerial). Whether this fairly represents the overall class composition of protesters is uncertain, since the latter has not been studied. Many protesters, particularly after the early weeks, travelled from outside Brightlingsea and this is reflected in the sample, eleven of whom lived outside Brightlingsea. As with the GST off-site sample, a majority (nineteen) had finished education at school, with seven attending work-related training colleges and two university.

As regards domestic media technology (N=22, calculated by household), access to some technologies was higher than the national average (video, 91 per cent; a computer, 41 per cent), but lower than the national average in other cases (cable or satellite television, 9 per cent). A very high proportion of the Brightlingsea sample were regular newspaper readers (89 per cent) (national average, 66 per cent: MORI poll, quoted *Guardian*, 3 March 1997 (Media section)) with 50 per cent reading a local paper, and 93 per cent were regular television news watchers (considerably higher in each case than in the GST samples). This interest in news probably reflects interviewees' experiences of being involved in a news event, but this cannot be proved.

## TRANSCRIPTION CONVENTIONS

Interview excerpts have been transcribed using the following conventions:

| | |
|---|---|
| pause in interview | ... |
| omission | ( ... ) |
| long omission | ( ... 2 pages) |
| interviewer's comments only omitted | [ ... ] |
| interviewee's emphasis | *underlined italics* |

# NOTES

1   Directed by Michael Myers, Paramount 1992.
2   For critiques of such assumptions, see Corner (1995: 43), Thompson (1993), Iris Marion Young (1990).
3   'It is not obvious why ordinary people go on television and little research has addressed this question' (Livingstone and Lunt, 1994: 116); 'virtually nothing is known about talk show participants' (Priest, 1995: 5).
4   On the distinction between different levels of naturalisation of the media's authority, see Silverstone (1983: 149).
5   For example, Callon and Latour (1981), Foucault (1979, 1981), Giddens (1984), Knorr-Cetina (1981).
6   For a parallel use of Garfinkel in studying spatial order, see Cresswell (1996: 21–2).
7   Note, however, that I use the term 'mediation' to cover any communicative medium, whether or not it has a mass audience. Hence, 'alternative forms of mediation' is used to mean any communicative practice which takes effect as an alternative to the communicative practices of 'the media' (as already defined).
8   Compare Bourdieu's point that symbolic power 'does not reside in "symbolic systems" in the form of an "illocutionary force" … but is defined in and through a given relation between those who exercise power and those who submit to it, i.e. in the very structure of the field in which belief is produced and reproduced' (1991: 70). For a more detailed discussion of how my argument relates to Bourdieu's work, see Chapter Three.
9   My emphasis. Melucci's use of the term 'naming' parallels Paolo Freire's earlier analysis of the 'Third World''s 'culture of silence' as an unequal share in the process of 'naming' (1972: 61–2).
10  Herbert Blumer long ago argued that the American 'mass media effects' tradition underestimated 'the interdependent connection of all forms of communication' (1969: 184).
11  One response to this problem is Cultivation Analysis' investigation of how long-term intense television viewing affects opinion formation (Signorielli and Morgan, 1990). However, the methodological problems with this approach have proved immense: McQuail (1994: 365–6), Silverstone (1994: 138–40).
12  Cf., for example, Morse (1990) on television's culture of 'everyday distraction' and Appadurai (1990) on 'mediascapes'.
13  Cf. Bausinger (1984), Comstock *et al.* (1978), Graber (1988), Kubey and Csikszentmihalyi (1990), Neuman and Pool (1986).
14  Cf. Raymond Williams's earlier argument that a dispersed society needs 'images … of what living is now like' (1975: 9).
15  Cf. Durkheim (1984) and Thompson (1995, ch. 6) on the development of de-traditionalised 'common consciousness' in contemporary societies.
16  Recall here the arguments of Wrong (1961) and Mann (1970) on the dangers of over-estimating levels of socialisation.

17  Gray (1992), Lindlof (1987), Lull (1990), Morley (1986), Petrie and Willis (1995), Silverstone (1994), Silverstone and Hirsch (1992).
18  Cf. Baudrillard's early statement that 'the symbolic has slipped from the order of the … production of meaning to that of its *re*production, which is always the order of power' (1981: 174, original emphasis).
19  For recent discussion of Silverstone's argument, see Rothenbuhler (1998: 90–2)
20  I say 'largely' to allow for the multiplication of channels on cable and satellite, and now digital, television: cf. Chapter Nine.
21  On the wider history of the term 'frame', see MacLachlan and Reid (1994), Silverstone (1981: 75–7).
22  Compare Negt and Kluge (1993: 1–2) on the media's dual nature as both material organisational form ('objective') and 'general social horizon of experience' ('subjective').
23  Buckingham (1987: 170, 180; 1993: 224–7), Willis (1990: 33–6), and cf. Chapter Five.
24  Although I mention Gamson (1998) in the main text, this book arrived too late for me to take detailed account of it. It offers (especially in chapter 3) a brilliant analysis of what I call 'interactions with the media frame' in the conflict-ridden world of the US talk show.
25  There are of course also hierarchies within and between media institutions, but that is a separate issue.
26  For parallel arguments outside geography, see Foucault (1986), Deleuze and Guattari (1988).
27  From within geography (Burgess and Gold, 1985; Jackson, 1989; Clarke, 1995) and within media studies (Moores, 1993a).
28  Cf. more generally Radway (1988).
29  Cf. important recent work on the symbolic aspects of how social space is organised (Sibley, 1995; Cresswell, 1996).
30  There is no room to discuss here the debates about whether the current period is best understood as 'postmodernity' or 'late modernity'; my sympathies lie with the latter position (cf. Fornas, 1995; Giddens, 1990).
31  For discussion of the 1990s Australian series *Sylvania Waters* along similar lines, see Stratton and Ang (1994).
32  The same, perhaps, could be argued of Vattimo's (1992) optimistic theory that mediated society is more 'transparent' than previous societies.
33  Cf. Schutz's (1973a) concept of 'multiple realities' in social interaction and cf. generally Ferguson (1990), Thompson (1995: 100–20).
34  Mintel survey quoted in *Guardian*, 11 September, 1997.
35  *The Times*, 23 July 1998.
36  There are similar tourist sites in other countries: for example, the Irish location for the television drama *Ballykissangel*, and the site where the German soap *Lindenstrasse* is filmed.
37  Tourism similarly is growing to fictional locations ('literary landscapes' such as 'Hardy's Wessex' and 'Catherine Cookson Country') (see Rojek, 1993) and locations associated with the music industry (from the Beatles' childhood homes to the tree where Marc Bolan crashed). Similarly, the British Tourist Authority issued in 1998 a map of 'Rock and Pop Locations'.
38  For brief comments on the second type, see Altheide (1985: 46–50). The largest relevant literature relates to Disney sites (for a review, see Bryman, 1995), but this gives very little attention to aspects directly linked to media production and filming (i.e. MGM Studios). Even the best discussion in this general area (Rojek,1993) does not discuss sites of media *production*. For important research on tourism to North American film locations, see Hills (1999).
39  Dayan and Katz (1992). Cf. Becker (1995), MacAloon (1984), Real (1975).
40  Moore (1980) discusses Disney sites in terms of pilgrimage, but with no mention of media aspects of this process. For the application of 'pilgrimage' to secular journeys more generally, see Reader and Walter (1993).
41  There are limited exceptions: The Project on Disney (1995), Real (1977), Wasko (1996: 364–6).
42  For the complexity and importance of this term, see Chapter Three.

43 The Umbrella Man's actions are a special case, explained further in Chapter Eight.

44 Gitlin (1980) on the 1960s/1970s US student movement; Halloran, Elliott and Murdock's (1970) study of a major London demonstration; Philo's (1990) study of the influence of media coverage of the 1984–5 Miners' Strike.

45 There are of course doubts about the validity of Bourdieu's deterministic model of social reproduction itself (Garnham, 1994: 179–83; R. Jenkins, 1992; cf. Couldry, 1995: 104–5).

46 On Bourdieu's neglect of the mass media, see Garnham (1994: 187), Silverstone (1994: 117). Bourdieu's recent analysis of television (1996) remains a partial, not a total, theory.

47 On which, see Lull (1991) (China), Sreberny-Mohammadi and Mohammadi (1994) (Iran), Wark (1994: 49–74) (East Germany), Downing (1995) (the former USSR).

48 I say 'more or less' to allow for videotaping 'off air'. In Chapter Nine, I argue that this does not necessarily undermine framing, and may in fact reinforce it.

49 They must become part of what Bourdieu calls *l'extraordinaire ordinaire* (1996: 19).

50 As one interviewee quoted by Livingstone and Lunt (1994: 119) put it.

51 Quoted in the *Independent on Sunday*, 16 July 1995.

52 Respectively: Granada Studios Tour ('GST') brochures (1988, 1989), BBC Experience leaflet (1997).

53 *New York Times*, 25 November 1963, quoted in Schwartz (1974: 865).

54 Brunsdon and Morley (1978: 22), Goldie (1977: 215), Hall (1973: 22–3), Root (1986: 91–4), Scannell and Cardiff (1991: 170).

55 Brunsdon and Morley (1978: 65–7), Hall (1973: 28).

56 Dahlgren (1981), Edelman (1988: 34–6, 97–9).

57 This was illustrated recently by a report of a British Medical Association survey which claimed that only 15 per cent of adults trusted 'journalists', but 74 per cent trusted 'newscasters': *Daily Mirror*, 26 January 1999.

58 On 'actuality', see Feuer (1983), Rath (1989: 86–8): cf. Brunsdon and Morley (1978: 27) on the 'myth of "the nation, now"' and Hall (1981: 242) on news photography's 'historic instantaneous'. On 'history', compare also Gamson's argument that it is media coverage that gives social groups the sense 'that they matter – they are making history' (1995: 94).

59 Ericson *et al.* (1987, 1991), Glasgow University Media Group (1976), Hall (1974), Young (1974).

60 Brooker-Gross (1983), Dominick (1977), Golding (1981).

61 The history of the 1920s BBC Radio Station in Manchester '2ZY' suggests a rather different type of audience involvement. Audience members, for instance, sometimes went into 2ZY, as if it was any other public space, a contrast with the distance between audiences and producers which soon became standard (Scannell and Cardiff, 1991: 311–14).

62 See, for UK television, Buckingham (1987), Burns (1977), Elliott (1972), Schlesinger (1978), Tunstall (1993); (for US news journalism) Gans (1980); and (for US TV entertainment) Espinosa (1982), Gamson (1994).

63 The studio audience is only an apparent exception to this since they have no control over the studio's production resources.

64 Magazines such as *Hello* and *OK* in Britain, and *People* in the USA, are interesting sites of exchange between categories of 'media people'.

65 Billig formulates a similar paradox in relation to royalty: '"we" might desire the privileges, but if "our" wish were granted "we" would not be "us"' (1992: 132).

66 As mentioned earlier, I will not attempt a full-scale analysis of the media as a 'field' in Bourdieu's sense. The concept of 'field' raises, as yet, too many unresolved questions (cf. R. Jenkins, 1992: 89): are 'the media' one field or many? If many, what is the relation between those fields? What is the relation between the media field(s) and other fields of symbolic capital (literature, art, music, and so on)? Are the media better understood as a general 'symbolic system' (Bourdieu, 1991: 168–70) like the educational system, which generates 'symbolic capital' (media status) for use in particular symbolic fields (cf. Mills, 1956: ch. 4; Priest, 1995:

169–70)? If so, how do we integrate the impacts of the media role in *representing* the whole social space? Have the media begun to redefine what is at stake in every field (as Bourdieu's recent (1996) work on the media suggests)? If that is true, what is the standing now of Bourdieu's earlier model of class and social reproduction?

67   Quoted in *Inside Soap*, April 1994.

68   Respectively by the programme's main star (quoted in H. Jenkins, 1992: 10) and the police (interview with author).

69   This incidentally raises the question of whether stories about fans who send wreaths to dead characters are quite the simple evidence of pathology they are normally taken for: see Chapter Five.

70   *Guardian*, 6–7 May 1998.

71   See Abercrombie *et al.* (1980) on the problems of arguments from 'dominant ideology'.

72   Note that it is specifically media power I am discussing – the authority of media institutions – not simply the habit of media consumption, although important issues arise about that too: see Lodziak (1987) for an excellent treatment.

73   Cf. Bill Bryson's comment in his popular English travel diary: '[it was] a profoundly thrilling experience to walk up and down this famous street' (1996: 229).

74   In GST's exhibition of video clips from the programme, a former cast member is scripted to say: 'I hope you enjoy your time on the Street as much as I did mine'.

75   On media-related performativity, see Abercrombie and Longhurst (1998: 78–96), Chaney (1994: 170–71, 197).

76   Depending on discounts, approximately £10–15 per adult.

77   Recalled by some visitors not as incidental background, but as 'memorabilia' (Julie), 'a history of the Street' (Susan).

78   Not surprisingly, Granada's (1996) brochure for the Blackpool 'Experience' has it both ways: offering a visit to 'the hallowed cobbles' (of the set replica), while encouraging people to visit afterwards the 'actual Street itself' at GST!

79   When John first visited the Street set you could *only* enter from the video room: it constituted the end of the 'tour'. Later, to John's dismay, you could approach the Street from any angle, without seeing the video footage first.

80   Admittedly, Smith's account of the ritual water/wine and my own (and John's) account of the rain on the set place the emphasis differently. The first emphasises the *change* in status which a ritual location has on the water/wine, while the second concentrates on the rain on the set and emphasises that it is *both* ordinary and (since on the set) special. This is simply to focus on different moments in structurally similar processes.

81   See for example this comment in John Urry's important book on the 'tourist gaze' (1990: 145, quoting Goodwin, 1989): 'as one commentator noted: "when we develop our photos of that Rovers' Return scenario we will consume a representation of a representation of a representation"'.

82   There is, however, nothing like the level of uncertainty found at Disney sites, which are so vast that even natural phenomena get interpreted as Disney constructions (Fjellman, 1992: ch. 13; The Project on Disney, 1995: 46).

83   Cf. accounts of standing speechless and motionless on meeting music stars (Vermorel and Vermorel, 1985: 122–4).

84   Cf. the Bay City Rollers fan quoted by the Vermorels (1985: 148): 'I don't think there's any chance I could go out with a Roller. Go up and talk to them maybe, and maybe sit in a cafe and see them around. '

85   John Langer has, quite independently, argued that news stories of royals spontaneously doing 'ordinary' things confirm our sense of royals' extraordinariness: the same things done by 'ordinary people' would not be noteworthy at all (1998: 60).

86   Cf. John Fiske's analysis of the 'popular cultural capital' of fandom which he argues is associated less with interest in the text than in the production process (1991: 49). Unlike Fiske,

however, I prefer to analyse such capital as part of the same field of capital involved in the media production process, rather than as a 'shadow cultural economy' (ibid.).

87  'Actual' and 'actually' are complex words. The relevant meanings here are: '*actual* . . . existing in act or fact; real . . .' ; and '*actually*. 1. as a fact; really . . . 4. as a matter of fact; indeed; even (strange as it may seem) . . .' (from the *New Shorter Oxford English Dictionary*, Oxford: Clarendon Press, 1993, vol. 1). Particularly relevant is the definition 'even (strange as it may seem)'. The usage I analyse marks off what is 'strange, but true' in precisely this way.

88  Cf. Bennett (1995: 243) on Blackpool Pleasure Beach and The Project on Disney (1995: 5) on Disney sites, for similar conclusions.

89  Again my emphasis here is rather different from Fiske (1991).

90  Cf. Schwartz (1974) on the connection between the differential value of people's or institutions' 'time', and wider power differentials.

91  Recall here television's professional ideology: its claim to present 'real life' with the 'boring bits' cut out.

92  Respectively: *Radio Times*, 24–30 May 1997; Vermorel and Vermorel (1985: 234–5); Gamson (1994: 134).

93  On the imaginary continuity of soaps, see Geraghty (1981).

94  For an unusual personal account by a non-media person of appearing on television, which has similar implications, see Gould (1984). Diana Gould is remembered in recent British political history as the woman who challenged Margaret Thatcher on a live phone-in about the location of the Argentinian warship, the *Belgrano*, when it was destroyed by the British navy during the Falklands War in 1982.

95  In March 1997 BBC2 broadcast a programme on people following *The Chris Evans Road Show*. Its title *Six Go Mad in Somerset* repeats the usual pathologisation.

96  The same applies to individual activists and Pure Genius residents discussed in Chapter Eight.

97  Cf. from Shoreham: 'every day we witness scenes which before many have only seen on television or in films' (Stephens and Shehata, 1995: 91).

98  For such sudden confrontations with 'reality', cf. the Jarrow Marches against unemployment in 1930s Britain which 'took poverty to the people that didn't know poverty existed' (marcher quoted in Pickard, 1982: 89).

99  Cf. comments from Shoreham in Stephens and Shehata (1995: 42, 91).

100 Almost half the interview sample commented on police surveillance. Cf. from Shoreham: Stephens and Shehata (1995: 8, 12, 14, 32, 91).

101 Those who mentioned this were all women and in all but one case working-class. I cannot deal here with the wider significance of the protests for gender relations. While anger at gender stereotyping was shown in some interviews (three cases), views on whether gender was important to the meaning of the protests were mixed: some women felt it important (four cases), others did not (three cases).

102 The first, third and fourth types correspond to Benton and Redfearn's useful, if brief, analysis (1996: 55–6).

103 Since Harry was in his seventies, this example may reflect the higher degree of trust in television news by older people which Philo suggests (1990: 149). The sample is not decisive on this. However, the general decline in trust in the media affected the whole sample, as we shall see.

104 Thanks to Dave Morley for lending me transcripts of interviews by Charles Parker given to him before the latter's death.

105 Cf. from Shoreham: 'instead of finding fanatics and thugs, I found people very like myself' (Stephens and Shehata, 1995: 3).

106 Cf. from Shoreham: 'We are judged by being down there. No thought is given to what we are as individuals' (ibid.: 23).

107 Ironically Brightlingsea's contradiction of stereotypes generated a new stereotype in the national press: the idea of 'Middle England' protesting or (a gendered version) 'middle-aged

housewives' (as Stephanie sardonically put it). Often, this simply reversed the original stereotype: instead of saying that the 'real' protesters weren't 'normal', it was implied that protesters who were 'normal' weren't 'real protesters'.

108  Differences in how particular media are trusted might have been significant here, but were not brought out by interviewees.

109  I say 'consumption of *news*' because this was the context in which such comments were made, although this was not a qualification people tended to make themselves.

110  The latter was in the room for part of the interview.

111  Four people said what they watched had changed since the protests, but to establish this would need further investigation: it was not, as already mentioned, my main concern.

112  On the sense that being in a mediated event gives you participation in 'history', see Gamson (1995: 94).

113  A colloquial English term for a woman who is employed to stop the traffic to allow schoolchildren to cross the road.

114  On the incompatibility of a protester's perspective on events with that of a viewer, cf. Ellis (1982: 166).

115  This might sound like a critique of the media, but I am not claiming there is a completely unmediated 'reality' underlying media representations. The point is how for Rachel the reality of the media as a mechanism of representation came to be articulated against the background of its usual naturalisation.

116  'Just do it' perhaps also echoes 'Do it', a catchphrase of the Yippies, media activists in 1960s America (Rubin, 1970).

117  Cf. Gamson (1995: 89) and more generally Goffman (1975). Note that different senses of the term 'frame' converge here: narrative 'frame', the 'frame' within which actions make sense, the (ritual) 'frame' of the social in Douglas' and Silverstone's sense, and my own particular usage of 'the media frame' as a more general social formation. Cf. Chapter One.

118  Approximately 40–60 people lived there at any one time, but with a considerable turnover; in the first week, numbers were higher (around 200), hence the overall phrase, 'a few hundred'. See Featherstone (1997).

119  Cf. Butler (1996: 342–53).

120  The image of 'tree-protesters' has been adopted as a (positive?) stereotype in advertising (for mobile phones, warming soups) and in soaps (Coronation Street).

121  The movement for media democratisation that followed the events of 1968, involving Godard, Agence-Presse Liberation, and so on (Barbrook, 1995: ch. 6).

122  Thompson (1995: 247).

123  For a fascinating study of relevant issues among young people in west London's South Asian community, see Gillespie (1995).

124  Cf. the important collection of essays in Silverstone and Hirsch (1992).

125  Few people use VCRs to record news (Levy and Gunter, 1988: 26–8).

126  Bondebjerg (1996), Dovey (1996: 124–31), Kilborn (1994), Langer (1998: 160–9), Schlesinger and Tumber (1994: Ch. 9).

127  'Television will change from a passive one-way street to an exciting two-way information tool and will revolutionise how viewers regard the television set' (BSkyB spokesman quoted, *Guardian*, 8 May 1997).

128  Office for National Statistics (1997: 151, 154), and more recently an ICM poll reported in the *Guardian*, 11 January 1999.

129  According to one Web users' survey, 70 per cent were male (quoted *Guardian*, 12 December 1996, Online section).

130  This shift is beginning to be reflected by, for example, film studies (Hansen, 1991).

131  See, for an interesting new approach to media 'textuality', Hartley (1996).

132  Ferguson and Golding (1997), Garnham (1995), Grossberg (1995).

133  Cf. Kellner's (1997) proposal for a 'multiperspectival' cultural study which includes both

approaches. We should, in any case, be sceptical about absolute divisions between the 'cultural' and the 'economic' or 'material' (Sahlins, 1976).

134  This was not my original intention: I had intended that many off-site interviews would be follow-ups of site interviews. But I had overestimated the extent to which visitors would make a time-commitment to a stranger in the course of what was a day *off* from commitments!

# BIBLIOGRAPHY

Abercrombie, Nicholas (1996) *Television and Society*, Cambridge: Polity Press.

Abercrombie, Nicholas, Hill, Stephen and Turner, Brian (1980) *The Dominant Ideology Thesis*, London: Allen & Unwin.

Abercrombie, Nicholas and Longhurst, Brian (1998) *Audiences: A Sociological Theory of Performance and Imagination,* London: Sage.

Agnew, John (1987) *Place and Politics: The Geographical Mediation of State and Society*, Winchester, Mass.: Allen & Unwin.

Alasuutari, Pertti (1995) *Researching Culture: Qualitative Method and Cultural Studies*, London: Sage.

Alberoni, Francesco (1972) 'The Powerless "Elite": Theory and Sociological Research on the Phenomenon of the Stars' in Denis McQuail (ed.) *Sociology of Mass Communications*, Harmondsworth: Penguin.

Altheide, David (1985) *Media Power*, Beverly Hills: Sage.

Altheide, David and Snow, Robert (1979) *Media Logic*, Beverly Hills: Sage.

Althusser, Louis (1969) 'Ideology and Ideological State Apparatuses (Notes Towards an Investigation)' in *Lenin and Philosophy and Other Essays* tr. B. Brewster, New York: Monthly Review Press.

Anderson, Christopher (1994) 'Disneyland' in Horace Newcomb (ed.) *Television: The Critical View* 5th edition, New York: Oxford University Press.

Ang, Ien (1996) *Living Room Wars: Rethinking Media Audiences For A Postmodern World*, London: Routledge.

Appadurai, Arjun (1990) 'Disjuncture and Difference in the Global Cultural Economy' in Mike Featherstone (ed.) *Global Culture: Nationalism, Globalisation, and Modernity*, London: Sage.

Auge, Marc (1995) *Non-Places: Introduction to an Anthropology of Supermodernity* tr. J. Howe, London: Verso.

Babcock, Barbara (ed.) (1978) *The Reversible World: Symbolic Inversion in Art and Society*, Ithaca and London: Cornell University Press.

Bacon-Smith, Camille (1992) *Enterprising Women: Television Fandom and The Creation of Popular Myth*, Philadelphia: University of Pennsylvania Press.

Bakhtin, Mikhail (1984) [o.p. 1965] *Rabelais and His World* tr. H. Iswolsky, Bloomington: Indiana University Press.

Barbrook, Richard (1995) *Media Freedom: The Contradictions of Communication in the Age of Modernity*, London: Pluto.

Barthes, Roland (1973) *Mythologies*, London: Paladin.
—— (1977) 'Rhetoric of the Image' in *Image-Music-Text*, London: Fontana.
Barwise, Patrick and Ehrenberg, Andrew (1988) *Television and its Audience*, London: Sage.
Baudrillard, Jean (1981) [1969] 'Requiem for the Media' in *For a Critique of the Political Economy of the Sign* tr. C. Nevin, St Louis: Telos Press.
—— (1983a) *Simulations* tr. P. Foss, P. Patton and P. Beitchman, New York: Semiotext[e].
—— (1983b) *In the Shadow of the Silent Majorities, Or, The End of the Social and Other Essays* tr. P. Foss, J. Johnston and P. Patton, New York: Semiotext[e].
Bausinger, Hermann (1984) 'Media, Technology and Daily Life', *Media, Culture and Society*, 6(4): 343–52.
Beck, Ulrich (1992) *Risk Society: Towards A New Modernity* tr. M. Ritter, London: Sage.
Becker, Karin (1995) 'Media and the Ritual Process', *Media, Culture and Society*, 17(4): 629–46.
Benhabib, Seyla (1992) 'Models of Public Space: Hannah Arendt, the Liberal Tradition and Jürgen Habermas' in Craig Calhoun (ed.) *Habermas and the Public Sphere*, Cambridge, Mass.: The MIT Press.
Benjamin, Walter (1968) 'The Work of Art in the Age of Mechanical Reproduction' in *Illuminations* tr. H. Zohn, New York: Schocken Books.
Bennett, Tony (1995) *The Birth of the Museum: History, Theory, Politics*, London: Routledge.
Benton, Ted and Redfearn, Simon (1996) 'The Politics of Animal Rights – Where is the Left?', *New Left Review*, 215: 43–58.
Billig, Michael (1992) *Talking of the Royal Family*, London: Routledge.
—— (1995) *Banal Nationalism*, London: Sage.
—— (1997) 'From Codes to Utterances: Cultural Studies, Discourse and Psychology' in Marjorie Ferguson and Peter Golding (eds) *Cultural Studies in Question*, London: Sage.
Blumer, Herbert (1969) [o.p. 1959] *Symbolic Interactionism: Perspective and Method*, Englewood Cliffs, NJ: Prentice Hall.
Blumler, Jay, and Gurevitch, Michael (1995) *The Crisis of Public Communication*, London: Routledge.
Bondebjerg, Ib (1996) 'Public Discourse/Private Fascination: Hybridisation in "True-life-story" Genres', *Media, Culture and Society*, 18(1): 27–45.
Boorstin, Daniel (1961) *The Image – Or What Happened to the American Dream*, London: Weidenfeld and Nicholson.
Bourdieu, Pierre (1973) 'Cultural Reproduction and Social Reproduction' in R. Brown (ed.) *Knowledge, Education and Cultural Change*, London: Tavistock.
—— (1977) *Outline of a Theory of Practice* tr. R. Nice, Cambridge: Cambridge University Press.
—— (1991) *Language and Symbolic Power* tr. G. Raymond and M. Adamson, Cambridge: Polity.
—— (1992) [with Terry Eagleton] 'Doxa and Common Life', *New Left Review*, 191: 111–121.
—— (1993) 'The Production of Belief' in *The Field of Cultural Production*, Cambridge: Polity Press.
—— (1996) *Sur la Télévision*, Paris: Liber.
—— (1998) *On Television and Journalism*, London: Pluto [English translation of Bourdieu (1996)]
Bourdieu, Pierre and Passeron, Jean-Claude (1977) *Reproduction in Education, Society and Culture*, London: Sage.

Brecht, Bertolt (1979–80) [o.p. 1932] 'Radio as a Means of Communication – A Talk on the Function of Radio' tr. S. Hood, *Screen* , 20(3–4): 24–28.

Brett, Guy (1986) *Through Our Own Eyes: Popular Art and Modern History*, London: GMP Publishers.

Brooker-Gross, Susan (1983) 'Spatial Aspects of Newsworthiness', *Geografisker Annaler*, 65B: 1–9.

Brown, Mary Ellen (1994) *Soap Opera and Women's Talk: The Pleasure of Resistance*, Beverly Hills: Sage.

Brunn, Stanley and Leinbach, Thomas (1991) 'Introduction' in Stanley Brunn and Thomas Leinbach (eds) *Collapsing Space and Time: Geographic Aspects of Communications and Information*, London: HarperCollins.

Brunsdon, Charlotte and Morley, David (1978) *Everyday Television: Nationwide*, London: British Film Institute.

Bryman, Alan (1988) *Quantity and Quality in Social Research*, London: Unwin Hyman.

—— (1995) *Disney and His Worlds*, London and New York: Routledge.

Bryson, Bill (1996) *Notes From a Small Island*, London: Black Swan.

Buckingham, David (1987) *Public Secrets: Eastenders and Its Audience*, London: BFI Publishing.

—— (1993) *Children Talking Television: The Making of Television Literacy*, London: The Falmer Press.

—— (1997) 'Dissin' Disney: Critical Perspectives on Children's Media Culture', *Media, Culture and Society*, 19(2): 285–93.

Burgess, Jacquelin and Gold, Peter (eds) (1985) *Geography, The Media and Popular Culture*, London: Croom Helm.

Burns, Tom (1977) *The BBC: Public Institution and Private World*, London: Macmillan.

Butler, Beverley (1996) 'The Tree, The Town and The Shaman – The Material Culture of Resistance of the No M11 Link Roads Protest of Wanstead and Leytonstone, London', *Journal of Material Culture*, 1(3): 337–64.

Caldwell, John (1996) *Televisuality: Style, Crisis, and Authority in American Television*, New Brunswick: Rutgers University Press.

Calhoun, Craig (ed.) (1992) *Habermas and the Public Sphere*, Cambridge, Mass.: The MIT Press.

Callon, Michel and Latour, Bruno (1981) 'Unscrewing the Big Leviathan: How Actors Macro-structure Reality and How Sociologists Help Them to Do So' in Karin Knorr-Cetina and Alvin Cicourel (eds) *Advances in Social Theory and Methodology: Toward an Integration of Micro- and Macro-sociologies*, London: Routledge & Kegan Paul.

Callon, Michel, Law, John and Rip, Arie (1986) 'Putting Texts in their Place' in Michel Callon, John Law and Arie Rip (eds.) *Mapping the Dynamics of Science and Technology: Sociology of Science in the Real World*, London: Macmillan, 221–30.

Camauer, Leonor (forthcoming) 'Women's Movements, Public Spheres and the Media' in Liesbet Van Zoonen and Annabelle Sreberny-Mohammadi (eds) *Women's Politics and Communication*, Cresskill, NJ: The Hampton Press.

Cantor, Muriel and Cantor, Joel (1992) *Prime Television: Content and Control* 2nd edition, Newbury Park: Sage.

Carey, James (1989) *Communications as Culture: Essays on Media and Society*, Boston: Unwin Hyman.

Castells, Manuel (1996) *The Rise of the Network Society*, Oxford: Blackwell.

Chaney, David (1994) *The Cultural Turn: Scene-Setting Essays in Contemporary Cultural History*, London: Routledge.

Christy, Desmond (1998) 'Confessions of a TV Reviewer', *Guardian*, 7 April 1998, G2: 19.

Clarke, David (1995) 'Space, Time and Media Theory: An Illustration from the Television-Advertising Nexus', *Environment and Planning D: Society and Space*, 13(5): 557–72.

Clifford, James (1990) 'Travelling Cultures' in Lawrence Grossberg, Cary Nelson, and Paula Treichler (eds) *Cultural Studies*, New York: Routledge.

Comstock, George, Chaffee, Steven, Katzman, Natan, McCombs, Maxwell and Roberts, Donald (1978) *Television and Human Behavior*, New York: Columbia University Press.

Connerton, Paul (1989) *How Societies Remember*, Cambridge: Cambridge University Press.

Cook, Alice and Kirk, Gwyn (1983) *Greenham Women Everywhere: Dreams, Ideas and Actions From the Women's Peace Movement*, London: Pluto Press.

Corcoran, Farrel (1987) 'Television as Ideological Apparatus: The Power and the Pleasure' in Horace Newcomb (ed.) *Television: The Critical View* 4th edition, New York: Oxford University Press.

Corner, John (1995) *Television Form and Public Address*, London: Edward Arnold.

—— (1997) 'Television in Theory', *Media, Culture and Society*, 19(2): 247–62.

Corner, John and Richardson, Kay (1986) 'Documentary Meanings and the Discourse of Interpretation' in John Corner (ed.) *Documentary and the Mass Media*, London: Edward Arnold.

Couldry, Nick (1995) 'Speaking Up in a Public Place: The Strange Case of Rachel Whiteread's *House*', *New Formations*, 25: 96–113.

—— (1998a) 'The View from Inside the Simulacrum: Visitors' Tales from the Set of *Coronation Street*', *Leisure Studies*, 17(2): 94–107.

—— (1998b) *Sites of Power, Journeys of Discovery: Place and Power in the Hierarchy of the Media Frame*, unpublished PhD dissertation, University of London.

—— (1999a) 'Remembering Diana: The Geography of Celebrity and the Politics of Lack', *New Formations*, 36: 77–91.

—— (1999b) 'Disrupting the Media Frame at Greenham Common: A New Chapter in the History of Mediations?', *Media, Culture and Society*, 21(3): 337–58.

—— (forthcoming) 'Media Organisations and Non-Media People' in James Curran (ed.) *Media Organisations*, London: Arnold.

Cresswell, Tim (1996) *In Place/Out of Place: Geography, Ideology and Transgression*, Minneapolis: University of Minnesota Press.

Cubitt, Sean (1991) *Timeshift: On Video Culture*, London: Routledge.

Curran, James (1982) 'Communications, Power and Social Order' in Michael Gurevitch, Tony Bennett, James Curran and Janet Woollacott (eds) *Culture, Society and the Media*, London and New York: Routledge.

—— (1998) 'Crisis of Public Communication: A Reappraisal' in Tamar Liebes and James Curran (eds) *Media, Ritual and Identity*, London: Routledge.

Curran, James and Seaton, Jean (1997) *Power Without Responsibility: The Press and Broadcasting in Britain* 5th edition, London: Routledge.

Dahlgren, Peter (1981) 'TV News and the Suppression of Reflexivity' in Elihu Katz and Tamas Szecsko (eds) *Mass Media and Social Change*, London: Sage.

—— (1995) *Television and The Public Sphere*, London: Sage.

Davis, Susan (1996) 'The Theme Park: Global Industry and Cultural Form', *Media, Culture and Society*, 18(3): 399–422.

Dayan, Daniel and Katz, Elihu (1992) *Media Events: The Live Broadcasting of History*, Cambridge, Mass.: Harvard University Press.

Debord, Guy (1983) [1967] *Society of the Spectacle* (various translators), Detroit: Black & Red.

de Certeau, Michel (1984) *The Practice of Everyday Life* tr. S. Rendall, Berkeley: University of California Press.

Deegan, Mary (1989) *American Ritual Dramas: Social Rules and Cultural Meanings*, New York: Greenwood Press.

Deleuze, Gilles and Felix Guattari (1988) *A Thousand Plateaus: Capitalism and Schizophrenia* tr. B. Massumi, London: Athlone Press.

Denzin, Norman (1978) *The Research Act: A Theoretical Introduction to Sociological Methods* 2nd edition, New York: McGraw Hill.

Dominick, Joseph (1977) 'Geographical Bias in National Television News', *Journal of Communication*, 27(4): 94–9.

Douglas, Mary (1984) [o.p. 1966] *Purity and Danger: An Analysis of Concepts of Pollution and Taboo,* London: Ark Paperbacks.

Dovey, John (1996) 'The Revelation of Unguessed Worlds' in Jon Dovey (ed.) *Fractal Dreams*, London: Lawrence & Wishart.

Dowmunt, Tony (1993) 'Introduction' in Tony Dowmunt (ed.) *Channels of Resistance*, London: British Film Institute.

Downing, John (1995) 'Media, Dictatorship and the Reemergence of "Civil Society"' in John Downing, Ali Mohammadi, and Annabelle Sreberny-Mohammadi (eds) *Questioning the Media: A Critical Introduction* 2nd edition, Thousand Oaks: Sage.

Drew, Jesse (1995) 'Media Activism and Radical Democracy' in James Brook and Iain Boal (eds) *Resisting the Virtual Life: The Culture and Politics of Information*, San Francisco: City Lights Books.

Drotner, Kirsten (1993) 'Media Ethnography: An Other Story?' in Ulla Carlsson (ed.) *Nordisk Forskning om Kvinnor och Medier*, Gothenberg: Nordicom.

Durkheim, Emile (1984) [1893] *The Division of Labour in Society* tr. W. Halls, London: Macmillan.

—— (1995) [o.p. 1912] *The Elementary Forms of Religious Life* tr. K. Fields, Glencoe: Free Press.

Dyer, Richard (1979) *Stars*, London: British Film Institute.

—— (1986) *Heavenly Bodies: Film Stars and Society*, London: Macmillan.

—— (1992) [1977] 'Entertainment and Utopia' in *Only Entertainment*, London and New York: Routledge.

Dyer, Richard, Geraghty, Christine, Jordan, Marion, Lovell, Terry, Paterson, Richard and Stewart, John (1981) *Coronation Street*, London: British Film Institute.

Eco, Umberto (1986) *Faith in Fakes*, London: Secker and Warburg.

Edelman, Murray (1988) *Constructing the Political Spectacle*, Chicago: University of Chicago Press.

Elliott, Philip (1972) *The Making of a Television Series: A Case Study in the Sociology of Culture*, London: Constable.

—— (1980) 'Press Performance as Political Ritual' in H. Christian (ed.) *The Sociology of Journalism and the Press* [Sociological Review Monograph 29], Keele: University of Keele.

Ellis, John (1982) *Visible Fictions: Cinema: Television: Video*, London: Routledge.

Engelman, Ralph (1996) *Public Radio and Television in America: A Political History*, Thousand Oaks: Sage.

Enzensberger, Hans Magnus (1972) 'Constituents of a Theory of the Media' in Denis McQuail (ed.) *Sociology of Mass Communications*, Harmondsworth: Penguin.

Ericson, Richard, Baranek, Patricia, and Chan, Janet (1987) *Visualising Deviance: A Study of News Organization*, Milton Keynes: Open University Press.

—— (1991) *Representing Order: Crime, Law, and Justice in the News Media*, Milton Keynes: Open University Press.

Espinosa, Paul (1982) 'The Audience in the Text: Ethnographic Observations of a Holly-wood Story Conference', *Media, Culture and Society*, 14(1): 77–86.

Essex County Council (1993) *1991 Census Ward Monitor – Tendring District*, Chelmsford: Essex County Council.

Fairclough, Norman (1989) *Language and Power*, London: Longman.

—— (1995) *Media Discourse*, London: Arnold.

Fairclough, Norman and Wodak, Ruth (1997) 'Critical Discourse Analysis' in Teun van Dijk (ed.) *Discourse as Social Interaction*, London: Sage.

Featherstone, Simon (1997) 'Reimagining the Inhuman City: The "Pure Genius" Land Occupation', *Soundings*, 7: 45–60.

Ferguson, Marjorie (1990) 'Electronic Media and the Redefining of Time and Space' in Marjorie Ferguson (ed.) *Public Communication: The New Imperatives: Future Directions for Media Research*, London: Sage.

Ferguson, Marjorie and Golding, Peter (1997) 'Cultural Studies and Changing Times: An Introduction' in M. Ferguson and P. Golding (eds) *Cultural Studies in Question*, London: Sage, xiii–xxvii.

Feuer, Jane (1983) 'The Concept of Live Television: Ontology as Ideology' in E. Ann Kaplan (ed.) *Regarding Television: Critical Approaches – An Anthology*, Los Angeles: The American Film Institute.

Fiske, John (1987) *Television Culture*, London: Methuen.

—— (1991) 'The Cultural Economy of Fandom' in Lisa Lewis (ed.) *The Adoring Audience*, London: Routledge.

Fjellman, Stephen (1992) *Vinyl Leaves: Walt Disney World and America*, Boulder: Westview Press.

Fornäs, Johan (1995) *Cultural Theory and Late Modernity*, London: Sage.

Foucault, Michel (1979) *Discipline and Punish: The Birth of the Prison* tr. A. Sheridan, Harmondsworth: Peregrine.

—— (1981) *The History of Sexuality: An Introduction* tr. R. Hurley, Harmondsworth: Penguin.

—— (1986) 'Of Other Places', *Diacritics*, 16(1): 22–7.

Fraser, Nancy (1992) 'Rethinking the Public Sphere: A Contribution to the Critique of Actually Existing Democracy' in Craig Calhoun (ed.) *Habermas and The Public Sphere*, Cambridge, Mass.: The MIT Press.

Frederick, Howard (1994) 'Networks and the Emergence of Global Civil Society' in Linda Harasim (ed.) *Global Networks: Computers and International Communication*, Cambridge, Mass.: The MIT Press.

Freire, Paolo (1972) *Pedagogy of the Oppressed* tr. M. Ramos, Harmondsworth: Penguin.

Fukuyama, Francis (1995) *Trust: The Social Virtues and the Creation of Prosperity*, Harmondsworth: Penguin.

Gamson, Joshua (1994) *Claims to Fame: Celebrity in Contemporary America*, Berkeley: University of California Press.

—— (1998) *Freaks Talk Back: Tabloid Talk Shows and Sexual Nonconformity*, Chicago: University of Chicago Press.

Gamson, William (1995) 'Constructing Social Protest' in Hank Johnston and Bert Klandermans (eds) *Social Movements and Culture*, London: UCL Press.

Gans, Herbert (1980) *Deciding What's News: A Study of CBS Evening News, NBC Nightly News, Newsweek and Time* 2nd edition, New York: Vintage.

Garfinkel, Harold (1967) *Studies in Ethnomethodology*, Englewood Cliffs, NJ: Prentice-Hall.

Garnham, Nicholas (1986) 'The Media and the Public Sphere' in P. Golding, G. Murdock, and P. Schlesinger (eds) *Communicating Politics: Mass Communications and the Political Process*, New York: Holmes and Meier.

—— (1992) 'The Media and the Public Sphere' in Craig Calhoun (ed.) *Habermas and the Public Sphere*, Cambridge, Mass.: The MIT Press.

—— (1994) 'Bourdieu, the Cultural Arbitrary and Television' in Craig Calhoun, Edward Lipuma and Moishe Postone (eds) *Bourdieu: Critical Perspectives*, Cambridge: Polity Press.

—— (1995) 'Political Economy and Cultural Studies: Reconciliation or Divorce?', *Critical Studies in Mass Communication*, 12(1): 62–71.

Geraghty, Christine (1981) 'The Continuous Serial – A Definition' in Richard Dyer, Christine Geraghty, Marion Jordan, Terry Lovell, Richard Paterson and John Stewart *Coronation Street*, London: British Film Institute.

—— (1991) *Women and Soap Opera: A Study of Prime-Time Soaps*, Cambridge: Polity Press.

Giddens, Anthony (1984) *The Constitution of Society*, Cambridge: Polity Press.

—— (1990) *The Consequences of Modernity*, Cambridge: Polity Press.

Gillespie, Marie (1995) *Television, Ethnicity and Cultural Change*, London: Routledge.

Gitlin, Todd (1980) *The Whole World is Watching: Mass Media in the Making and Unmaking of the New Left*, Berkeley: University of California Press.

—— (1987) 'Prime-Time Ideology: The Hegemonic Process in Television Entertainment' in Horace Newcomb (ed.) *Television: The Critical View* 4th edition, New York: Oxford University Press.

Glaser, Barney and Strauss, Anselm (1967) *The Discovery of Grounded Theory: Strategies for Qualitative Research*, London: Weidenfeld and Nicholson.

Glasgow University Media Group (1976) *Bad News*, London: Routledge & Kegan Paul.

Gledhill, Christine (ed.) (1991) *Stardom: Industry of Desire*, London: Routledge.

Goffman, Erving (1972) 'Where The Action Is' in *Interaction Ritual*, London: Allen Lane.

—— (1975) *Frame Analysis: An Essay on the Organisation of Experience*, Harmondsworth: Penguin.

Goldie, Grace Wyndham (1977) *Facing the Nation: Television and Politics 1936–1976*, London: Bodley Head.

Golding, Peter (1981) 'The Missing Dimensions: News Media and the Management of Social Change' in Elihu Katz and Tamas Szeksko (eds) *Mass Media and Social Change*, London: Sage.

Goodwin, Andrew (1989) 'Nothing Like the Real Thing', *New Statesman and Society*, 12 August.

Gould, Diana (1984) *On the Spot: The Sinking of the "Belgrano"*, London: Cecil Woolf.

Gouldner, Alvin (1962) '"Anti-Minotaur": The Myth of a Value-Free Sociology', *Social Problems*, 9: 199–213.

Graber, Doris (1988) *Processing the News: How People Tame the Information Tide* 2nd edition, London: Longman.

Gray, Ann (1992) *Video Playtime: The Gendering of a Leisure Technology*, London: Comedia/Routledge.

Gray, Herman (1995) *Watching Race: Television and the Struggle for "Blackness"*, Minneapolis and London: University of Minnesota Press.

Grindstaff, Laura (1997) 'Producing Trash, Class, and the Money Shot: A Behind-the-Scenes Account of Daytime TV Talk Shows' in James Lull and Stephen Hinerman (eds) *Media Scandals: Morality and Desire in the Popular Culture Marketplace*, Cambridge: Polity Press.

Gripsrud, Jostein (1995) *The Dynasty Years: Hollywood Television and Critical Media Studies*, London: Comedia/Routledge.

Grossberg, Lawrence, (1987) 'The In/Difference of Television', *Screen*, 28(2): 28–46.

—— (1995) 'Cultural Studies Versus Political Economy: Is Anyone Else Bored with This Debate?', *Critical Studies in Mass Communication*, 12(1): 72–81.

Gunter, Barrie and Winstone, Paul (1993) *Television: The Public's View (1992)*, London: John Libbey.

Habermas, Jürgen (1989) [1962] *The Structural Transformation of the Public Sphere* tr. T. Bürger, Cambridge: Polity Press.

Hagerstrand, Torsten (1975) 'Space, Time and Human Conditions' in A. Karlquist, L. Lundquist, and F. Snickars (eds) *Dynamic Allocation of Urban Space*, Farnborough: Saxon House.

—— (1978) 'Survival and Arena: On the Life History of Individuals in Relation to Their Environment' in Tommy Carlstein, Don Parkes, and Nigel Thrift (eds) *Human Activity and Time Geography* vol. 2, London: Edward Arnold.

Halbwachs, Maurice (1992) [o.p. 1924] *On Collective Memory* tr. L. Coser, Chicago: University of Chicago Press.

Hall, Stuart (1973) 'The "Structured Communication" of Events', Stencilled Occasional Paper no. 5, Birmingham: Centre for Contemporary Cultural Studies.

—— (1974) 'Deviance, Politics and the Media' in Paul Rock and Mary Mackintosh (eds) *Deviance and Social Control*, London: Tavistock.

—— (1977) 'Culture, The Media and "The Ideological Effect"' in James Curran, Michael Gurevitch and Janet Woollacott (eds) *Mass Communications and Society*, London: Edward Arnold.

—— (1980) 'Encoding/Decoding' in Stuart Hall, Dorothy Hobson, Andrew Lowe and Paul Willis (eds) *Culture, Media, Language*, London: Unwin Hyman.

—— (1981) 'The Determination of News Photographs' in S. Cohen and J. Young (eds) *The Manufacture of News*, 2nd edition, London: Constable.

—— (1982) 'The Rediscovery of "Ideology": Return of the Repressed in Media Studies' in Michael Gurevitch, Tony Bennett, James Curran and Janet Woollacott (eds) *Culture, Society and the Media*, London: Routledge.

Hall, Stuart, Critcher, Chas, Jefferson, Tony, Clarke, John and Roberts, Brian (1978) *Policing the Crisis: Mugging, The State, and Law and Order*, London: Macmillan.

Halloran, J., Elliott, Philip and Murdock, Graham (1970) *Demonstrations and Communication: A Case Study*, Harmondsworth: Penguin.

Hammersley, Martin (1989) *The Dilemma of Qualitative Method: Herbert Blumer and the Chicago Tradition*, London: Routledge.

Hammersley, Martin and Atkinson, Paul (1995) *Ethnography: Principles in Practice* 2nd edition, London: Routledge.

Handelman, Don (1990) *Models and Mirrors: Towards an Anthropology of Public Events*, Cambridge: Cambridge University Press.

Hansen, Miriam (1991) *Babel and Babylon: Spectatorship in American Silent Film*, Cambridge, Mass.: Harvard University Press.

Harding, Thomas (1997) *The Video Activist's Handbook*, London: Pluto.

Harford, Barbara and Hopkins, Sarah (1984) *Greenham Common: Women at the Wire*, London: The Women's Press.

Harrington, C. Lee, and Bielby, Denise (1995) *Soap Fans: Pursuing Pleasure and Making Meaning in Everyday Life*, Philadelphia: Temple University Press.

Hartley, John (1996) *Popular Reality*, London: Arnold.

Harvey, David (1989) *The Condition of Postmodernity: An Inquiry into the Origins of Cultural Change*, Oxford: Basil Blackwell.

Hay, James (1992) 'Afterword' in Robert Allen (ed.) *Channels of Discourse, Revisited: Television and Contemporary Criticism*, London: Routledge, 354–85.

—— (1996) 'Afterword' in James Hay, Lawrence Grossberg, and Ellen Wartella (eds) *The Audience and Its Landscape*, Boulder: Westview Press.

—— (1997) 'Piecing Together What Remains of the Cinematic City' in David Clarke (ed.) *The Cinematic City*, London: Routledge.

Hay, James, Grossberg, Lawrence and Wartella, Ellen (eds) (1996) *The Audience and Its Landscape*, Boulder: Westview Press.

Hayden, Dolores (1995) *The Power of Place: Urban Landscapes as Public History*, Cambridge, Mass.: The MIT Press.

Heidegger, Martin (1962) [o.p. 1927] *Being and Time* tr. J. Macquarie and E. Robinson, Oxford: Basil Blackwell.

Heritage, John (1984) *Garfinkel and Ethnomethodology*, Cambridge: Polity Press.

Hetherington, Kevin (1998) *Expressions of Identity*, London: Sage.

Hewison, Robert (1987) *The Heritage Industry*, London: Methuen.

Higson, Andrew (1984) 'Space, Place and Spectacle', *Screen*, 25(4–5): 2–21.

Hill, Christopher (1975) *The World Turned Upside Down: Radical Ideas During the English Revolution*, Harmondsworth: Pelican.

Hills, Matthew (1999) *The Dialectic of Value: The Sociology and Psychoanalysis of Cult Media*, unpublished PhD dissertation, University of Sussex.

Hooper-Greenhill, Eilean (1988) 'Counting Visitors or Visitors Who Count?' in Robert Lumley (ed.) *The Museum Time-Machine: Putting Cultures on Display*, London: Comedia.

Hornby, Nick (1992) *Fever Pitch*, London: Gollancz.

Horton, Donald and Wohl, R. Richard (1956) 'Mass Communications and Para-social Interaction: Observations on Intimacy at a Distance', *Journal of Psychiatry*, 19(3): 215–29.

Huyssen, Andreas (1995) *Twilight Memories: Marking Time in a Culture of Amnesia*, New York and London: Routledge.

Jack, Ian (1997) 'Those Who Felt Differently', *Guardian*, 27 December 1997, Weekend, 4–10.

Jackson, Peter (1989) *Maps of Meaning: An Introduction to Cultural Geography*, London: Unwin Hyman.

Jameson, Frederic (1984) 'Postmodernism, or the Cultural Logic of Late Capitalism', *New Left Review*, 146: 53–93.

Janelle, Donald (1991) 'Global Interdependence and its Consequences' in Stanley Brunn and Thomas Leinbach (eds) *Collapsing Space and Time: Geographic Aspects of Communications and Information*, London: HarperCollins.

Jeffries, Stuart (1997) 'Tune In, Turn On, Freak Out' *Guardian*, 4 January, G2: 5.

—— (1998) 'Surreal Side of the Street', *Guardian*, 2 October 1998, G2: 2–3.

Jenkins, Henry (1992) *Textual Poachers: Television Fans and Participating Culture*, New York and London: Routledge.

Jenkins, Richard (1992) *Pierre Bourdieu*, London: Routledge.

Jordan, Marion (1981) 'Realism and Convention' in Richard Dyer, Christine Geraghty, Marion Jordan, Terry Lovell, Richard Paterson and John Stewart *Coronation Street*, London: British Film Institute.

Junor, Beth (1995) *Greenham Common Women's Peace Camp: A History of Non-Violent Resistance 1984–1995*, London: Working Press.

Kellner, Douglas (1990) *Television and the Crisis of Democracy*, Boulder: Westview Press.

—— (1995) *Media Culture: Cultural Studies, Identity and Politics Between the Modern and the Postmodern*, London and New York: Routledge.

—— (1997) 'Overcoming the Divide: Cultural Studies and Political Economy' in Marjorie Ferguson and Peter Golding (eds) *Cultural Studies in Question*, London: Sage.

Kilborn, Richard (1994) '"How Real Can you Get?" Recent Developments in "Reality" Television', *European Journal of Communication*, 9(4): 421–40.

Knorr-Cetina, Karin (1981) 'The Micro-sociological Challenge of Macro-sociology: Towards a Reconstruction of Social Theory and Methodology' in Karin Knorr-Cetina and Alvin Cicourel (eds) *Advances in Social Theory and Methodology: Toward an Integration of Micro- and Macro-sociologies*, Boston: Routledge & Kegan Paul.

Kraus, Sidney, Davis, Dennis, Lang, Gladys, and Lang, Kurt (1975) 'Critical Events Analysis' in Steven Chaffee (ed.) *Political Communication: Issues and Strategies for Research*, Beverly Hills and London: Sage.

Kubey, Robert and Csikszentmihalyi, Mikhail (1990) *Television and the Quality of Life: How Viewing Shapes Everyday Experience*, New Jersey: Lawrence Erlbaum.

Lacan, Jacques (1977) 'The Mirror Stage as Formative of the Function of the I' in *Ecrits: A Selection* tr. A. Sheridan, London: Tavistock.

Lakoff, George and Johnson, Mark (1980) *Metaphors We Live By*, Chicago: University of Chicago Press.

Lang, Kurt and Gladys Lang (1969) 'The Unique Perspective of Television and Its Effects: A Pilot Study' in Wilbur Schramm (ed.) *Mass Communications* 2nd edition, Urbana: University of Illinois Press.

—— (1991) 'Studying Events in Their Natural Settings' in Klaus Bruhn Jensen and Nicholas Jankowski (eds) *A Handbook of Qualitative Methodologies for Mass Communication Research*, London: Routledge.

Langer, John (1998) *Tabloid Television: Popular Journalism and the 'Other News'*, London: Routledge.

Lash, Scott (1990) *Sociology of Postmodernism*, London: Routledge.

Lash, Scott and Urry, John (1994) *Economies of Signs and Space*, London: Sage.

Law, John (1994) *Organising Modernity*, Oxford: Blackwell.

Lefebvre, Henri (1991a) [1947] *Critique of Everyday Life Volume 1* tr. J. Moore, London: Verso.

—— (1991b) *The Production of Space* tr. D. Nicholson-Smith, Oxford: Basil Blackwell.

Levi-Strauss, Claude (1981) *The Naked Man* tr. J. and D. Weightman, London: Jonathan Cape.

Levy, Mark and Gunter, Barry (1988) *Home Video and the Changing Nature of the Television Audience*, London: John Libbey.

Lewis, Justin (1991) *The Ideological Octopus: An Exploration of Television and Its Audience*, London: Routledge.

Lewis, Lisa (ed.) (1993) *The Adoring Audience: Fan Culture and Popular Media*, London: Routledge.

Liddington, Jill (1989) *The Long Road To Greenham: Feminism and Anti-Militarism in Britain Since 1920*, London: Virago.

Liebes, Tamar and Katz, Elihu (1990) *The Export of Meaning: Cross-Cultural Readings of Dallas*, Oxford: Oxford University Press.

Lindlof, Thomas (ed.) (1987) *Natural Audiences: Qualitative Research of Media Uses and Effects*, Norwood, NJ: Ablex Publishing.

Lindlof, Thomas and Grodin, Debra (1990) 'When Media Use Can't Be Observed: Some Problems and Tactics of Collaborative Audience Research', *Journal of Communication*, 40(4): 8–28.

Lipsitz, George (1990) *Time Passages: Collective Memory and American Popular Culture*, Minneapolis: University of Minnesota Press.

Livingstone, Sonia and Lunt, Peter (1994) *Talk on Television: Audience Participation and Public Debate*, London: Routledge.

Lockwood, David (1964) 'Social Integration and System Integration' in George Zollschan and Walter Hirsch (eds) *Explorations in Social Change*, London: Routledge & Kegan Paul.

Lodziak, Konrad (1987) *The Power of Television: A Critical Appraisal*, London: Frances Pinter.

Lofland, John and Lofland, Lyn (1984) *Analysing Social Settings: A Guide to Qualitative Observation and Analysis* 2nd edition, Belmont: Wadsworth.

Lull, James (1990) *Inside Family Viewing: Ethnographic Research on Television's Audiences*, London: Comedia/Routledge.

—— (1991) *China Turned On: Television, Reform and Resistance*, London: Routledge.

Lull, James and Hinerman, Stephen (eds.) (1998) *Media Scandals: Morality and Desire in the Popular Culture Marketplace*, Cambridge: Polity Press.

MacAloon, John (1984) 'Olympic Games and the Theory of Spectacle in Modern Societies' in John MacAloon (ed.) *Rite, Drama, Festival, Spectacle: Rehearsals Toward a Theory of Cultural Performance*, Philadelphia: ISHI Press.

MacCannell, Dean (1976) *The Tourist: A New Theory of the Leisure Class*, London: Macmillan.

—— (1992) *Empty Meeting Grounds: The Tourist Papers*, London: Routledge.

Mackay, George (1996) *Senseless Acts of Beauty: Cultures of Resistance Since the Sixties*, London: Verso.

MacLachlan, Gale and Reid, Ian (1994) *Framing and Interpretation*, Melbourne: Melbourne University Press.

Maffesoli, Michel (1996) *The Time of the Tribes: The Decline of Individualism in Mass Society* tr. D. Smith, London: Sage.

Mann, Michael (1970) 'The Social Cohesion of Liberal Democracy', *American Sociological Review*, 35(3): 423–39.

Marshall, P. David (1997) *Celebrity and Power: Fame in Contemporary Culture*, Minneapolis: University of Minnesota Press.

Martin-Barbero, Jesus (1993) *Communication, Culture and Hegemony: From the Media to Mediations* tr. E. Fox and R. White, London: Sage.

Marx, Karl (1973) *Grundrisse: Foundations of the Critique of Political Economy (Rough Draft)* tr. M. Nicolaus, Harmondsworth: Penguin.

Massey, Doreen (1994) *Space, Place, and Gender*, Cambridge: Polity Press.

—— (1995) 'Places and Their Pasts', *History Workshop Journal*, 39: 182–92.

Mattelart, Armand (1996) *The Invention of Communication* tr. S. Emanuel, Minneapolis: University of Minnesota Press.

McCombs, M. and Shaw, D. (1972) 'The Agenda-setting Function of the Mass Media', *Public Opinion Quarterly*, 36: 176–87.

McGuigan, Jim (1996) *Culture and the Public Sphere*, London: Routledge.

McLuhan, Marshall and Fiore, Quentin (1967) *The Medium is the Message: An Inventory of Effects*, New York: Bantam Books.

McQuail, Denis (1994) *Mass Communications Theory* 2nd edition, London: Sage.

McRobbie, Angela (1991) *Feminism and Youth Culture: From 'Jackie' to 'Just Seventeen'*, London: Routledge.

Melucci, Alberto (1985) 'The Symbolic Challenge of Contemporary Movements', *Social Research*, 52(4): 781–816.

—— (1989) *Nomads of the Present: Social Movements and Individual Needs in Contemporary Society*, London: Hutchinson Radius.

—— (1996) *Challenging Codes*, Cambridge: Cambridge University Press.

Merriman, Nick (1989) 'Museum Visiting as a Cultural Phenomenon' in Peter Vergo (ed.) *The New Museology*, London: Reaktion Books.

Meyrowitz, Joshua (1985) *No Sense of Place: The Impact of Electronic Media on Social Behavior*, New York: Oxford.

—— (1989) 'The Generalized Elsewhere', *Critical Studies in Mass Communication*, 6(3): 326–34.

Michaels, Eric (1994) *Bad Aboriginal Art: Tradition, Media and Technological Horizons*, Minneapolis: University of Minnesota Press.

Mills, C. Wright (1956) *The Power Elite*, Oxford: Oxford University Press.

Moore, Alexander (1980) 'Walt Disney World: Bounded Ritual Space and the Playful Pilgrimage Centre', *Anthropological Quarterly*, 53: 207–18.

Moores, Sean (1993a) 'Television, Geography and "Mobile Privatisation"', *European Journal of Communication*, 8(3): 365–79.

—— (1993b) 'Satellite Television as Cultural Sign: Consumption, Embedding and Articulation', *Media, Culture and Society*, 15(4): 621–39.

Morley, David (1980) *The 'Nationwide' Audience*, London: British Film Institute.

—— (1986) *Family Television: Cultural Power and Domestic Leisure*, London: Comedia/Routledge.

—— (1992) *Television, Audiences and Cultural Studies*, London: Routledge.

—— (1997) 'Theoretical Orthodoxies: Textualism, Constructivism and the "New Ethnography" in Cultural Studies' in Marjorie Ferguson and Peter Golding (eds) *Cultural Studies in Question*, London: Sage.

Morse, Margaret (1990) 'An Ontology of Everyday Distraction: The Freeway, The Mall, and Television' in Patricia Mellencamp (ed.) *Logics of Television: Essays in Cultural Criticism*, Bloomington and London: Indiana University Press and British Film Institute.

Negroponte, Nicholas (1995) *Being Digital*, London: Hodder & Stoughton.

Negt, Oskar and Kluge, Alexander (1993) [o.p. 1972] *Public Sphere and Experience: Towards an Analysis of the Bourgeois and Proletarian Public Sphere* tr. P. Labanyi *et al.,* Minneapolis: University of Minnesota Press.

Neuman, W. Russell (1991) *The Future of the Mass Audience*, Cambridge: Cambridge University Press.

Neuman, W. Russell and Pool, Ithiel de Sola (1986) 'The Flow of Communications into the Home' in Sandra Ball-Rokeach and Muriel Cantor (eds) *Media, Audience and Social Structure*, Newbury Park: Sage.

Nichols, Bill (1994) *Blurred Boundaries: Questions of Meaning in Contemporary Culture*, Bloomington: Indiana University Press.

Nightingale, Virginia (1996) *Studying Audiences: The Shock of the Real*, London: Routledge.

Noelle-Neuman, Elizabeth (1974) 'The Spiral of Silence: A Theory of Public Opinion', *Journal of Communication*, 24: 43–51.

Nora, Pierre (1989) 'Between Memory and History: *Les Lieux de Mémoire*', *Representations*, 26: 7–25.

Nora, Pierre (ed.) (1984) *Les Lieux de Mémoire* 3 vols, Paris: Gallimard.

O'Connor, Paul (1995) 'Talking Turkey with Television' in booklet accompanying *Undercurrents* [video magazine] 4, Oxford: Undercurrents Productions.

Offe, Claus (1985) 'New Social Movements: Challenging the Boundaries of Institutional Politics', *Social Research*, 52(4): 817–68.

Office for National Statistics (1997) *Family Spending: A Report on the 1996–97 Family Expenditure Survey*, London: HMSO.

Parker, Charles (1974) unpublished interviews with participants in the 1971–2 Miners' Strike.

Parker, Tony (1986) *Red Hill: A Mining Community*, London: Heinemann.

Parkin, Frank (1972) *Class Inequality and Political Order*, London: Granada.

Petrie, Duncan and Willis, Janet (eds) (1995) *Television and The Household: Reports From the BFI's Audience Tracking Study*, London: British Film Institute.

Philo, Greg (1990) *Seeing and Believing: The Influence of Television*, London: Routledge.

Pickard, Tom (1982) *Jarrow March*, London: Allison and Busby.

Pool, Ithiel de Sola (1983) *Technologies of Freedom*, Cambridge, Mass.: Harvard University Press.

Poster, Mark (1995) 'Postmodern Virtualities' in Mike Featherstone and Roger Burrows (eds) *Cyberspace / Cyberbodies / Cyberpunk: Cultures of Technological Embodiment*, London: Sage.

Potter, Jonathan and Wetherall, Margaret (1987) *Discourse and Social Psychology: Beyond Attitudes and Behaviour*, London: Sage.

Priest, Patricia (1995) *Public Intimacies: Talk Show Participants and Tell-All TV*, Cresskill, NJ: Hampton Press.

—— (1996) '"Gilt by Association": Talk Show Participants' Televisually Enhanced Status and Self-Esteem' in Debra Grodin and Thomas Lindlof (eds) *Constructing the Self in a Mediated World*, London: Sage.

Project on Disney, The (1995) *Inside the Mouse: Work and Play at Disney World*, Durham and London: Duke University Press.

Radway, Janice (1988) 'Reception Study: Ethnography and the Problems of Dispersed Audiences and Nomadic Subjects', *Cultural Studies*, 2(3): 359–76.

Rath, Claus-Dieter (1985) 'The Invisible Network: Television as an Institution in Everyday Life' in Philip Drummond and Richard Paterson (eds) *Television in Transition*, London: British Film Institute.

—— (1989) 'Live TV and its Audiences: Challenges of Media Reality' in Ellen Seiter, Hans Borches, Gabriele Kreutzner and Eva-Maria Warth (eds) *Remote Control: Television, Audiences and Cultural Power*, London: Routledge.

Reader, Ian and Walter, Tony (eds) (1993) *Pilgrimage and Popular Culture*, London: Macmillan.

Real, Michael (1975) 'Superbowl: Mythic Spectacle', *Journal of Communication*, 25(1): 31–43.

—— (1977) *Mass-mediated Culture*, Englewood Cliffs, NJ: Prentice Hall.

—— (1996) *Exploring Media Culture: A Guide*, Thousand Oaks: Sage.

Reeves, Jimmie (1988) 'Television Stardom: A Ritual of Social Typification and Individualization' in James Carey (ed.) *Media, Myths and Narratives: Television and the Press*, Newbury Park: Sage.

Relph, Edward (1976) *Place and Placelessness*, London: Pion.

Rheingold, Howard (1994) *The Virtual Community: Finding Connection in a Computerised World*, London: Secker and Warburg.

Rice, Jenny and Saunders, Carol (1996) 'Consuming *Middlemarch*: The Construction and Consumption of Nostalgia in Stamford' in Deborah Cartmell, I. Q. Hunter, Heidi Kaye and Imelda Whelehan (eds) *Pulping Fictions: Consuming Culture Across the Literature/Media Divide*, London: Pluto.

Riggs, Karen (1996) 'Television Use in a Retirement Community', *Journal of Communication*, 46(1): 144–56.

Road Alert! (1997) *Road Raging: Top Tips for Wrecking Roadbuilding*, Newbury: Road Alert!

Robins, Kevin and Webster, Frank (1986) 'Broadcasting Politics: Communications and Consumption', *Screen*, 27(3–4): 30–44.

Rojek, Chris (1993) *Ways of Escape: Modern Transformations in Leisure and Travel*, London: Macmillan.

Root, Jane (1986) *Open The Box*, London: Comedia.

Roseneil, Sasha (1995) *Disarming Patriarchy: Feminism and Political Action at Greenham*, Buckingham: Open University Press.

Rothenbuhler, Eric (1998) *Ritual Communication: From Everyday Conversation to Mediated Ceremony*, Thousand Oaks: Sage.

Routledge, Paul (1997) 'The Imagineering of Resistance: Pollok Free State and the Practice of Postmodern Politics', *Transactions of the Institute of British Geographers*, 22(3): 359–76.

Rowe, William and Schelling, Vivian (1991) *Memory and Modernity: Popular Culture in Latin America*, London: Verso.

Rubin, Jerry (1970) *Do It!*, New York: Simon and Schuster.

Sack, Robert, (1986) *Human Territoriality: Its Theory and History*, Cambridge: Cambridge University Press.

—— (1992) *Place, Modernity and the Consumer's World: A Relational Framework for Geographical Analysis*, Baltimore: The Johns Hopkins Press.

Saenz, Michael (1994) 'Television Viewing as a Cultural Practice' in Horace Newcomb (ed.) *Television: The Critical View* 4th edition, New York: Oxford University Press.

Sahlins, Marshall (1976) *Culture and Practical Reason*, Chicago: University of Chicago Press.

Said, Edward (1978) *Orientalism*, London: Routledge & Kegan Paul.

Sallnow, Michael (1981) 'Communitas Reconsidered: The Sociology of Andean Pilgrimage', *Man* (N.S.), 16: 163–82.

—— (1987) *Pilgrims of the Andes: Regional Cults in Cusco*, Washington DC: Smithsonian Press.

Samuel, Raphael (1994) *Theatres of Memory, Volume 1: Past and Present in Contemporary Culture*, London: Verso.

Scannell, Paddy, (1988a) 'Radio Times: The Temporal Arrangements of Broadcasting in the Modern World' in Philip Drummond and Richard Paterson (eds) *Television and its Audiences: International Research Perspectives*, London: British Film Institute.

—— (1988b) 'The Communicative Ethos of Broadcasting', paper delivered to the British Film Institute/University of London International Television Studies conference, 1988.

—— (1989) 'Public Service Broadcasting and Modern Public Life', *Media, Culture and Society*, 11(1): 135–166.

—— (1996) *Radio, Television and Modern Life*, Oxford: Basil Blackwell.

Scannell, Paddy and Cardiff, David (1991) *History of British Broadcasting, Volume 1: 1922–39 Serving The Nation*, Oxford: Basil Blackwell.

Schickel, Richard (1985) *Intimate Strangers: The Culture of Celebrity*, Garden City, NJ: Doubleday.

Schivelbusch, Wolfgang (1978) 'Railroad Space and Railroad Time', *New German Critique*, 14: 31–40.

Schlesinger, Philip (1978) *Putting 'Reality' Together: BBC News*, London: Methuen.

Schlesinger, Philip and Tumber, Howard (1994) *Reporting Crime: The Media Politics of Criminal Justice*, Oxford: Oxford University Press.

Schrag, Peter (1978) 'Heeere's Johnny!' in James Monaco (ed.) *Celebrity: The Media as Image Makers*, New York: Delta.

Schutz, Alfred (1973a) 'On Multiple Realities' in *Collected Papers Volume 1*, The Hague: Martinus Nijhoff, 207–59.

—— (1973b) 'The Stranger' in *Collected Papers Volume 2*, The Hague: Martinus Nijhoff, 90–105.

Schwartz, Barry (1974) 'Waiting, Exchange and Power: The Distribution of Time in Social Systems', *American Journal of Sociology*, 79(4): 841–70.

Sennett, Richard and Cobb, Jonathan (1972) *The Hidden Injuries of Class*, Cambridge: Cambridge University Press.

Shields, Rob (1991) *Places on the Margin: Alternative Geographies of Modernity*, London: Routledge.

Sibley, David (1995) *Geographies of Exclusion: The Exclusion of Geographies*, London: Routledge.

Signorielli, Nancy and Morgan, David (eds) (1990) *Cultivation Analysis: New Directions in Media Effects Research*, Newbury Park: Sage.

Silverstone, Roger (1981) *The Message of Television: Myth and Narrative in Contemporary Culture*, London: Heinemann Educational Books.

—— (1983) 'The Right to Speak: A Poetic for Documentary', *Media, Culture and Society*, 5(2): 137–54.

—— (1988) 'Television Myth and Culture' in James Carey (ed.) *Media, Myths and Narratives: Television and the Press*, Newbury Park: Sage.

—— (1994) *Television and Everyday Life*, London: Routledge.

Silverstone, Roger and Hirsch, Eric (eds) (1992) *Consuming Technologies: Media and Information in Domestic Spaces*, London: Routledge.

Simmel, Georg (1971) [o.p. 1911] 'The Adventurer' in *On Individuality and Social Forms* (various translators), Chicago: University of Chicago Press, 187–98.

Smith, Jonathan Z. (1987) *To Take Place: Toward Theory in Ritual*, Chicago: University of Chicago Press.

Snow, Robert (1983) *Creating Media Culture*, Beverly Hills: Sage.

Soja, Edward (1989) *Postmodern Geographies: The Reassertion of Space in Critical Social Theory*, London: Verso.

Sorkin, Michael (ed.) (1992) *Variations on a Theme Park: The New American City and the End of Public Space*, New York: Hill and Wang.

Sparks, Colin (1998) *Communication, Capitalism and the Mass Media*, London: Sage.

Sperber, Dan (1985) *On Anthropological Knowledge*, Cambridge: Cambridge University Press.

Sreberny-Mohammadi, Annabelle and Mohammadi, Ali (1994) *Small Media, Big Revolution: Communication, Culture and the Iranian Revolution*, Minneapolis: University of Minnesota Press.

Stacey, Jackie (1994) *Star Gazing: Hollywood Cinema and Female Spectatorship*, London: Routledge.

Stallybrass, Peter and White, Allon (1986) *The Politics and Poetics of Transgression*, London: Methuen.

Stephens, Fiona and Shehata, Wendy (eds) (1995) *The Siege of Shoreham: Reflections From The Front Line*, Brighton: Hatagra.

Stratton, Jon and Ang, Ien (1994) '*Sylvania Waters* and the Spectacular Exploding Family', *Screen* 35(1): 1–21.

Swallow, Norman (1966) *Factual Television*, London and New York: The Focal Press.

Swyngedouw, Eric (1989) 'The Heart of the Place: The Resurrection of Locality in an Age of Hyperspace', *Geografisker Annaler*, 71(B)(1): 31–42.

Tannenbaum, Eric (1995) *Animal Transport through Brightlingsea: Report of an Opinion Survey*, Colchester: Department of Politics, University of Essex.

Thompson, E. P. (1971) 'The Moral Economy of the Crowd', *Past and Present*, 50: 76–136.

Thompson, John (1990) *Ideology and Modern Culture: Critical Social Theory in the Era of Mass Communications*, Cambridge: Polity Press.

—— (1993) 'The Theory of the Public Sphere', *Theory, Culture and Society*, 10(3): 173–89.

—— (1995) *The Media and Modernity: A Social Theory of the Media*, Cambridge: Polity Press.

Thrift, Nigel (1985) 'Flies and Germs: A Geography of Knowledge' in Derek Gregory and John Urry (eds) *Social Relations and Spatial Structures*, London: Macmillan.

Tichi, Cecelia (1991) *Electronic Hearth: Creating an American Television Culture*, New York: Oxford University Press.

Tocqueville, Alexis de (1994) [o.p. 1835–40] *Democracy in America* (various translators), London: David Campbell.

Toffler, Alvin (1980) *The Third Wave*, London: Pan Books.

Tolson, Andrew (1991) 'Televised Chat and the Synthetic Personality' in Paddy Scannell (ed.) *Broadcast Talk*, London: Sage.

Traudt, Paul and Lont, Cynthia (1987) 'Media-Logic-In-Use: The Family as Locus of Study' in Thomas Lindlof (ed.) *Natural Audiences: Qualitative Research of Media Uses and Effects*, Norwood, NJ: Ablex Publishing.

Tunstall, Jeremy (1993) *Television Producers*, London: Routledge.

Turner, Victor (1973) 'The Center Out There: Pilgrim's Goal', *History of Religions*, 12: 191–230.

—— (1974) *Dramas, Fields and Metaphors: Symbolic Action in Human Society*, Ithaca and London: Cornell University Press.

—— (1977) 'Variations on a Theme of Liminality' in Sally Moore and Barbara Myerhoff (eds) *Secular Ritual*, Assen/Amsterdam: Van Gorcum.

Turner, Victor and Turner, Edith (1978) *Image and Pilgrimage in Christian Culture: Anthropological Perspectives*, Oxford: Basil Blackwell.

Tusa, John (1993) 'Live Broadcasting' in Nod Miller and Rod Allen (eds) *It's Live But Is It Real?*, London: John Libbey.

Urry, John (1990) *The Tourist Gaze: Leisure and Travel in Contemporary Societies*, London: Sage.

—— (1995) *Consuming Places*, London: Routledge.

van Dijk, Teun (1996) 'Power and the News Media' in David Paletz (ed.) *Political Communication in Action: States, Institutions, Movements, Audiences*, New Jersey: Hampton Press.

van Gennep, Arnold (1960) [o.p. 1908] *The Rites of Passage* tr. M. Vizedom and G. Caffee, London: Routledge & Kegan Paul.

Vaneigem, Raoul (1989) [o.p. 1963] 'Basic Banalities (II)' in Inona Blazwick (ed.) *A Situationist Scrapbook: An Endless Passion ... an Endless Banquet*, London: ICA/Verso.

van Zoonen, Liesbet (1992) The Women's Movement and the Media: Constructing a Public Identity', *European Journal of Communication*, 7(4): 453–76.

—— (1996) 'A Dance of Death: New Social Movements and the Mass Media' in David Paletz (ed.) *Political Communication in Action: States, Institutions, Movements, Audiences*, New Jersey: Hampton Press.

Vattimo, Gianni (1992) *The Transparent Society*, Cambridge: Polity Press.

Vermorel, Fred and Vermorel, Julie (1985) *Starlust: The Secret Life of Fans*, London: W.H. Allen.

Vidal, John (1998) 'Swampy Goes to Ground', *Guardian*, 1 April, G2: 2–3.

Virilio, Paul (n.d.) 'The Overexposed City' in Jonathan Crary, Michael Feher, Hal Foster and Sanford Kwinter (eds) *Zone 1 and 2*, New York: Urzone, Inc.

—— (1986) *Speed and Politics: An Essay on Dromology*, New York: Semiotext(e).

Walkerdine, Valerie (1995) 'Subject to Change Without Notice' in Steve Pile and Nigel Thrift (eds) *Mapping the Subject: Geographies of Cultural Transformation*, London and New York: Routledge.

Walsh, Kevin (1992) *The Representation of the Past: Museums and Heritage in the Post-Modern World*, London and New York: Routledge.

Wark, McKenzie (1994) *Virtual Geography: Living with Global Media Events*, Bloomington: Indiana University Press.

Wasko, Janet (1994) *Hollywood and the Information Age*, Cambridge: Polity Press.

—— (1996) 'Understanding the Disney Universe' in James Curran and Michael Gurevitch (eds) *Mass Media and Society* 2nd edition, London: Arnold.

Webster, Frank and Robins, Kevin (1989) 'Plan and Control: Towards a Cultural History of the Information Society', *Theory and Society*, 18: 323–51.

Wernick, Andrew (1991) *Promotional Culture: Advertising, Ideology and Symbolic Expression*, London: Sage.

Williams, Raymond (1961) *Culture and Society: 1780–1950*, Harmondsworth: Penguin.

—— (1973) *The Country and the City*, London: The Hogarth Press.

—— (1975) *Drama in a Dramatised Society*, Cambridge: Cambridge University Press.

229

—— (1983) *Keywords* 2nd edition, London: Fontana.

—— (1989) [o.p. 1958] 'Culture is Ordinary' in *Resources of Hope: Culture, Democracy, Socialism*, London: Verso.

—— (1990) [o.p. 1974] *Television: Technology and Cultural Form* 2nd edition, London: Routledge.

Willis, Paul (1980) 'Notes on Method' in Stuart Hall, Dorothy Hobson, Andrew Lowe and Paul Willis (eds) *Culture, Media, Language*, London: Unwin Hyman.

—— (1990) *Common Culture: Symbolic Work and Play in the Everyday Cultures of the Young*, Milton Keynes: Open University Press.

Wilson, Tony (1993) *Watching Television: Hermeneutics, Reception and Popular Culture*, Cambridge: Polity Press.

Winston, Brian (1998) *Media Technology and Society – A History: From the Telegraph to the Internet*, London: Routledge.

Worth, Sol and John Adair (1972) *Through Navaho Eyes: An Exploration in Film Communications and Anthropology*, Bloomington: Indiana University Press.

Wright, Patrick (1985) *On Living in an Old Country: The National Past in Contemporary Britain*, London: Verso.

Wrong, Dennis (1961) 'The Oversocialised Conception of Man', *American Sociological Review*, 26(2): 183–93.

Young, Alison (1990) *Femininity in Dissent*, London: Routledge.

Young, Iris Marion (1990) 'The Ideal of Community and the Politics of Difference' in Linda Nicholson (ed.) *Feminism/Postmodernism*, London and New York: Routledge.

Young, Jock (1974) 'Mass Media, Drugs and Deviance' in Paul Rock and Mary Mackintosh (eds) *Deviance and Social Control*, London: Tavistock.

Zizek, Slavoj (1989) *The Sublime Object of Ideology*, London: Verso.

# INDEX

Rheingold, Howard 189
ritual action: and protests 160
ritual contact 102
ritual place: *see under* place
road protests 35; *see also* Newbury
    anti-road; protest
Robins, Kevin 53
Rojek, Chris 70

Sack, Robert 106
sacred/profane distinction 12, 14, 15, 26,
    41–3 *passim*, 47, 54
Sallnow, Michael 73
sampling, interview: snowballing method
    200
Samuel, Raphael 31
satellite television: impact of 11; use of
    185, 187, 203
Scannell, Paddy 10–12, 30, 192
scepticism, public: of media 138
Schickel, Richard 114
Schwartz, Barry 48
self-reflexive tactics 181
Sennett, Richard 22
sensationalism: by media 137, 142
'showing': act of 170, 171
Sibley, David 25
significance, framework of: and *Coronation
    Street* set 72
silence: media 160–1; mode of 49; of
    'ordinary' world 174
Silverstone, Roger 10, 12–13, 14, 50
Simmel, Georg 119
simultaneity: in television 185
sites, media 33, 181; and consumption
    sites 25, 54; of mediated conflict 34–6;
    size of 113; of witnessing 128–34; *see
    also* tourist sites, media
Situationists 26, 28, 114, 194
size: symbolic 113
Smith, Jonathan 85
Snow, Robert 18–19
soaps: and media tourist sites 66
social activism 7
social authority: of media 5, 12, 29, 127,
    138, 139, 167 rejection of 174, 181
social effects: of media 5
social facts 13
social knowledge: media as sources of 4;
    *see also* knowledge-generation
social life: mediation of 3
social memory 30, 75–8; changing 31

social ontology 13
social realities 13, 14, 82; and 'media' and
    'ordinary' worlds 20
social relations: and spatial organisaton 25
space, media 23, 25, 38, 113, 194; of
    action 167; complexity of 24; collapse
    through mediation 24; and electronic
    media 24; intervention in 167; and
    place 23, 40
spacing, of media frame 52–5, 178
spatial boundaries 105–6; and restrictions
    110
spatial differentiation 27
spatial intensity 113
spatial logic: in media frame 26
spatial order 205 n.6
spatial process: media as 52
spatial relation: map 30; territory 30
spectacle: alienating 114
spiral of silence 160; *see also* silence, media
Stallybrass, Peter 6
stars, of *Coronation Street*: as characters 92;
    meeting 91–7, 180 and spontaneity 96,
    97; and 'ordinary' world 114;
    promotion of 91–2; quality of contact
    95–7 *passim*; status 94
state: force of 132
status, of media 7; legitimation of 61; of
    stars 94
stereotyping 209 n.107; and
    de-naturalisation 137; of protestors, by
    media 136, 137, 143, 172 impact of 150
    power of 165
Strauss, Anselm 196
studios: and *Coronation Street* set 81; for
    media resources 52–3
Swyngedouw, Eric 27
symbolic disruption: and protestor
    experience 152, 153
symbolic division: of world 46–8
symbolic hierarchy, of media frame: *see
    under* media frame
symbolic interactionism 197
symbolic power: competition for 58, 134,
    179 masked 179; future of 184;
    inequality of 16, 20; in institutions 13;
    and Internet 191; of media 3–22
    *passim*, 38, 44, 205 n.8 differential 13,
    174, 177, 209 n.90; of media
    institutions, reproduction 124, 182;
    naturalised 18, 157, 201
symbolic production: witnessing 18

symbolic reversal 57, 89, 106–8 *passim*, 180

tactics: self-reflexive 181; spatial 167
talk: ethnomethodological approaches to 197
talk shows, television 193; non-media people's experiences, appearing on 19, 37; US participants 47, 117, 205 n.3
technology, media: changes in 18, 182, 185–91; domestic, and interviewees 203, 204; in-use 184
Telestars booth: *see under* Granada Studios Tour
teletext 185
television 6; authority, and availability 14, 15; 'being on' 116–19; changes in 184; digital 188; disillusionment with 102; falseness 180; framing function 42; live 42–3; locations, and tourism 31–4; 'magic' of 112; 'mythic' dimension of 12, 13; naturalisation 100; news, mediation by 50; power of, and falsity 102–3; production costs 112–13; as ritual 'frame' 14; segregation with 'ordinary' 100; sense of glamour 101; transformative nature of 118; trust in 50; visual deception 98; *see also* cable television; satellite television; trust, in media
'territory': and 'map' 129; media 38, 40, 106, 119, 194; spatial relation 30
textual analysis 191–2
*The Big Breakfast*, 118
*The Chris Evans Road Show* 118
*The Real World*, 47
Thompson, John 8, 30, 40
Thrift, Nigel 53
Tichi, Cecelia 47
timeshifting: and VCRs 185
time-space compression 27
time-space convergence 27
TLIO, The Land Is Ours 169–71
Tocqueville, Alexis de 193
Tolson, Andrew 45
touching: the medium 55, 57
tourist sites, media 31, 65–87, 179, 181–2,

206 n.36; fictive 88; as ritual place 82–7; 'Break into the World of Broadcasting' 48; 'Step Inside the World of Television' 48; *see also* Granada Studios Tour
tracking: *see* witnessing, active
trust, in media 34, 50–1, 138, 151, 178, 207 n.57; loss of 51, 137, 139, 145–8 *passim*, 150, 180–1, 209 n.103
Turner, Victor 73, 108

Umbrella Man, The 123, 156, 164–5, *166*, 167, 172, 181, 207 n.43
Urry, John, 32–3, 38, 72, 182, 191, 208 n.81
US: network television 186; talk show participants 47, 117, 118–19

van Gennep, Arnold 86
Vaneigem, Raoul 114
video 6; cameras, portable 53; inputs 185–6; news, non-mainstream 173; recorders, use of 185, 203, 210 n. 125
*Video Diaries* 186
*Video Nation* 186
viewers: interactivity with 188; as 'ordinary' people 47
viewing patterns 187
Virilio, Paul 30
visitors' talk 34
visual deception: in media world 98

Wark, McKenzie 30, 129
Web broadcasting 189
Webster, Frank 53
White, Allon 6
Wilby, Maria: and BALE 124, 127, 135, 137, 142, 144, 161, 168
Williams, Raymond 23, 26, 45, 137
Willis, Paul 75
witnessing 29, 37, 186; active 37, 156; false, by media 146; site of 128–34; symbolic production 18

Yorkshire Television Official Holiday 65

Zizek, Slavoj 45